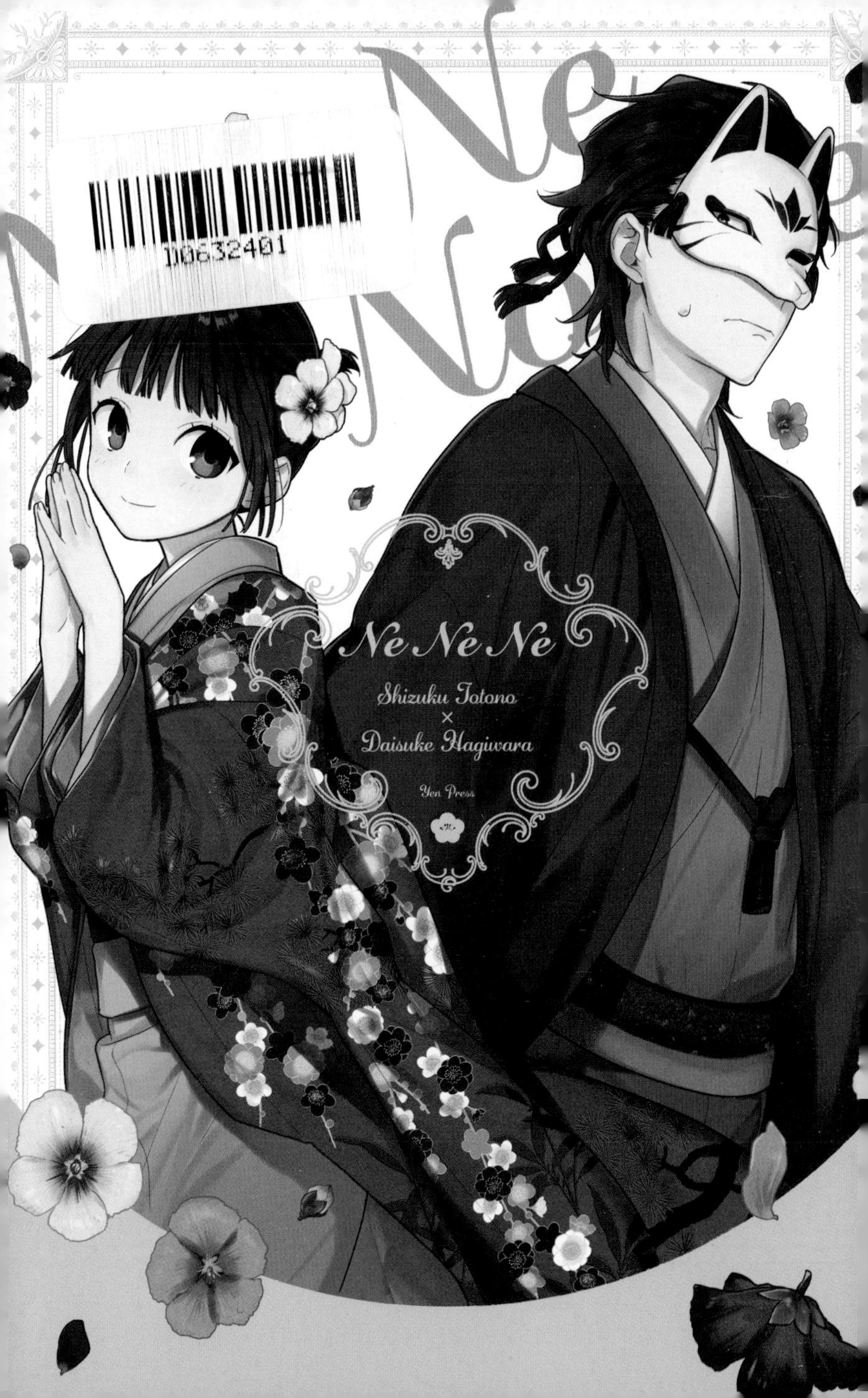
Ne Ne Ne
Shizuku Totono
×
Daisuke Hagiwara
Yen Press

Contents

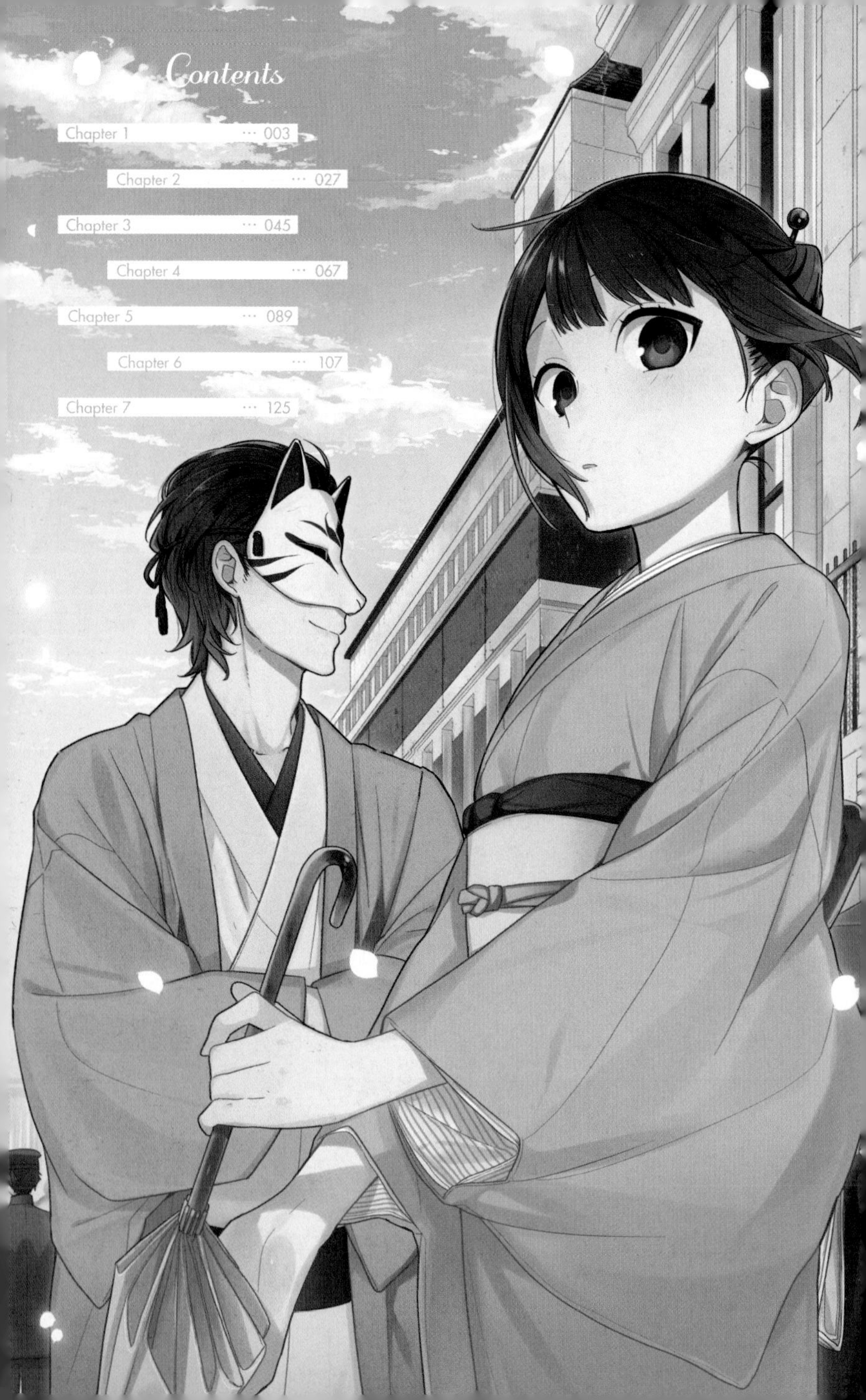

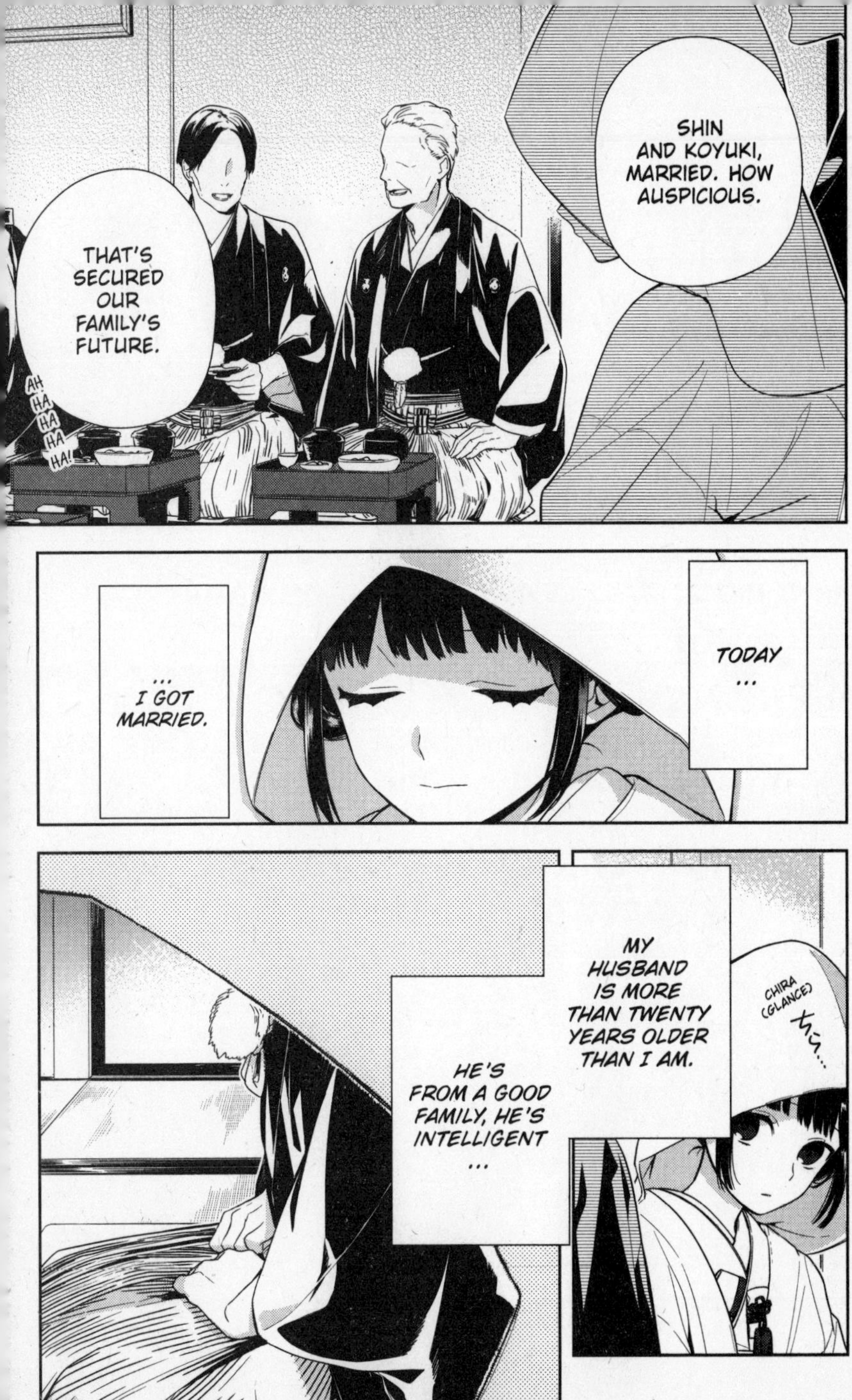
SHIN AND KOYUKI, MARRIED. HOW AUSPICIOUS.
THAT'S SECURED OUR FAMILY'S FUTURE.
AH HA HA HA HA!
TODAY ...
... I GOT MARRIED.
MY HUSBAND IS MORE THAN TWENTY YEARS OLDER THAN I AM.
HE'S FROM A GOOD FAMILY, HE'S INTELLIGENT ...
CHIRA (GLANCE)

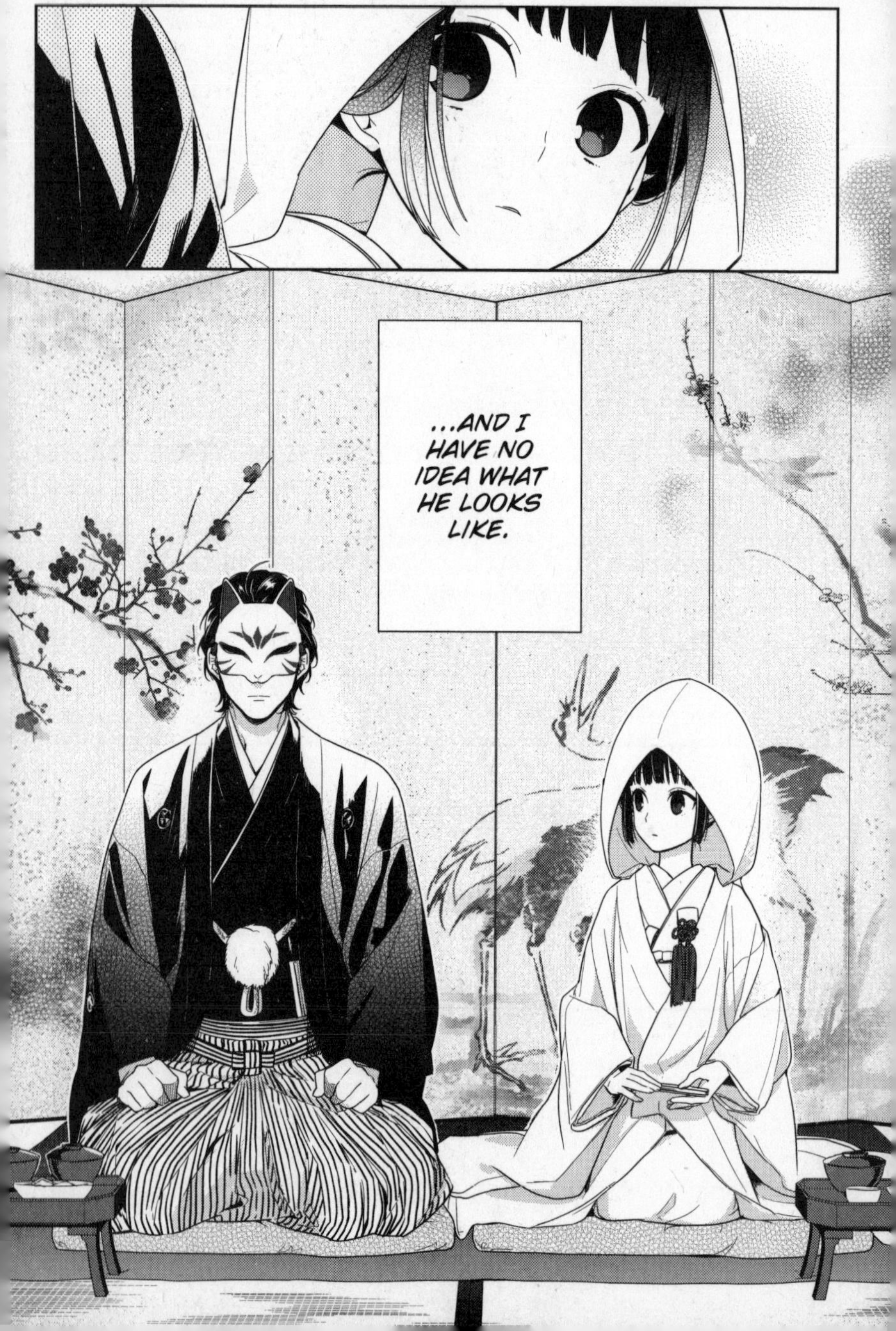
...AND I HAVE NO IDEA WHAT HE LOOKS LIKE.

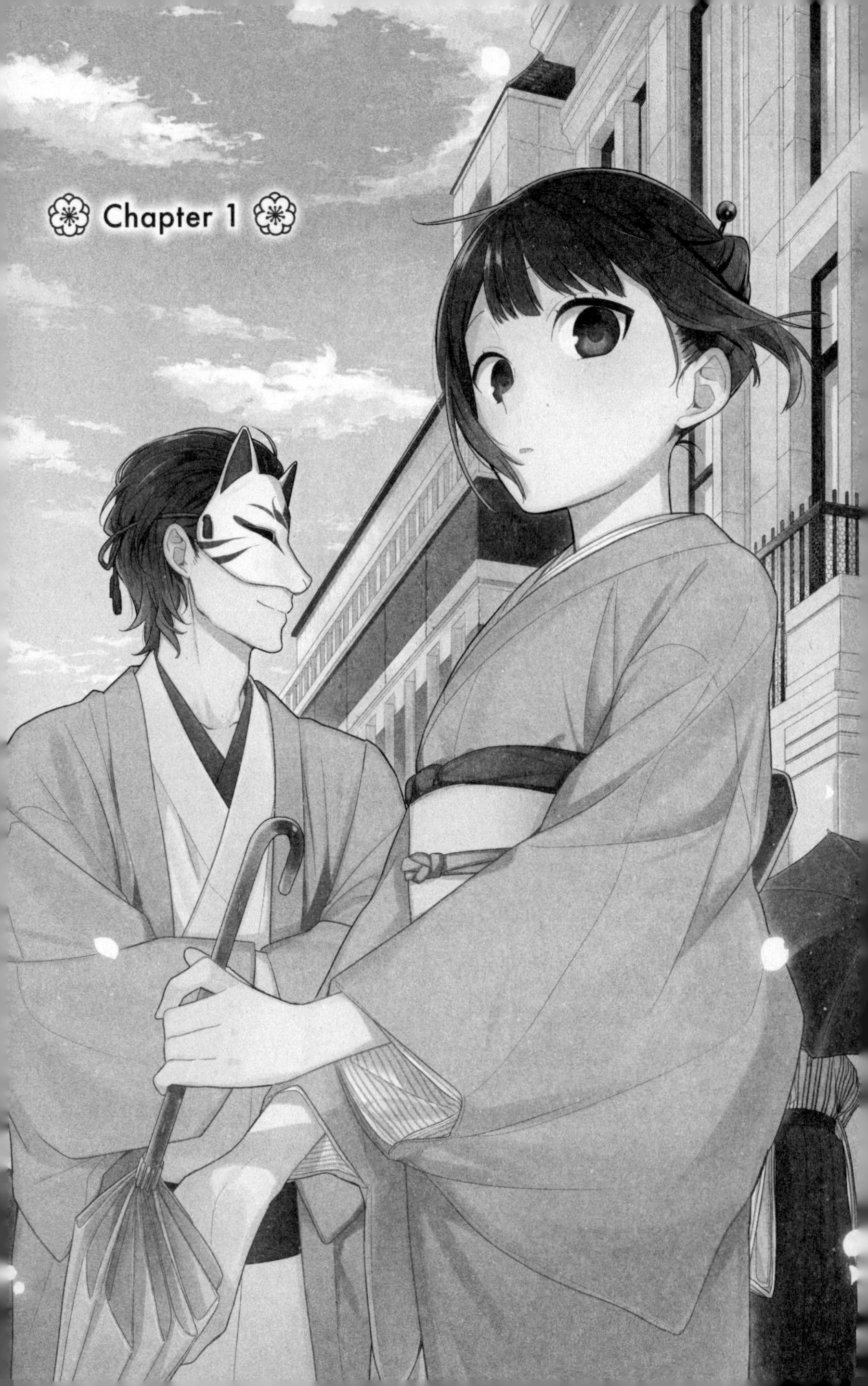

Chapter 1

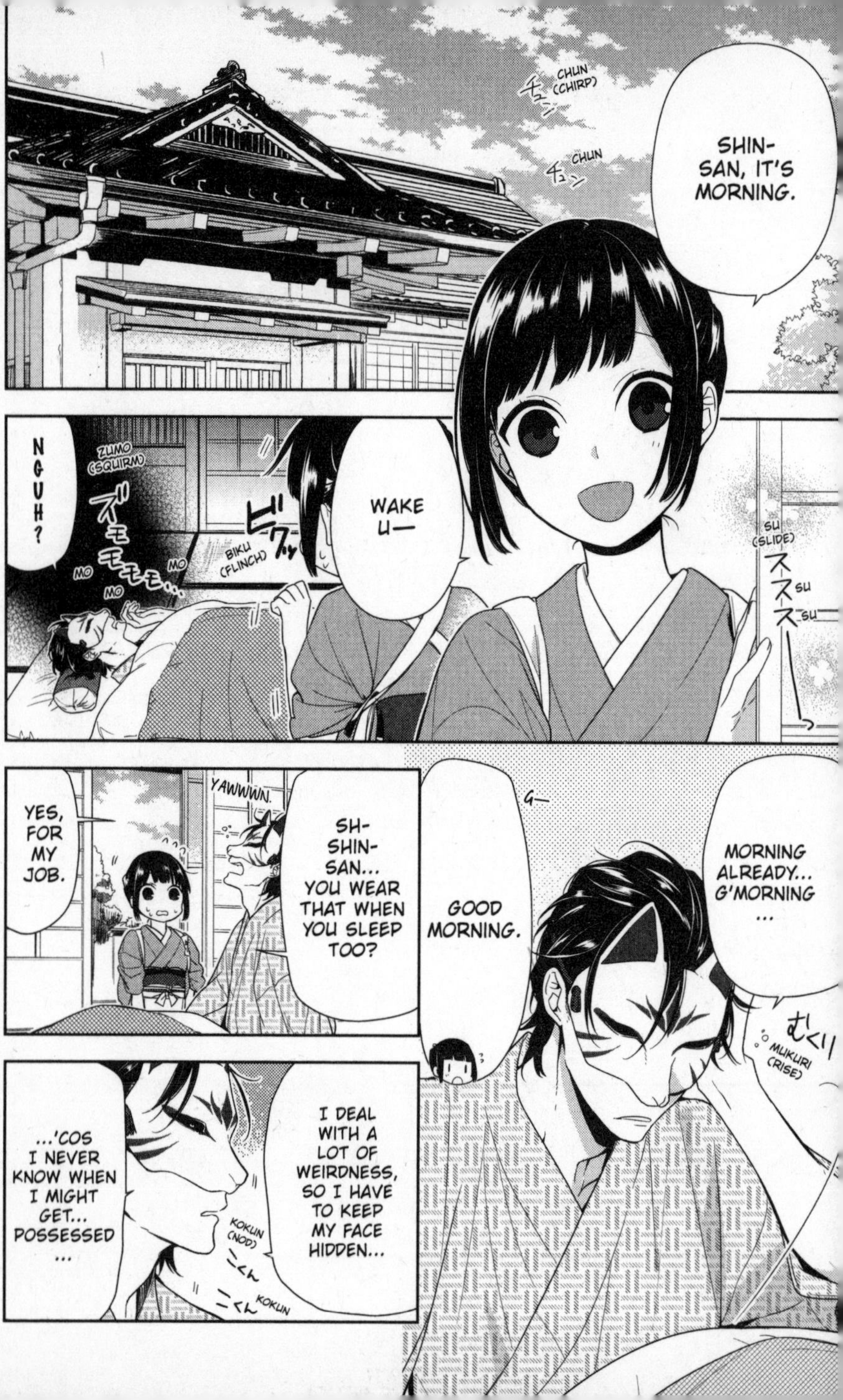
SHIN-SAN, IT'S MORNING.
CHUN (CHIRP)
チュン
CHUN
チュン
SU (SLIDE)
スススー
SU
SU
WAKE U—
BIKU (FLINCH)
ビクッ
ZUMO (SQUIRM)
ズモモモ...
MO
MO
MO
NGUH?
MORNING ALREADY... G'MORNING...
MUKURI (RISE)
むくり
G—
GOOD MORNING.
SH-SHIN-SAN... YOU WEAR THAT WHEN YOU SLEEP TOO?
YAWWWN.
YES, FOR MY JOB.
I DEAL WITH A LOT OF WEIRDNESS, SO I HAVE TO KEEP MY FACE HIDDEN...
KOKUN (NOD)
こくん
こくん
KOKUN
...'COS I NEVER KNOW WHEN I MIGHT GET... POSSESSED...

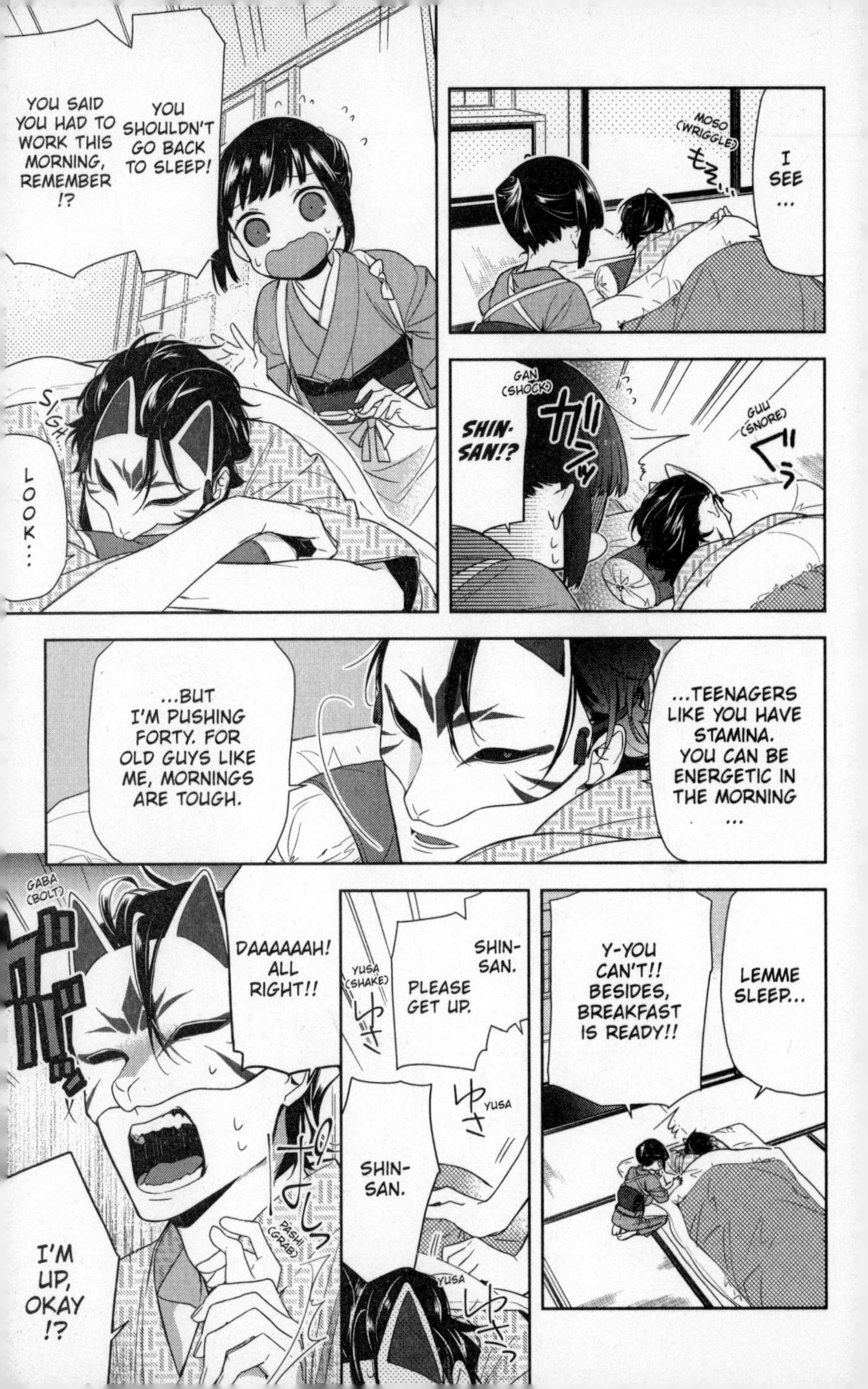
I SEE...
MOSO (WRIGGLE)
GUU (SNORE)
SHIN-SAN!?
GAN (SHOCK)
YOU SHOULDN'T GO BACK TO SLEEP!
YOU SAID YOU HAD TO WORK THIS MORNING, REMEMBER!?
SIGH...
LOOK...
...TEENAGERS LIKE YOU HAVE STAMINA. YOU CAN BE ENERGETIC IN THE MORNING...
...BUT I'M PUSHING FORTY. FOR OLD GUYS LIKE ME, MORNINGS ARE TOUGH.
LEMME SLEEP...
Y-YOU CAN'T!! BESIDES, BREAKFAST IS READY!!
SHIN-SAN.
PLEASE GET UP.
YUSA (SHAKE)
YUSA
SHIN-SAN.
YUSA
DAAAAAAH! ALL RIGHT!!
GABA (BOLT)
PASHI (GRAB)
I'M UP, OKAY!?

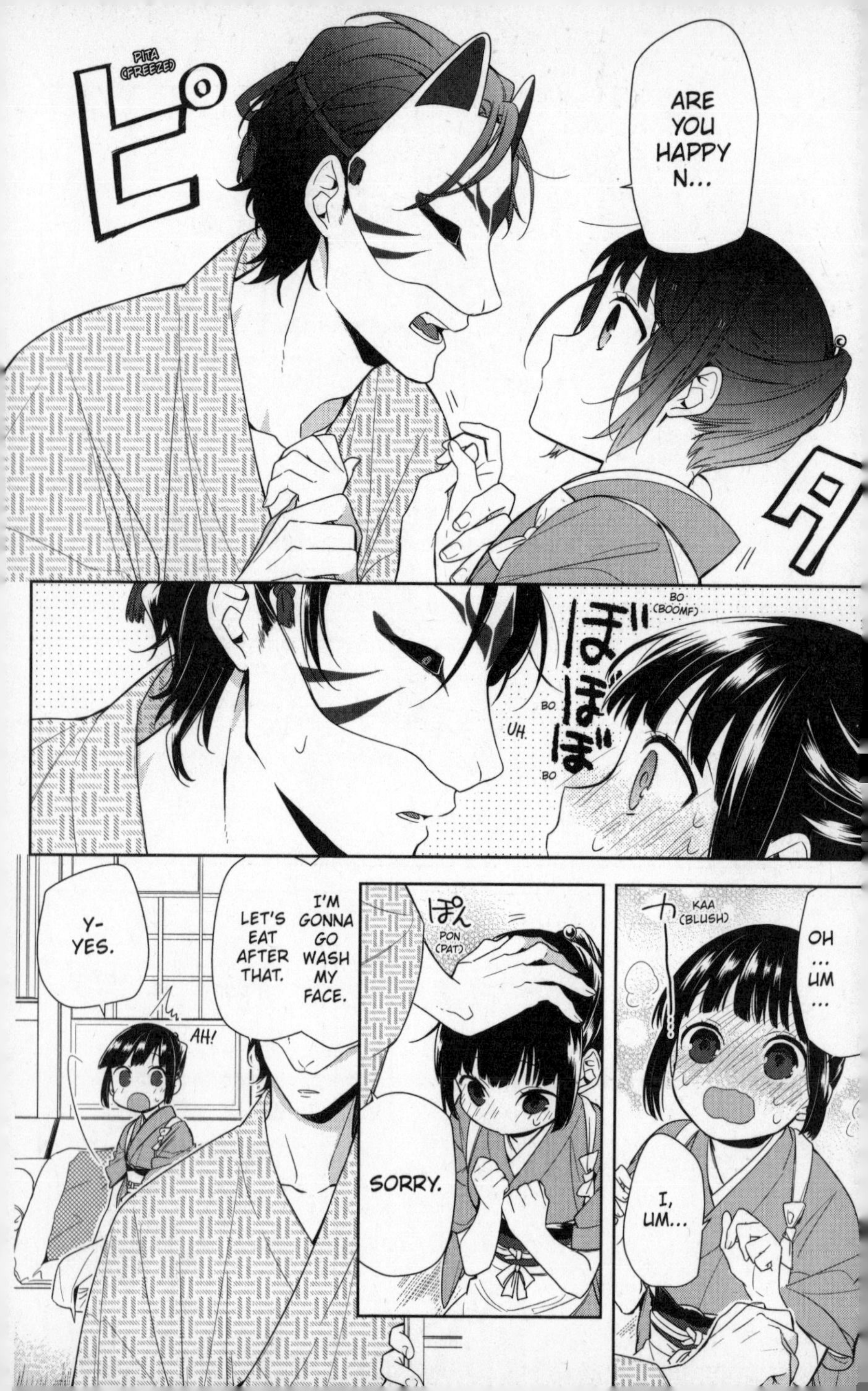
ARE YOU HAPPY N...
ピ
PITA (FREEZE)
タ
ぼぼぼぼ
BO (BOOMF)
BO
BO
UH.
か
KAA (BLUSH)
OH ... UM ...
I, UM...
ぽん
PON (PAT)
SORRY.
I'M GONNA GO WASH MY FACE.
LET'S EAT AFTER THAT.
Y- YES.
AH!

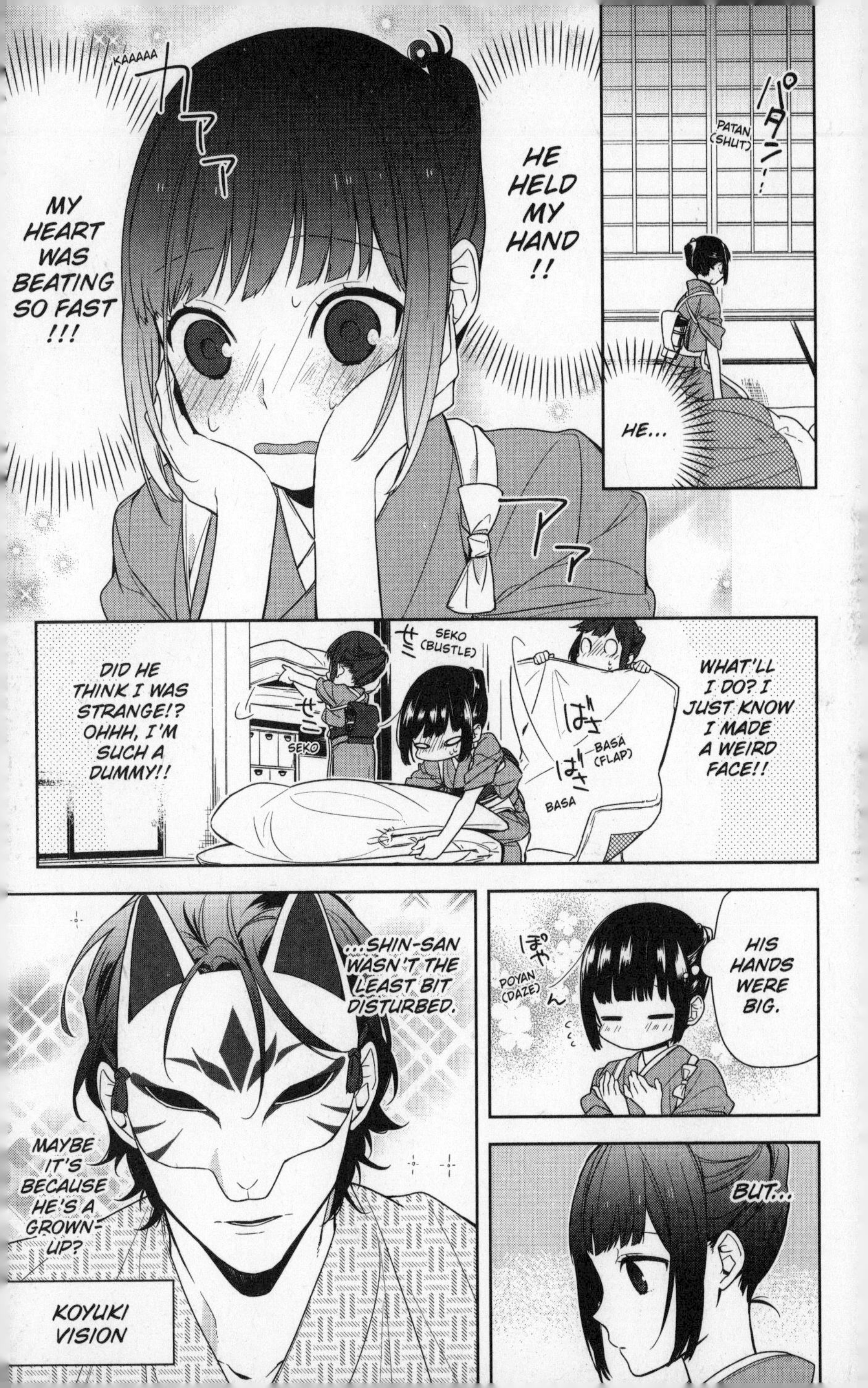
パタン
PATAN (SHUT)
HE...
HE HELD MY HAND!!
MY HEART WAS BEATING SO FAST!!!
KAAAAA
WHAT'LL I DO? I JUST KNOW I MADE A WEIRD FACE!!
BASA (FLAP)
BASA
SEKO (BUSTLE)
SEKO
DID HE THINK I WAS STRANGE!? OHHH, I'M SUCH A DUMMY!!
HIS HANDS WERE BIG.
POYAN (DAZE)
BUT...
...SHIN-SAN WASN'T THE LEAST BIT DISTURBED.
MAYBE IT'S BECAUSE HE'S A GROWN-UP?
KOYUKI VISION

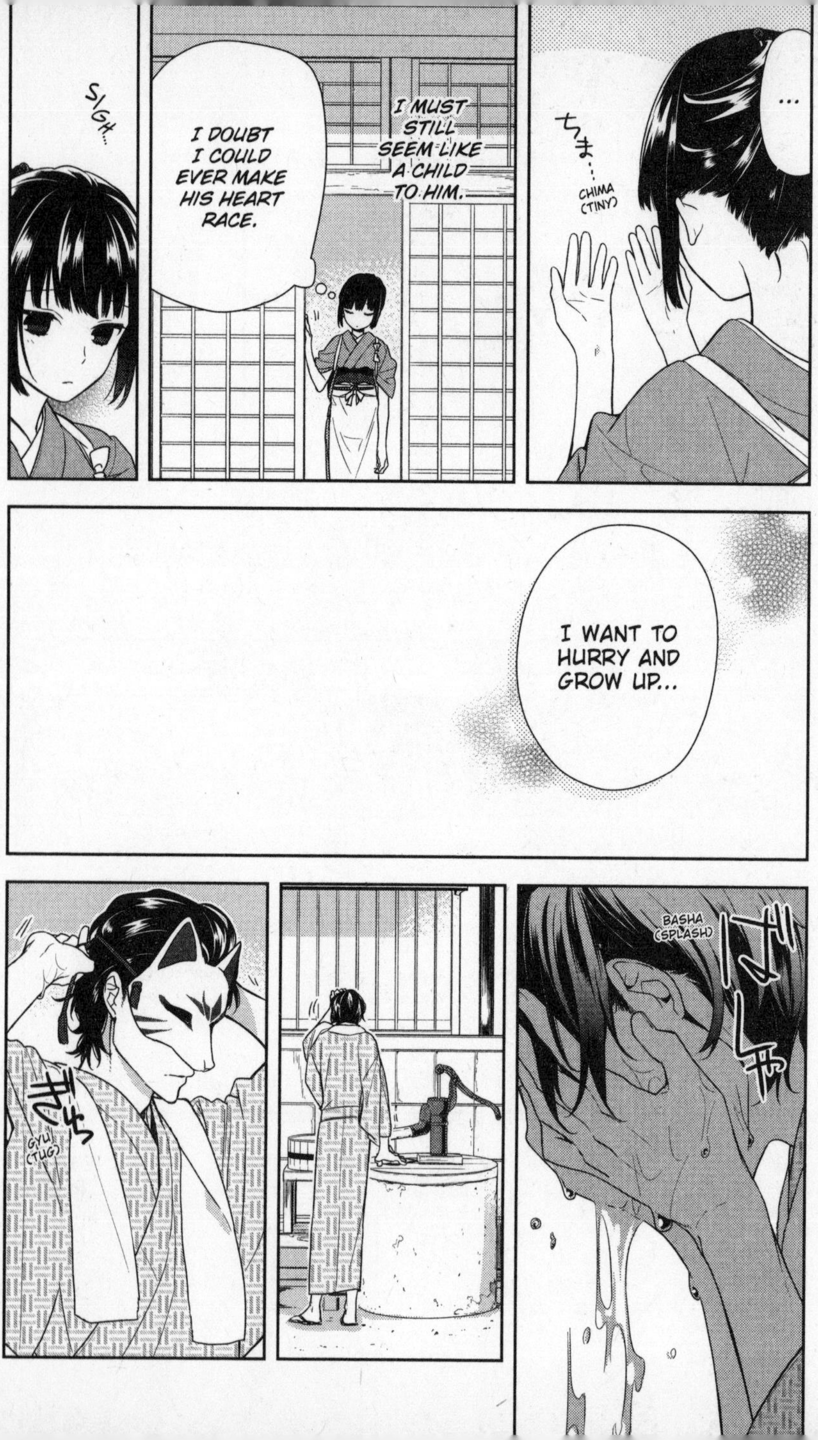
...
ちま…
CHIMA (TINY)
I MUST STILL SEEM LIKE A CHILD TO HIM.
I DOUBT I COULD EVER MAKE HIS HEART RACE.
SIGH...
I WANT TO HURRY AND GROW UP...
BASHA (SPLASH)
GYU (TUG)

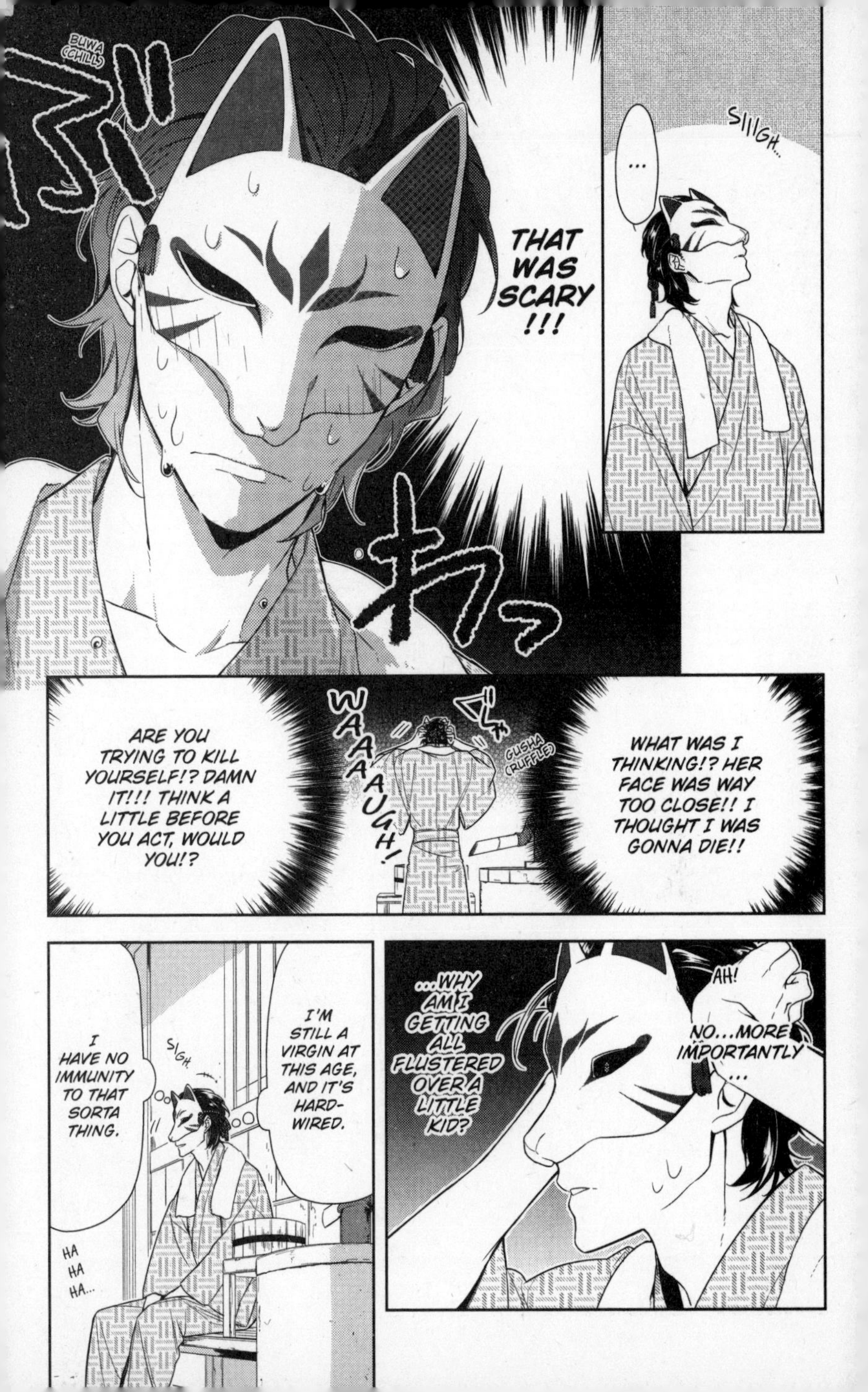
...
SIIIGH...
BUWA (CHILL)
THAT WAS SCARY!!!
WHAT WAS I THINKING!? HER FACE WAS WAY TOO CLOSE!! I THOUGHT I WAS GONNA DIE!!
GUSHA (RUFFLE)
WAAAAUGH!
ARE YOU TRYING TO KILL YOURSELF!? DAMN IT!!! THINK A LITTLE BEFORE YOU ACT, WOULD YOU!?
AH!
NO...MORE IMPORTANTLY...
...WHY AM I GETTING ALL FLUSTERED OVER A LITTLE KID?
I'M STILL A VIRGIN AT THIS AGE, AND IT'S HARD-WIRED.
SIGH
I HAVE NO IMMUNITY TO THAT SORTA THING.
HA HA HA...

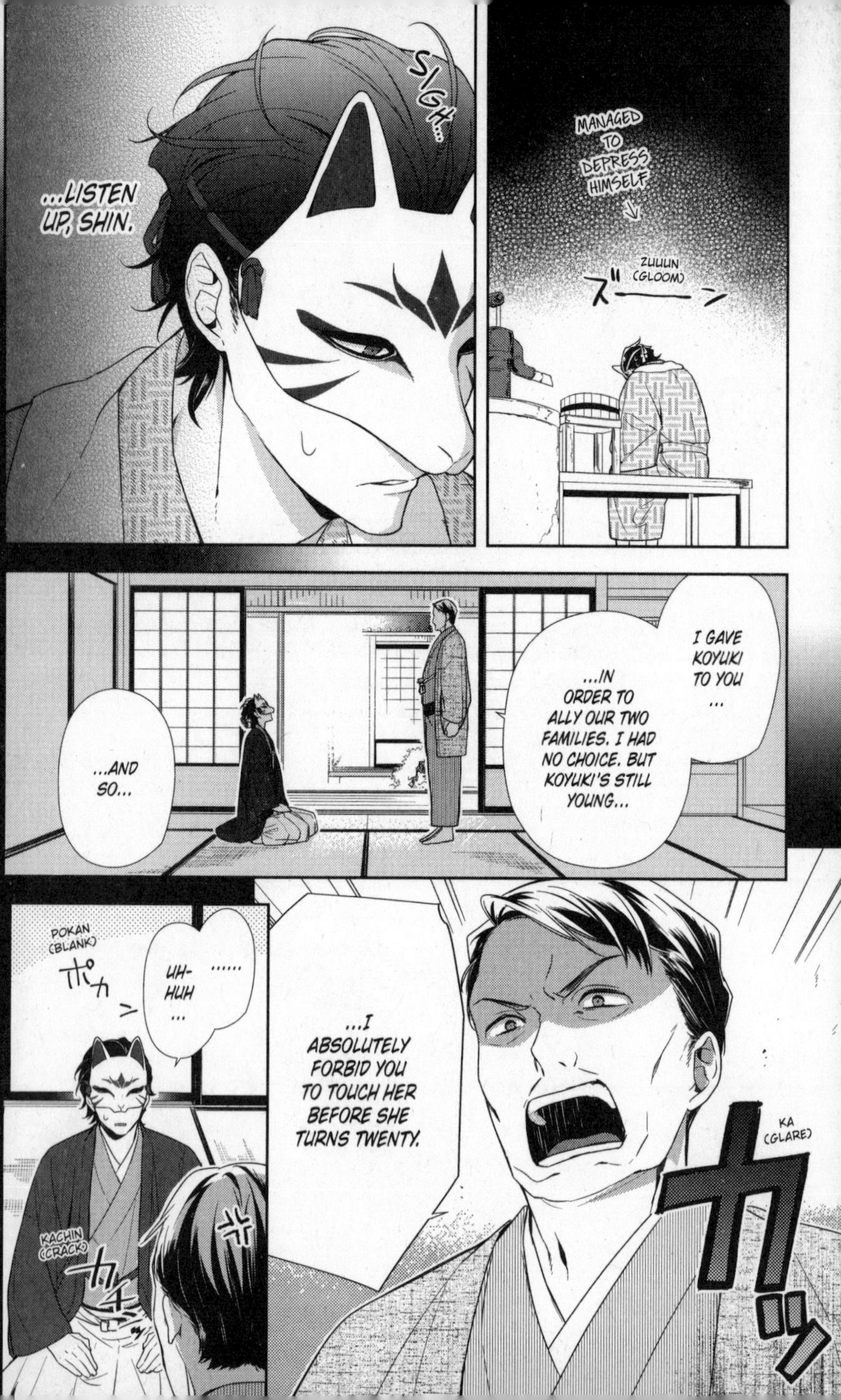
MANAGED TO DEPRESS HIMSELF
ZUUUN (GLOOM)
ズーーン
SIGH...
...LISTEN UP, SHIN.
I GAVE KOYUKI TO YOU ...
...IN ORDER TO ALLY OUR TWO FAMILIES. I HAD NO CHOICE. BUT KOYUKI'S STILL YOUNG...
...AND SO...
...I ABSOLUTELY FORBID YOU TO TOUCH HER BEFORE SHE TURNS TWENTY.
KA (GLARE)
POKAN (BLANK)
ポカン
UH-HUH ...
......
KACHIN (CRACK)

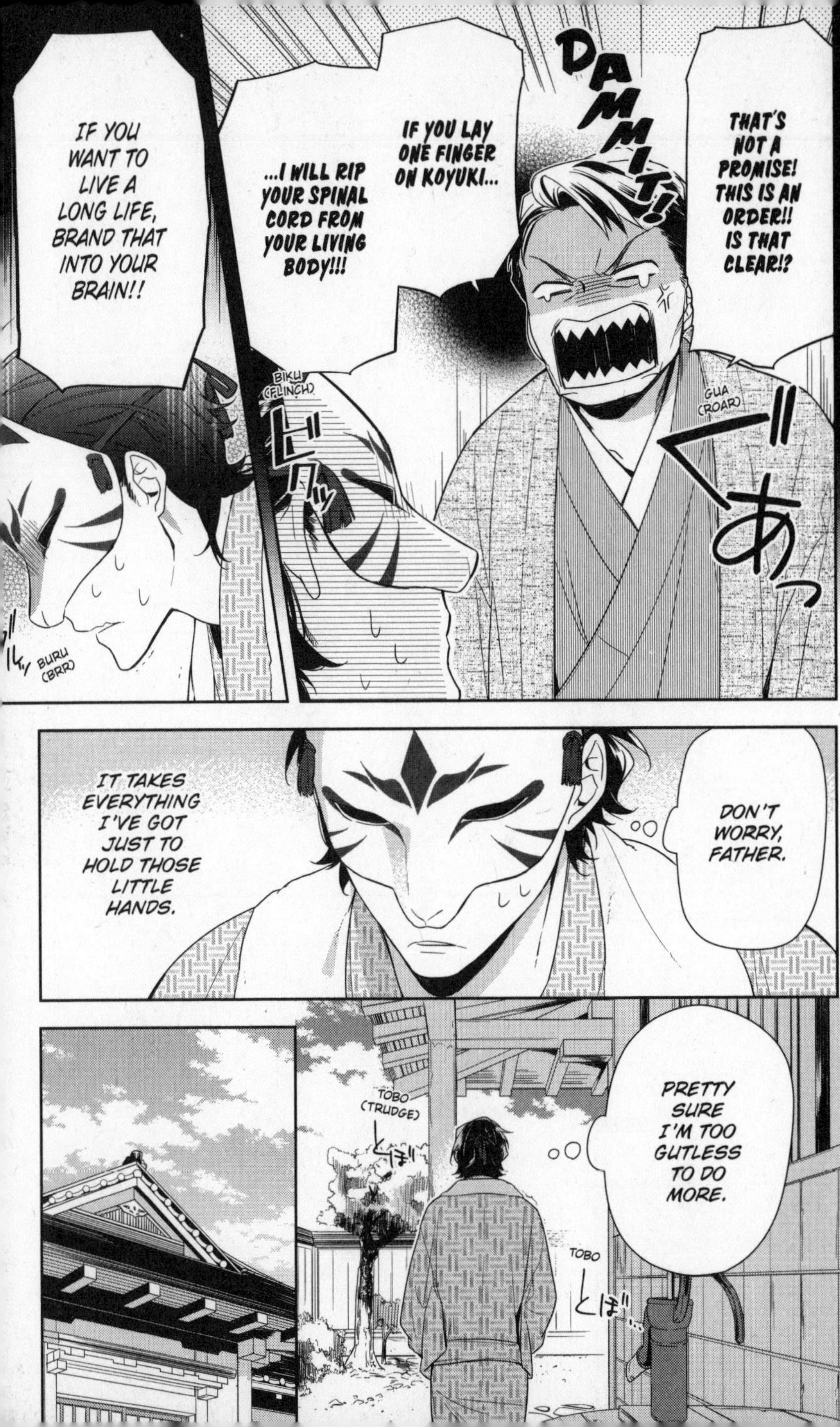
DAMMIT!
THAT'S NOT A PROMISE! THIS IS AN ORDER!! IS THAT CLEAR!?
IF YOU LAY ONE FINGER ON KOYUKI...
...I WILL RIP YOUR SPINAL CORD FROM YOUR LIVING BODY!!!
IF YOU WANT TO LIVE A LONG LIFE, BRAND THAT INTO YOUR BRAIN!!
GUA (ROAR)
ぐあっ
BIKU (FLINCH)
ビクッ
BURU (BRR)
DON'T WORRY, FATHER.
IT TAKES EVERYTHING I'VE GOT JUST TO HOLD THOSE LITTLE HANDS.
PRETTY SURE I'M TOO GUTLESS TO DO MORE.
TOBO (TRUDGE)
とぼ
TOBO
とぼ...

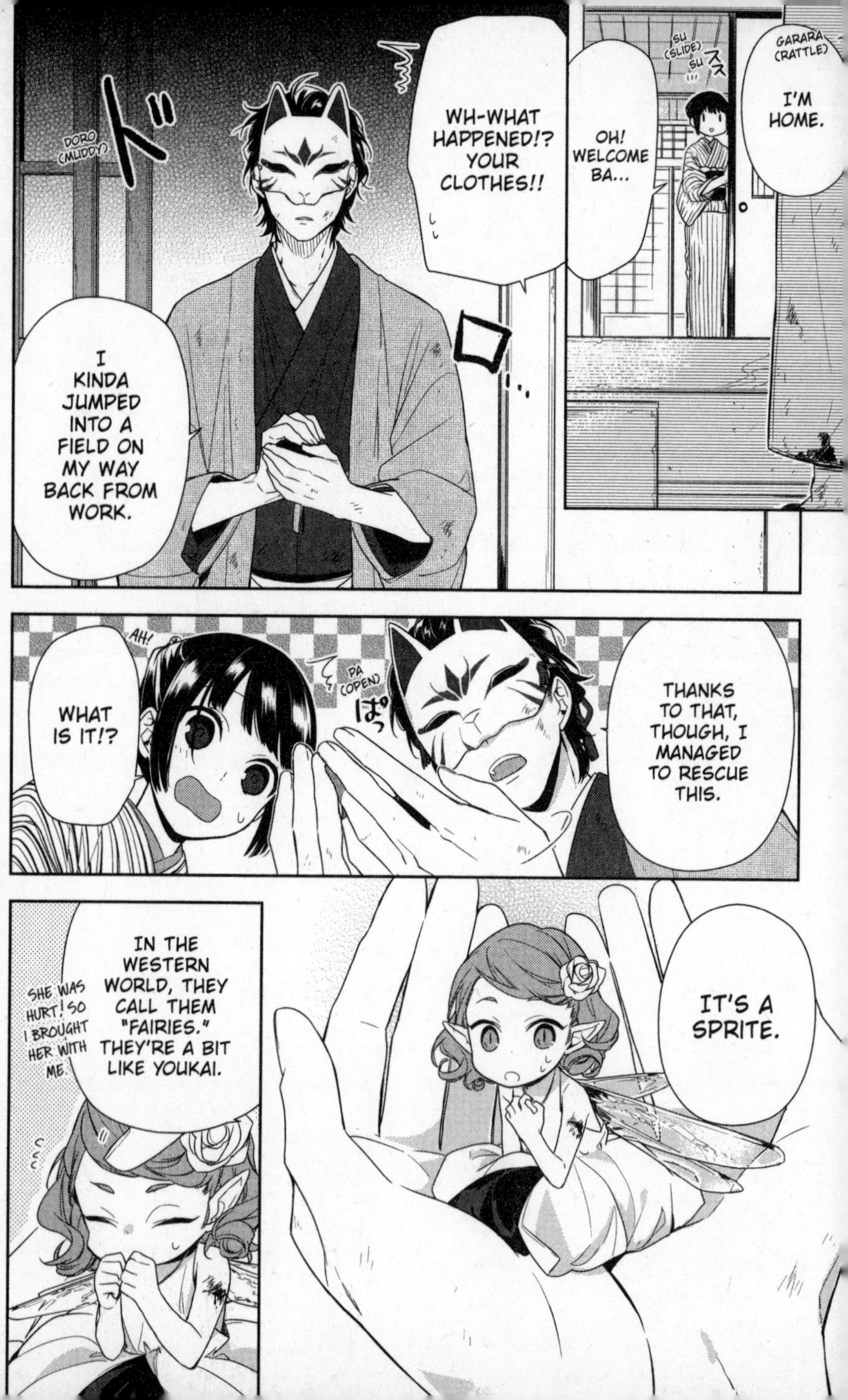
GARARA (RATTLE)
I'M HOME.
SU (SLIDE) SU
スス
OH! WELCOME BA...
WH-WHAT HAPPENED!? YOUR CLOTHES!!
DORO (MUDDY)
ド
I KINDA JUMPED INTO A FIELD ON MY WAY BACK FROM WORK.
THANKS TO THAT, THOUGH, I MANAGED TO RESCUE THIS.
PA (OPEN)
ぱっ
AH!
WHAT IS IT!?
IT'S A SPRITE.
IN THE WESTERN WORLD, THEY CALL THEM "FAIRIES." THEY'RE A BIT LIKE YOUKAI.
SHE WAS HURT, SO I BROUGHT HER WITH ME.

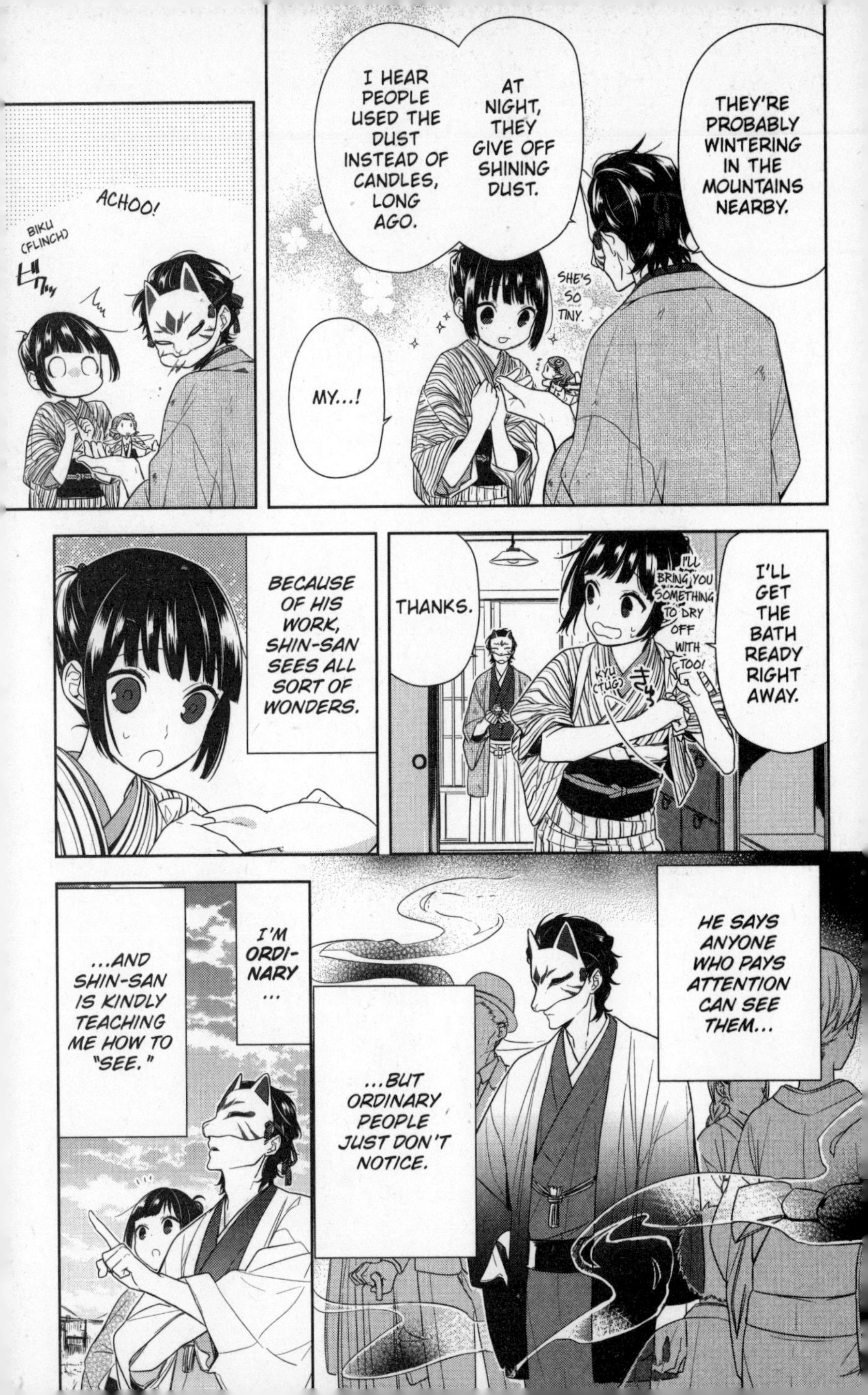
THEY'RE PROBABLY WINTERING IN THE MOUNTAINS NEARBY.
AT NIGHT, THEY GIVE OFF SHINING DUST.
I HEAR PEOPLE USED THE DUST INSTEAD OF CANDLES, LONG AGO.
SHE'S SO TINY.
MY...!
ACHOO!
BIKU (FLINCH)
I'LL GET THE BATH READY RIGHT AWAY.
I'LL BRING YOU SOMETHING TO DRY OFF WITH TOO!
KYU (TUG)
THANKS.
BECAUSE OF HIS WORK, SHIN-SAN SEES ALL SORT OF WONDERS.
HE SAYS ANYONE WHO PAYS ATTENTION CAN SEE THEM...
...BUT ORDINARY PEOPLE JUST DON'T NOTICE.
I'M ORDI-NARY...
...AND SHIN-SAN IS KINDLY TEACHING ME HOW TO "SEE."

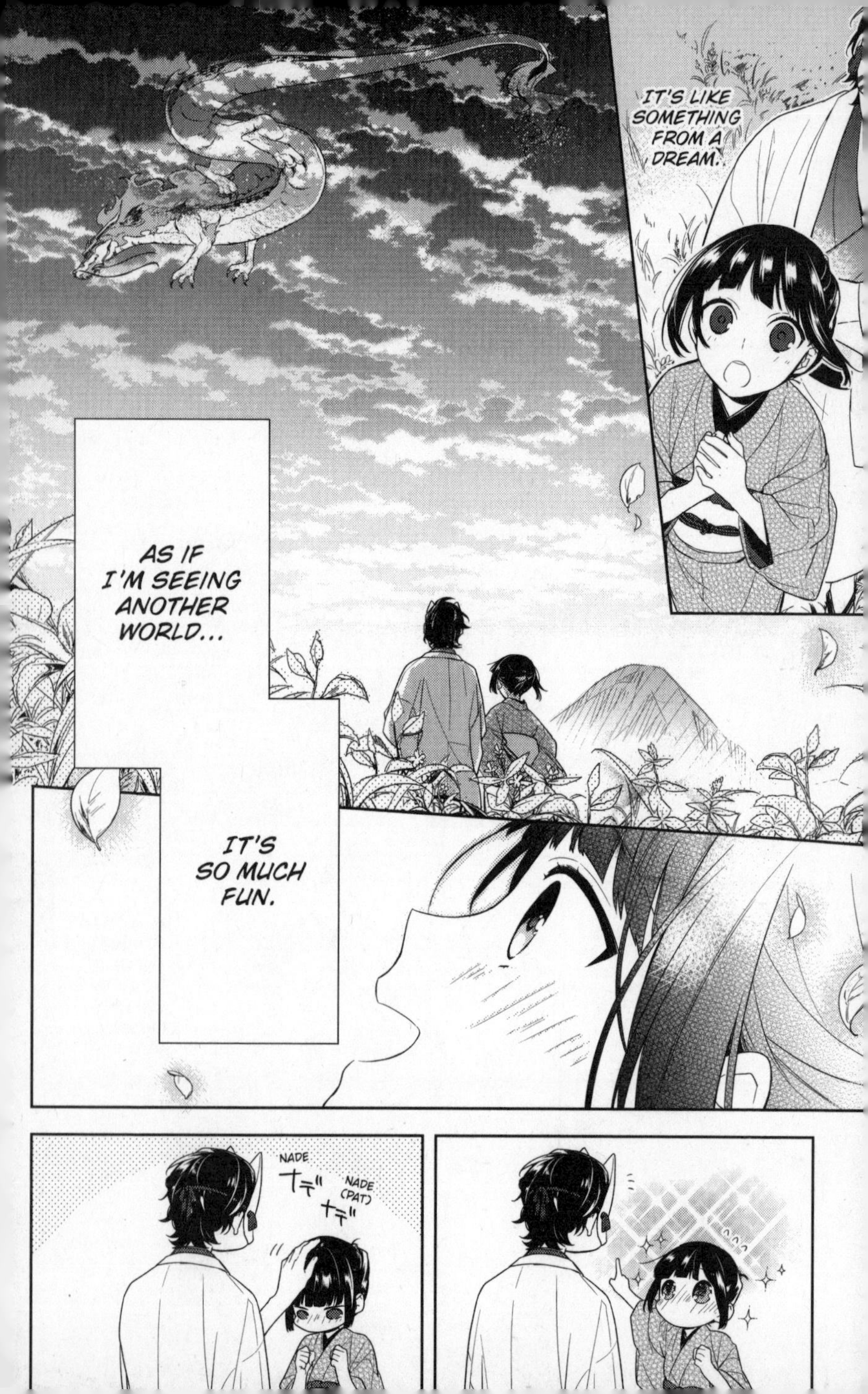
IT'S LIKE SOMETHING FROM A DREAM.
AS IF I'M SEEING ANOTHER WORLD...
IT'S SO MUCH FUN.
NADE
ナデ
NADE (PAT)
ナデ

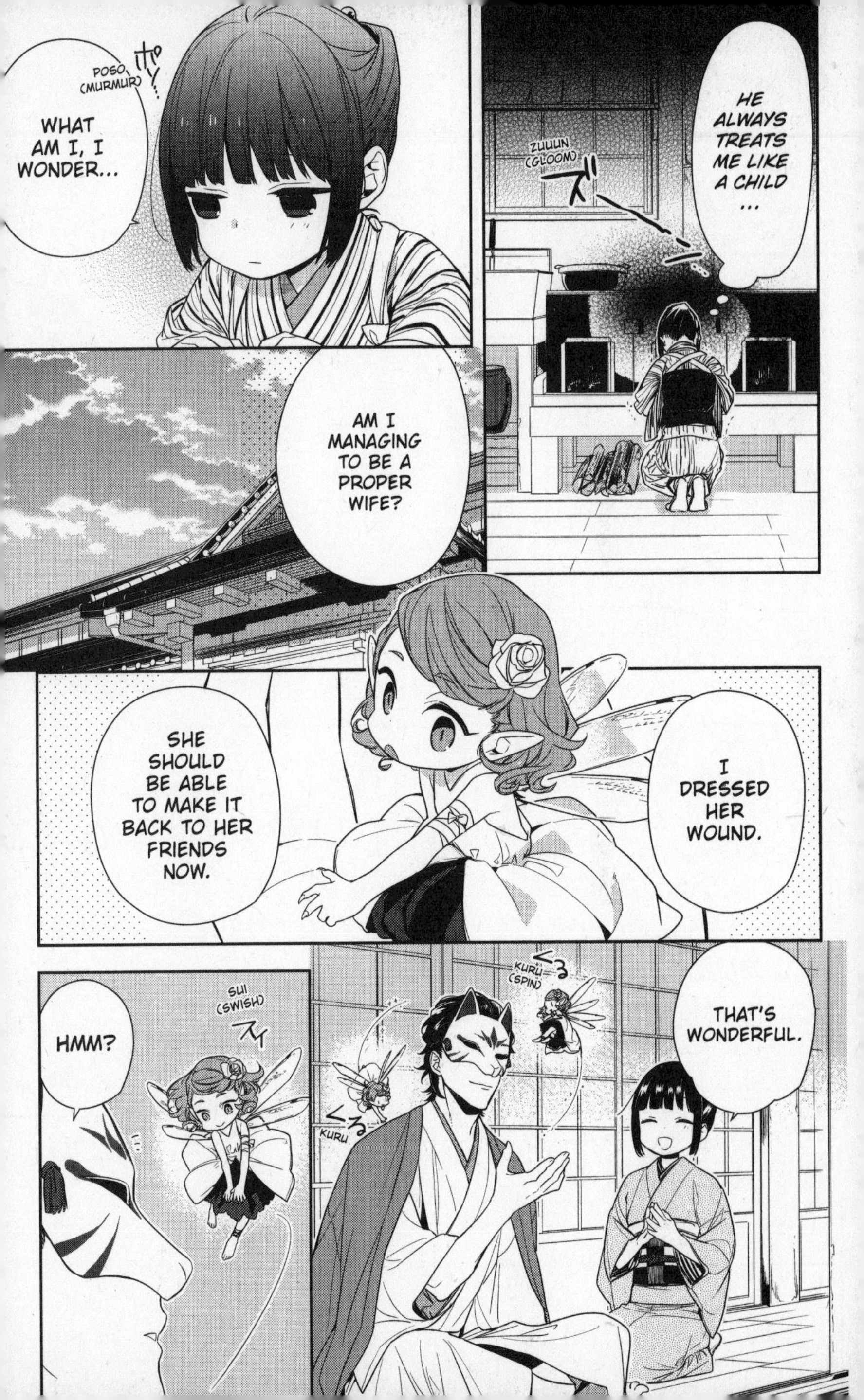
HE ALWAYS TREATS ME LIKE A CHILD ...
ZUUUN (GLOOM)
POSO (MURMUR)
WHAT AM I, I WONDER...
AM I MANAGING TO BE A PROPER WIFE?
I DRESSED HER WOUND.
SHE SHOULD BE ABLE TO MAKE IT BACK TO HER FRIENDS NOW.
THAT'S WONDERFUL.
KURU (SPIN)
KURU
SUI (SWISH)
HMM?

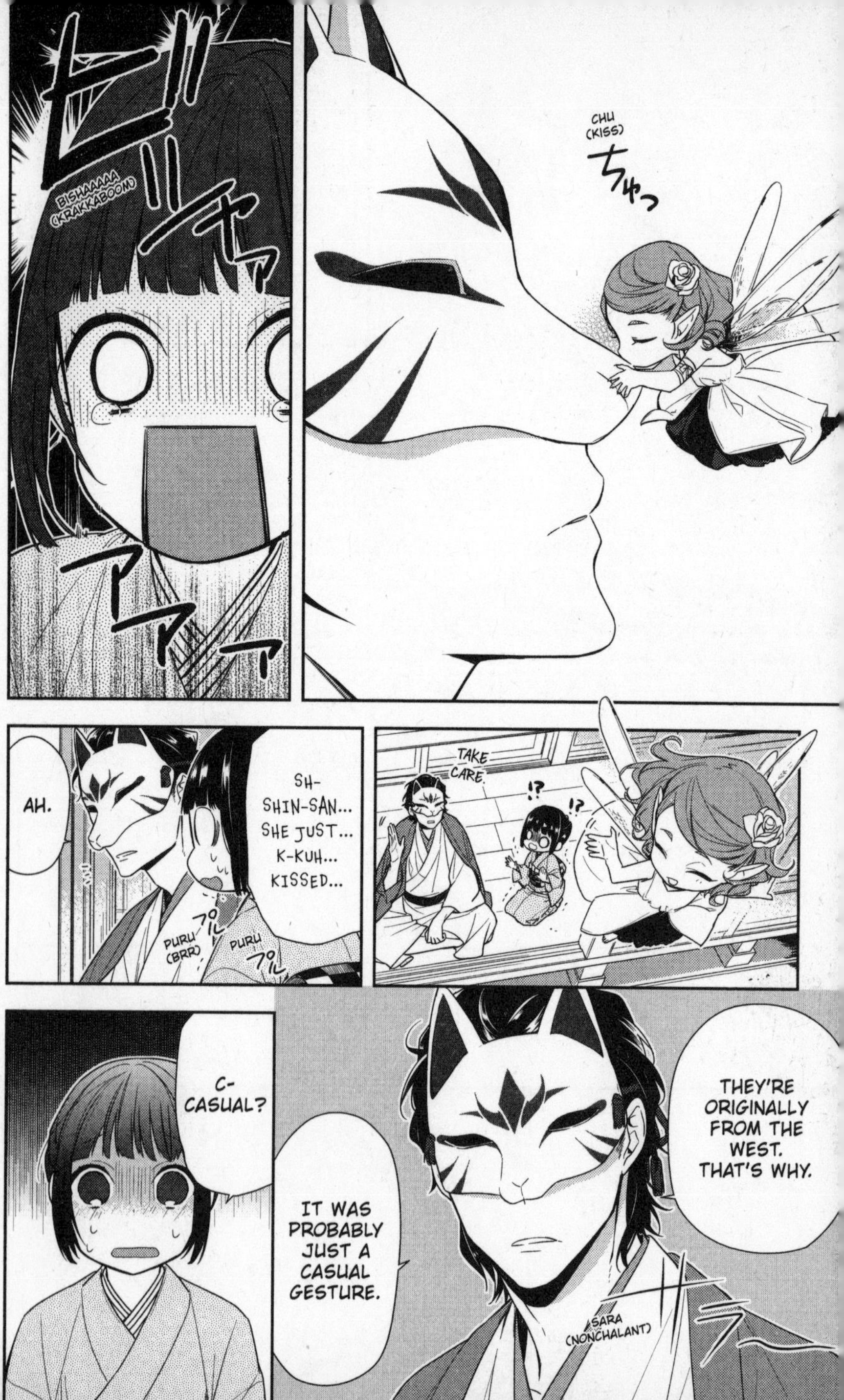
CHU (KISS)
ちゃっ
BISHAAAAA (KRAKKABOOM)
TAKE CARE.
!?
!?
SH-SHIN-SAN... SHE JUST... K-KUH... KISSED...
AH.
PURU (BRR)
プル
PURU
プル
THEY'RE ORIGINALLY FROM THE WEST. THAT'S WHY.
IT WAS PROBABLY JUST A CASUAL GESTURE.
SARA (NONCHALANT)
C-CASUAL?

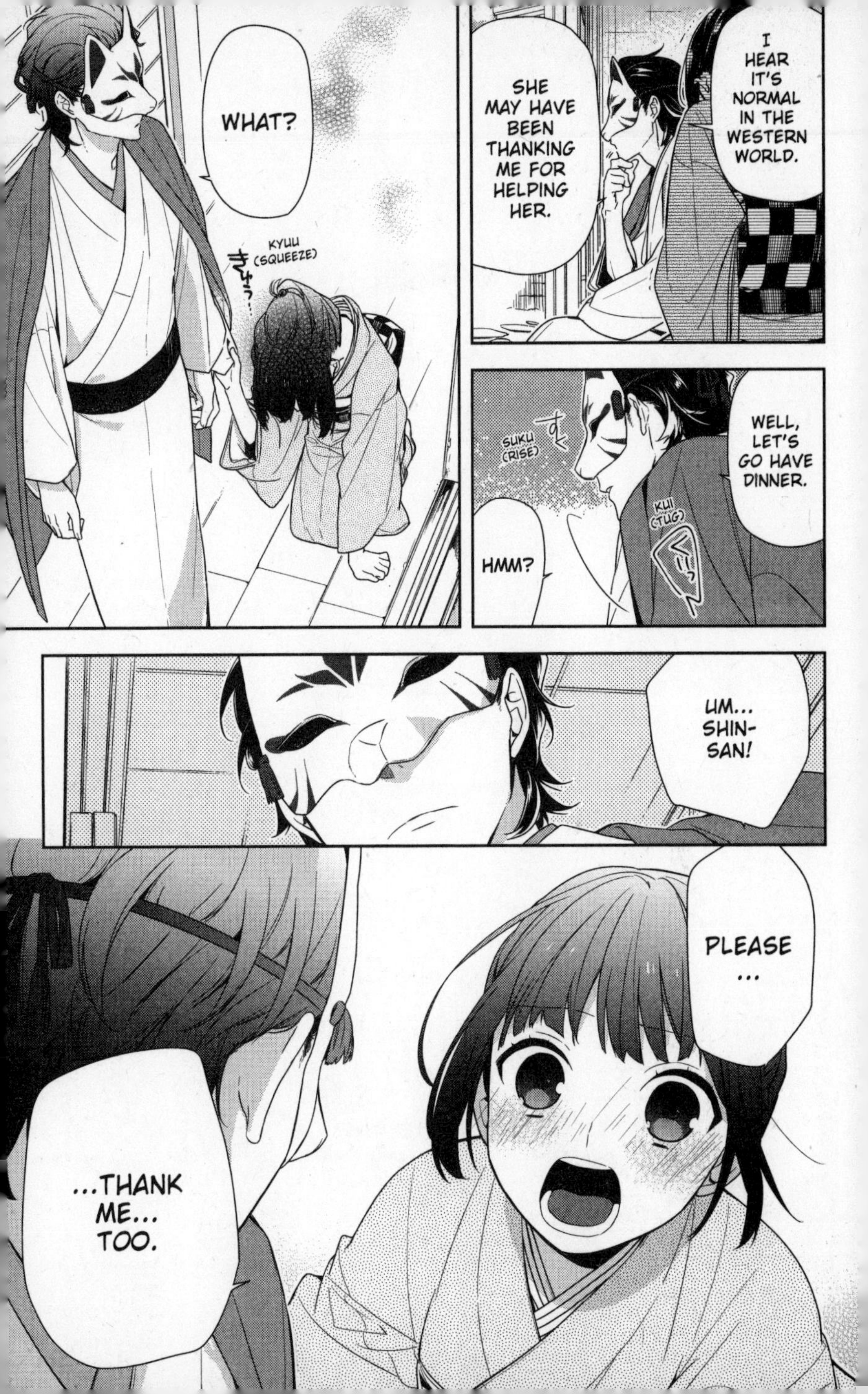
I HEAR IT'S NORMAL IN THE WESTERN WORLD.
SHE MAY HAVE BEEN THANKING ME FOR HELPING HER.
WELL, LET'S GO HAVE DINNER.
SUKU (RISE)
KUI (TUG)
HMM?
WHAT?
KYUU (SQUEEZE)
UM... SHIN-SAN!
PLEASE...
...THANK ME... TOO.

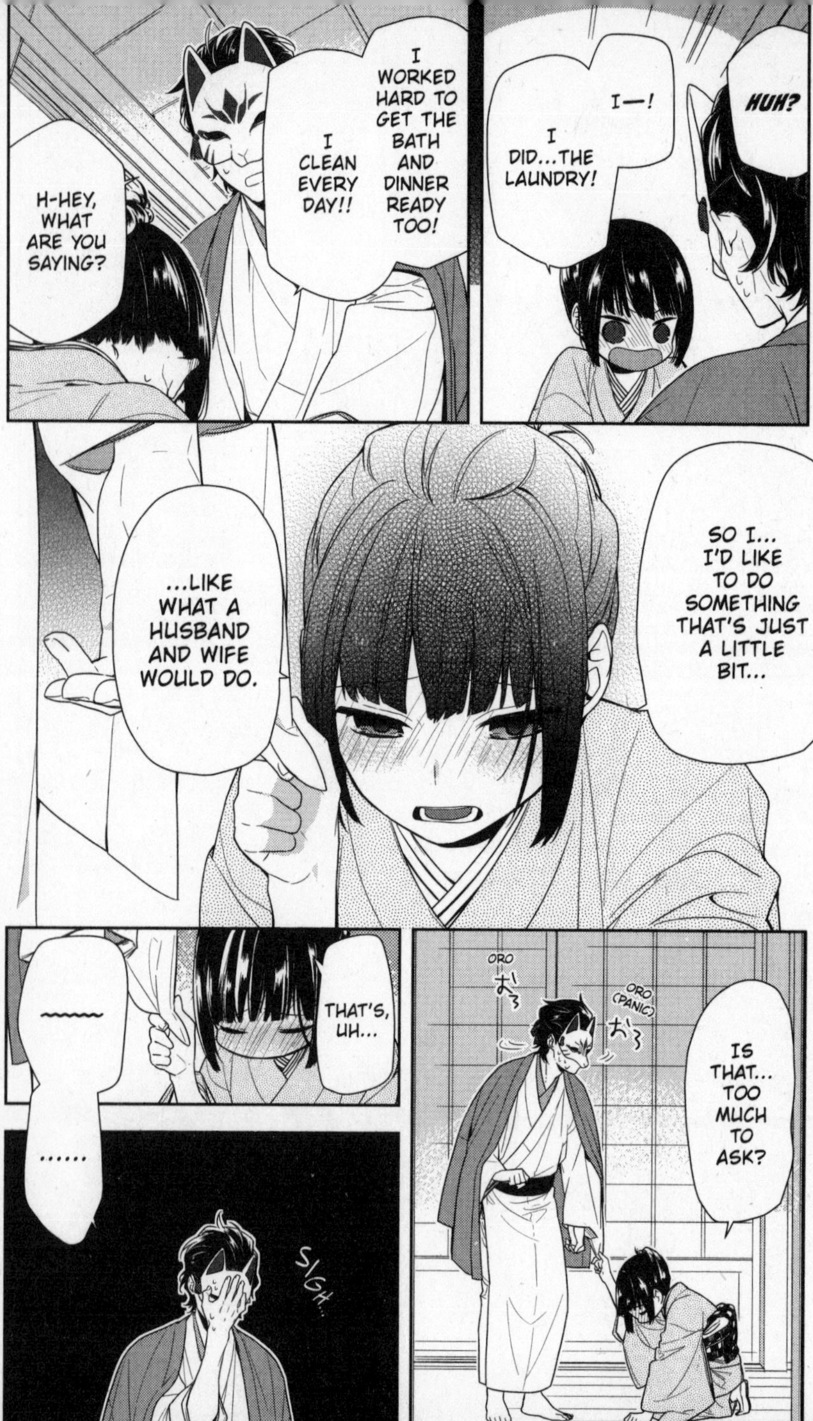
HUH?
I—!
I DID...THE LAUNDRY!
I WORKED HARD TO GET THE BATH AND DINNER READY TOO!
I CLEAN EVERY DAY!!
H-HEY, WHAT ARE YOU SAYING?
SO I... I'D LIKE TO DO SOMETHING THAT'S JUST A LITTLE BIT...
...LIKE WHAT A HUSBAND AND WIFE WOULD DO.
ORO
おろ
ORO (PANIC)
おろ
IS THAT... TOO MUCH TO ASK?
THAT'S, UH...
~~~~~
......
SIGH...
~~~~~

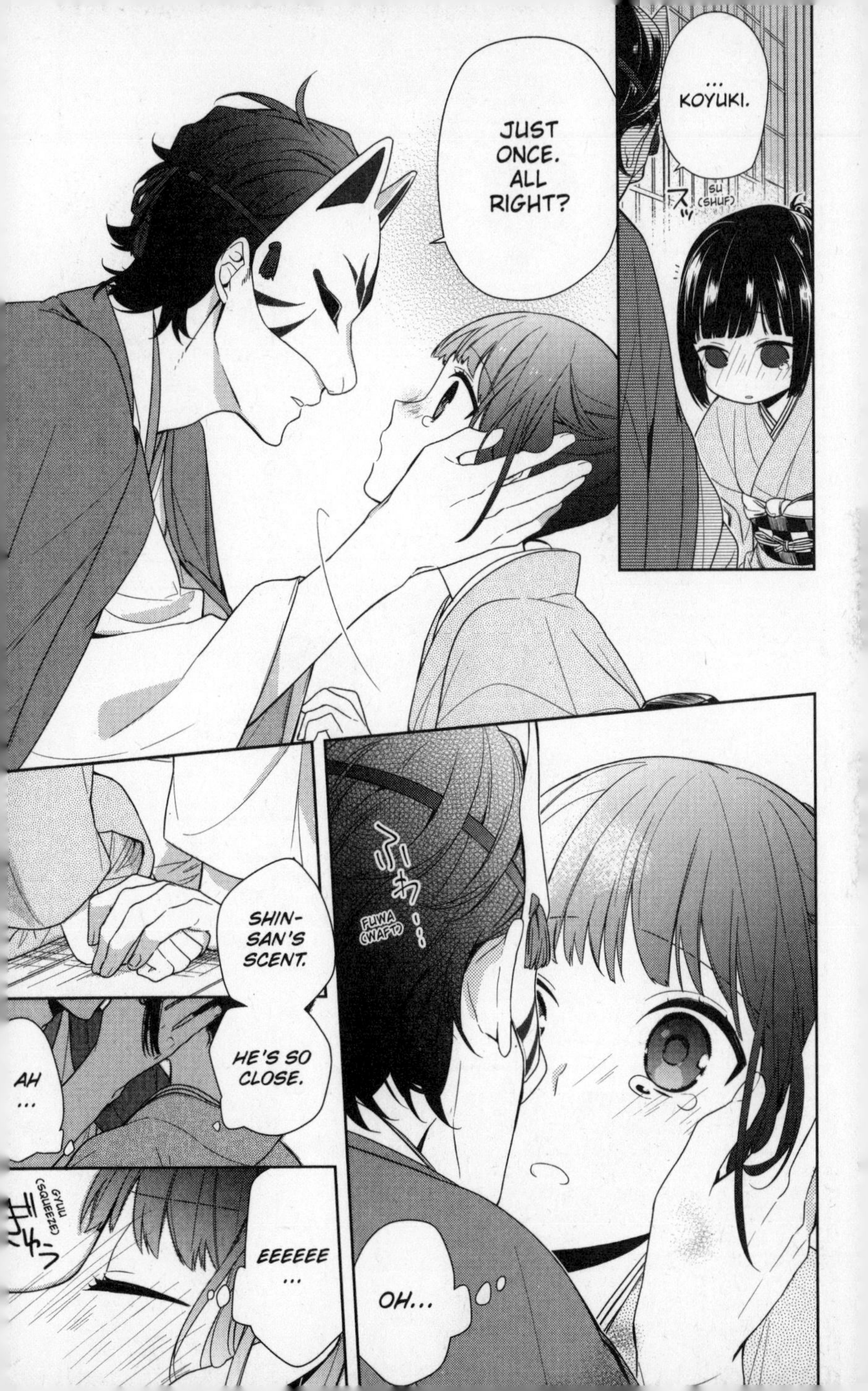
... KOYUKI.
SU (SHUF)
JUST ONCE. ALL RIGHT?
FUWA (WAFT)
SHIN-SAN'S SCENT.
HE'S SO CLOSE.
OH...
AH ...
GYUU (SQUEEZE)
EEEEEE ...

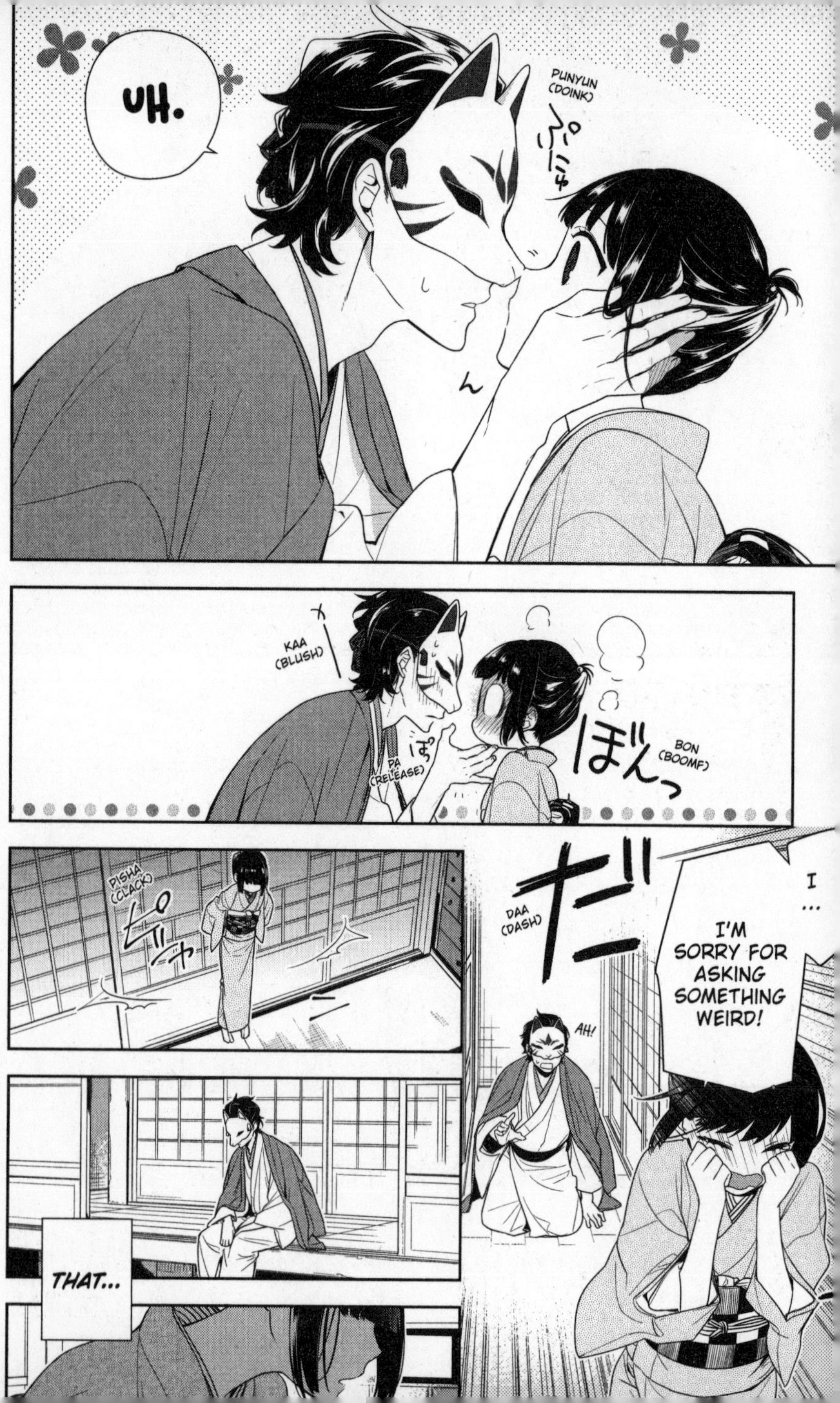
PUNYUN (DOINK)
ぷにゅ
UH.
ん
BON (BOOMF)
ぼんっ
KAA (BLUSH)
カー
PA (RELEASE)
ぱっ
DAA (DASH)
だー
I...
I'M SORRY FOR ASKING SOMETHING WEIRD!
AH!
PISHA (CLACK)
ピシャ
THAT...

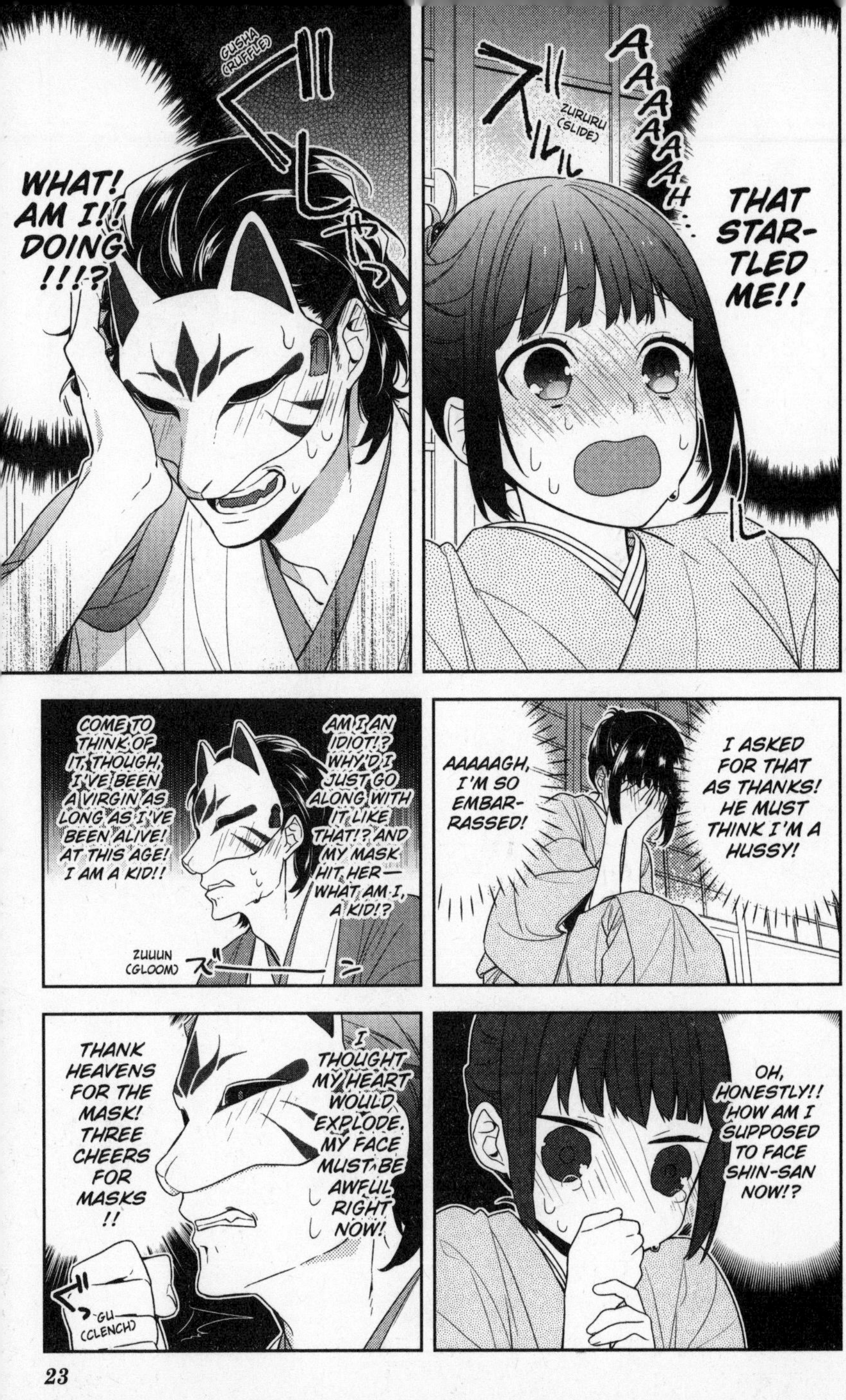
AAAAAAH...
ZURURU (SLIDE)
THAT STARTLED ME!!
GUSHA (RUFFLE)
WHAT! AM I!! DOING !!!?
I ASKED FOR THAT AS THANKS! HE MUST THINK I'M A HUSSY!
AAAAAGH, I'M SO EMBARRASSED!
AM I AN IDIOT!? WHY'D I JUST GO ALONG WITH IT LIKE THAT!? AND MY MASK HIT HER— WHAT AM I, A KID!?
COME TO THINK OF IT, THOUGH, I'VE BEEN A VIRGIN AS LONG AS I'VE BEEN ALIVE! AT THIS AGE! I AM A KID!!
ZUUUN (GLOOM)
OH, HONESTLY!! HOW AM I SUPPOSED TO FACE SHIN-SAN NOW!?
I THOUGHT MY HEART WOULD EXPLODE. MY FACE MUST BE AWFUL RIGHT NOW!
THANK HEAVENS FOR THE MASK! THREE CHEERS FOR MASKS !!
GU (CLENCH)

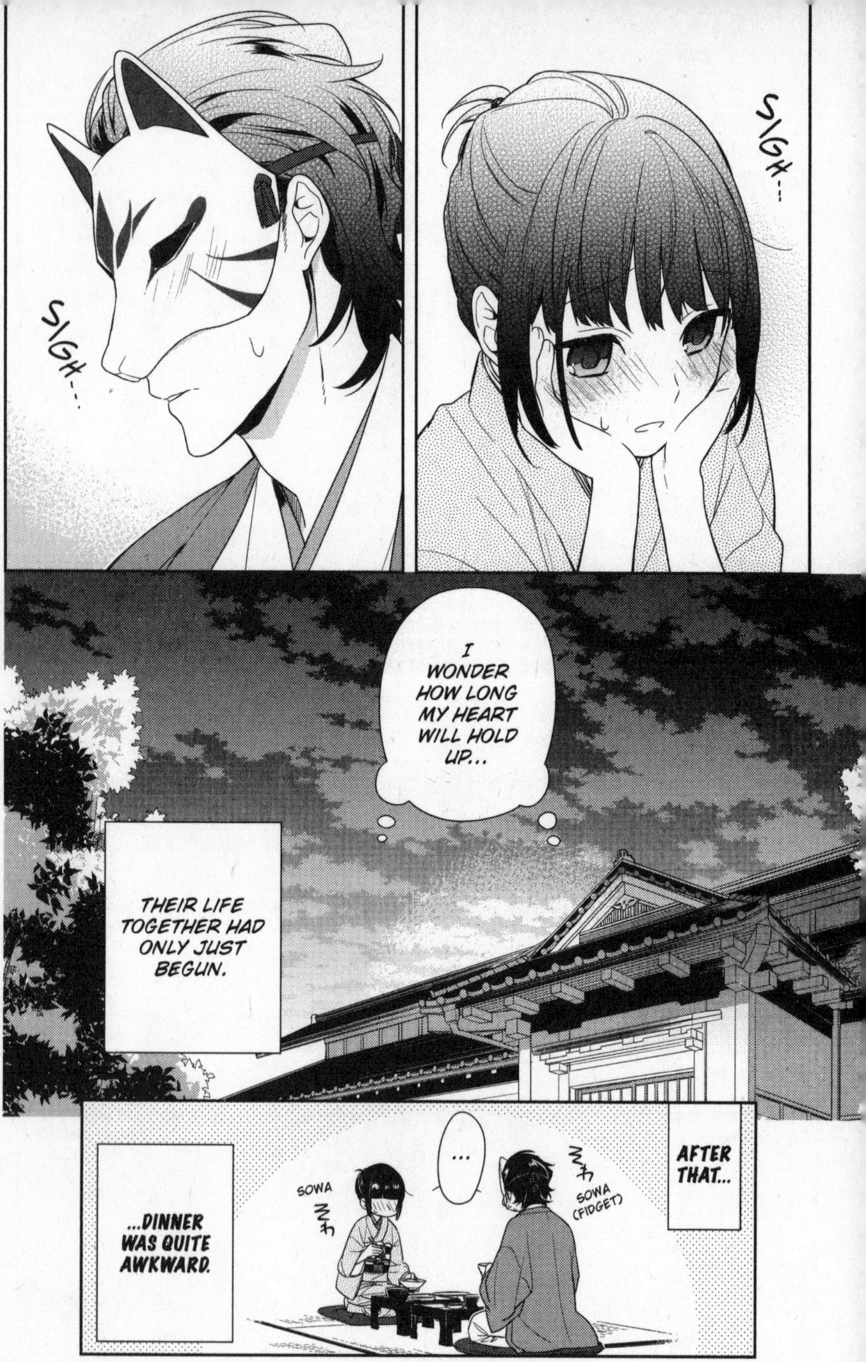
SIGH...
SIGH...
I WONDER HOW LONG MY HEART WILL HOLD UP...
THEIR LIFE TOGETHER HAD ONLY JUST BEGUN.
AFTER THAT...
SOWA (FIDGET)
...
SOWA
...DINNER WAS QUITE AWKWARD.

Ne Ne Ne

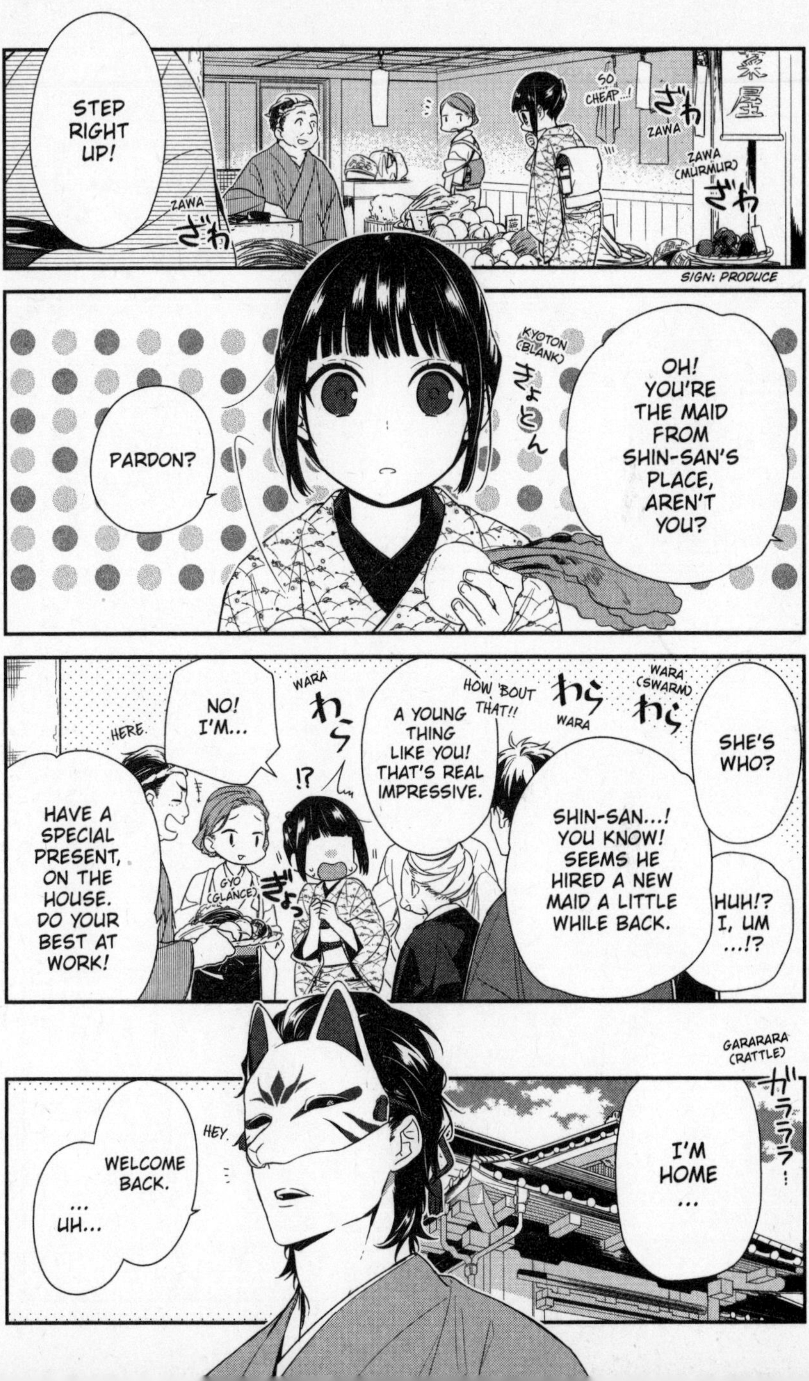
SO CHEAP...!
ZAWA ざわ
ZAWA (MURMUR) ざわ
STEP RIGHT UP!
ZAWA ざわ
SIGN: PRODUCE
OH! YOU'RE THE MAID FROM SHIN-SAN'S PLACE, AREN'T YOU?
KYOTON (BLANK) きょとん
PARDON?
SHE'S WHO?
HUH!? I, UM ...!?
WARA (SWARM) わら
WARA わら
SHIN-SAN...! YOU KNOW! SEEMS HE HIRED A NEW MAID A LITTLE WHILE BACK.
HOW 'BOUT THAT!!
A YOUNG THING LIKE YOU! THAT'S REAL IMPRESSIVE.
WARA わら
!?
NO! I'M...
HERE.
GYO (GLANCE) ぎょっ
HAVE A SPECIAL PRESENT, ON THE HOUSE. DO YOUR BEST AT WORK!
GARARARA (RATTLE) ガラララ…
I'M HOME ...
HEY.
WELCOME BACK. ... UH...

Chapter 2

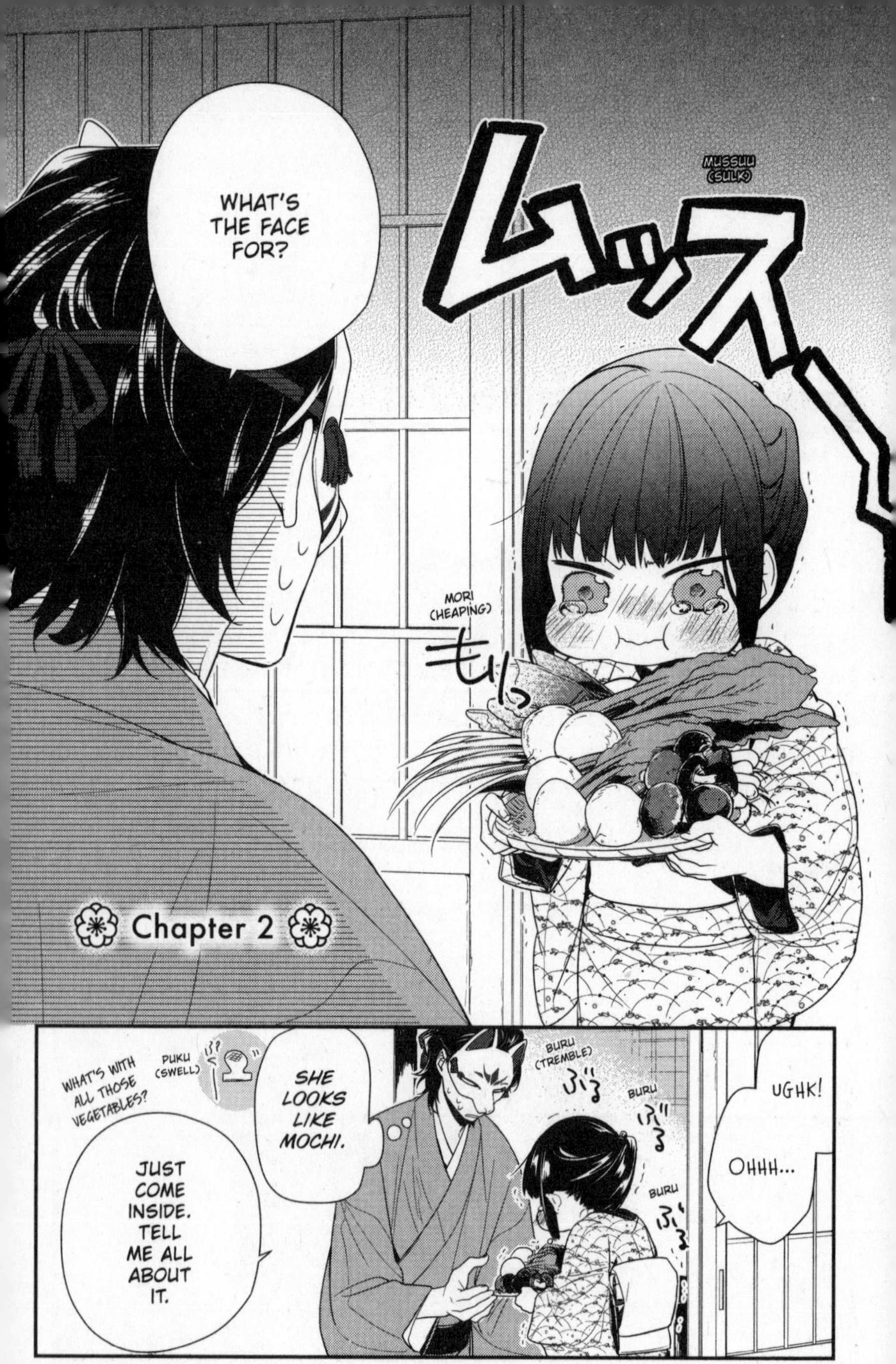
MUSSUU (SULK)
ムッスー
WHAT'S THE FACE FOR?
MORI (HEAPING)
もりっ
UGHK!
OHHH...
BURU (TREMBLE)
ぶる
BURU
ぶる
BURU
ぶる
SHE LOOKS LIKE MOCHI.
PUKU (SWELL)
WHAT'S WITH ALL THOSE VEGETABLES?
JUST COME INSIDE. TELL ME ALL ABOUT IT.

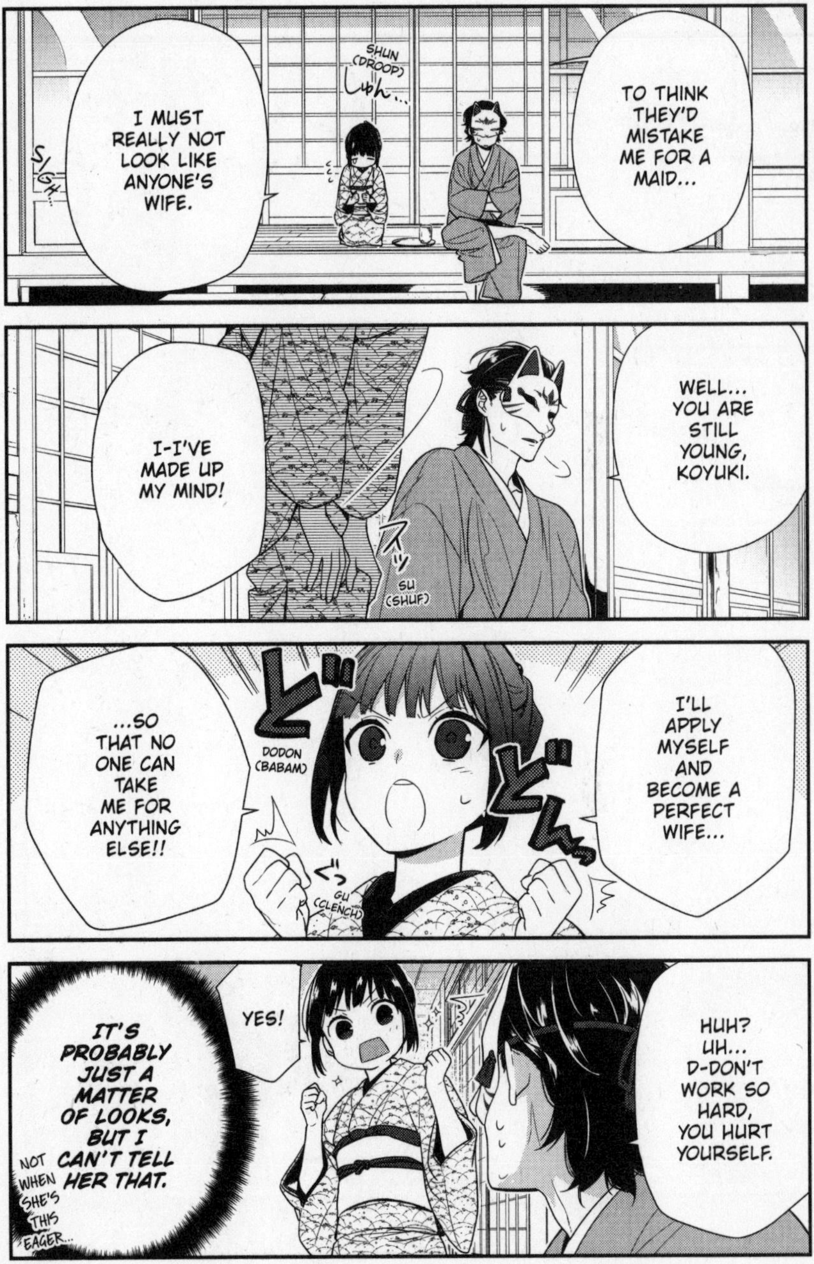
TO THINK THEY'D MISTAKE ME FOR A MAID...
SHUN (DROOP)
I MUST REALLY NOT LOOK LIKE ANYONE'S WIFE.
SIGH...
WELL... YOU ARE STILL YOUNG, KOYUKI.
SU (SHUF)
I-I'VE MADE UP MY MIND!
I'LL APPLY MYSELF AND BECOME A PERFECT WIFE...
DODON (BABAM)
...SO THAT NO ONE CAN TAKE ME FOR ANYTHING ELSE!!
GU (CLENCH)
HUH? UH... D-DON'T WORK SO HARD, YOU HURT YOURSELF.
YES!
IT'S PROBABLY JUST A MATTER OF LOOKS, BUT I CAN'T TELL HER THAT.
NOT WHEN SHE'S THIS EAGER...

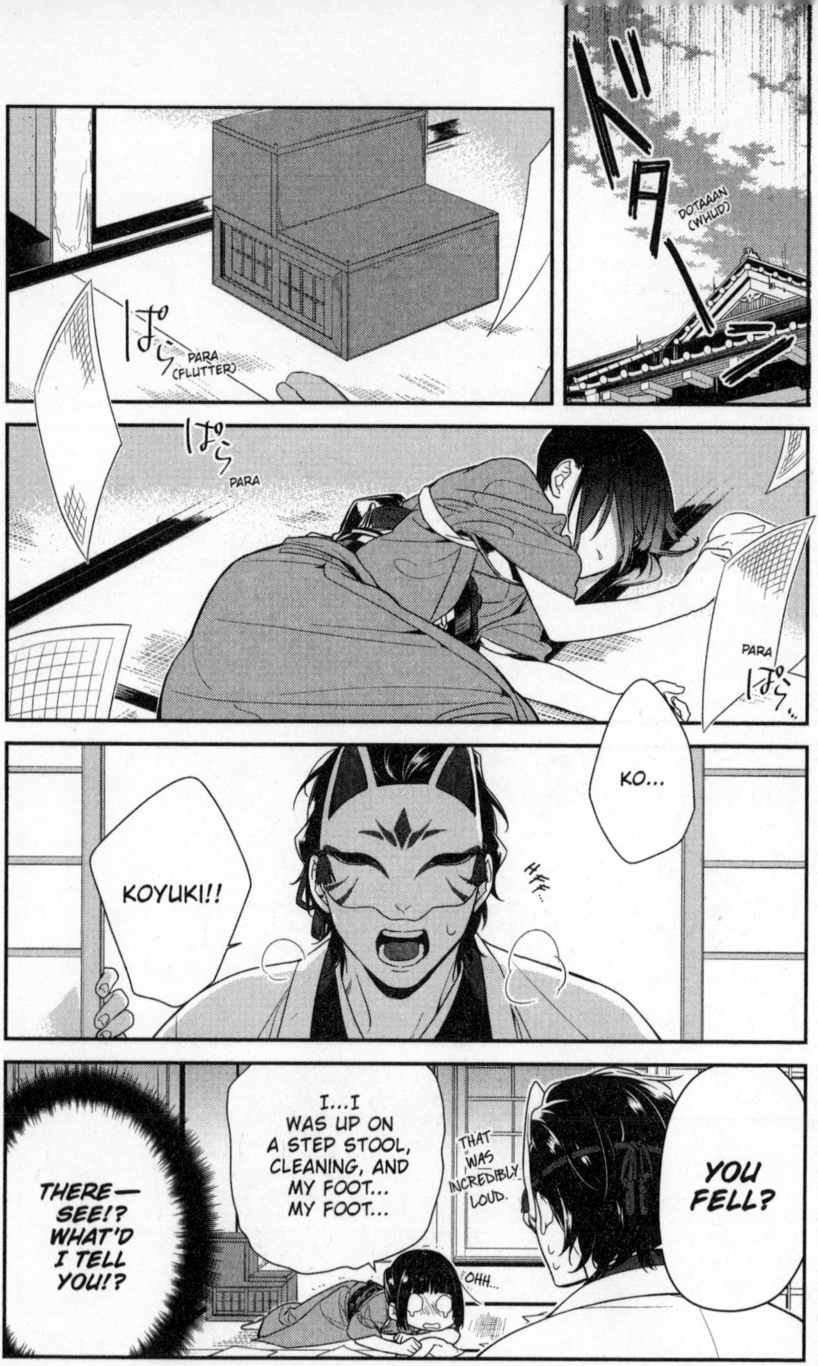
ドタ
DOTAAAN (WHUD)
ぱら
PARA (FLUTTER)
PARA
ぱら
ぱら
PARA
KO...
HFF...
KOYUKI!!
YOU FELL?
THAT WAS INCREDIBLY LOUD.
I...I WAS UP ON A STEP STOOL, CLEANING, AND MY FOOT... MY FOOT...
OHH...
THERE—SEE!? WHAT'D I TELL YOU!?

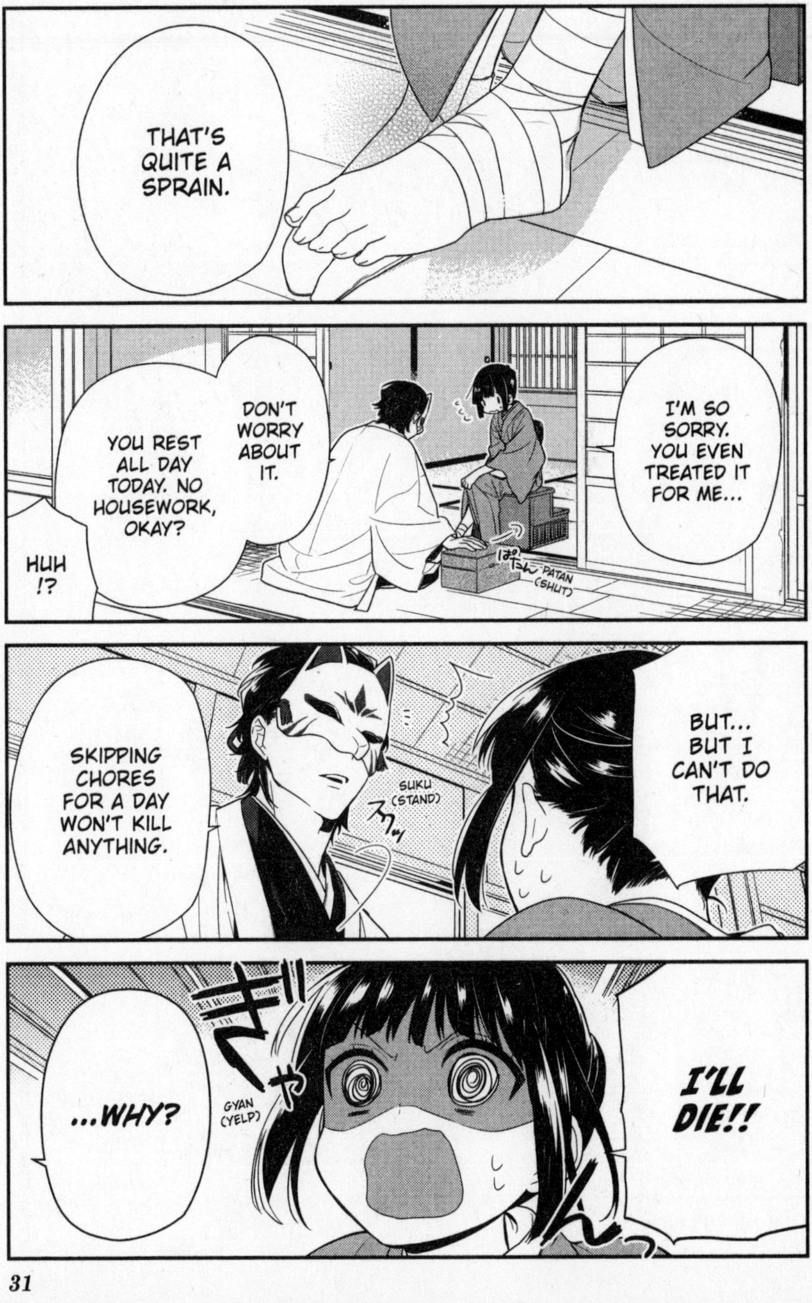
THAT'S QUITE A SPRAIN.
I'M SO SORRY. YOU EVEN TREATED IT FOR ME...
PATAN (SHUT)
DON'T WORRY ABOUT IT.
YOU REST ALL DAY TODAY. NO HOUSEWORK, OKAY?
HUH!?
BUT... BUT I CAN'T DO THAT.
SUKU (STAND)
SKIPPING CHORES FOR A DAY WON'T KILL ANYTHING.
I'LL DIE!!
GYAN (YELP)
...WHY?

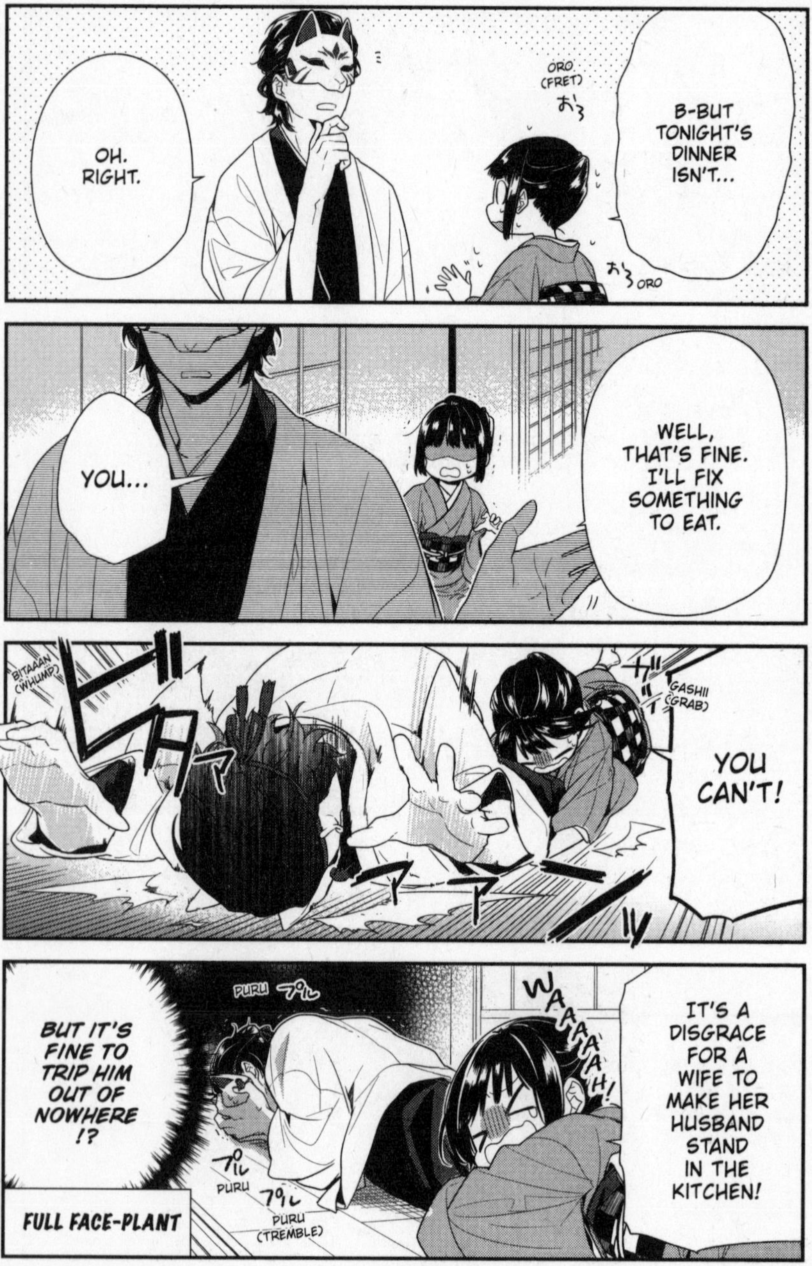
B-BUT TONIGHT'S DINNER ISN'T...
ORO (FRET)
おろ
おろ ORO
OH. RIGHT.
WELL, THAT'S FINE. I'LL FIX SOMETHING TO EAT.
YOU...
GASHII (GRAB)
YOU CAN'T!
BITAAAN (WHUMP)
IT'S A DISGRACE FOR A WIFE TO MAKE HER HUSBAND STAND IN THE KITCHEN!
WAAAAAH!
PURU プル
BUT IT'S FINE TO TRIP HIM OUT OF NOWHERE!?
プル PURU
プル PURU (TREMBLE)
FULL FACE-PLANT

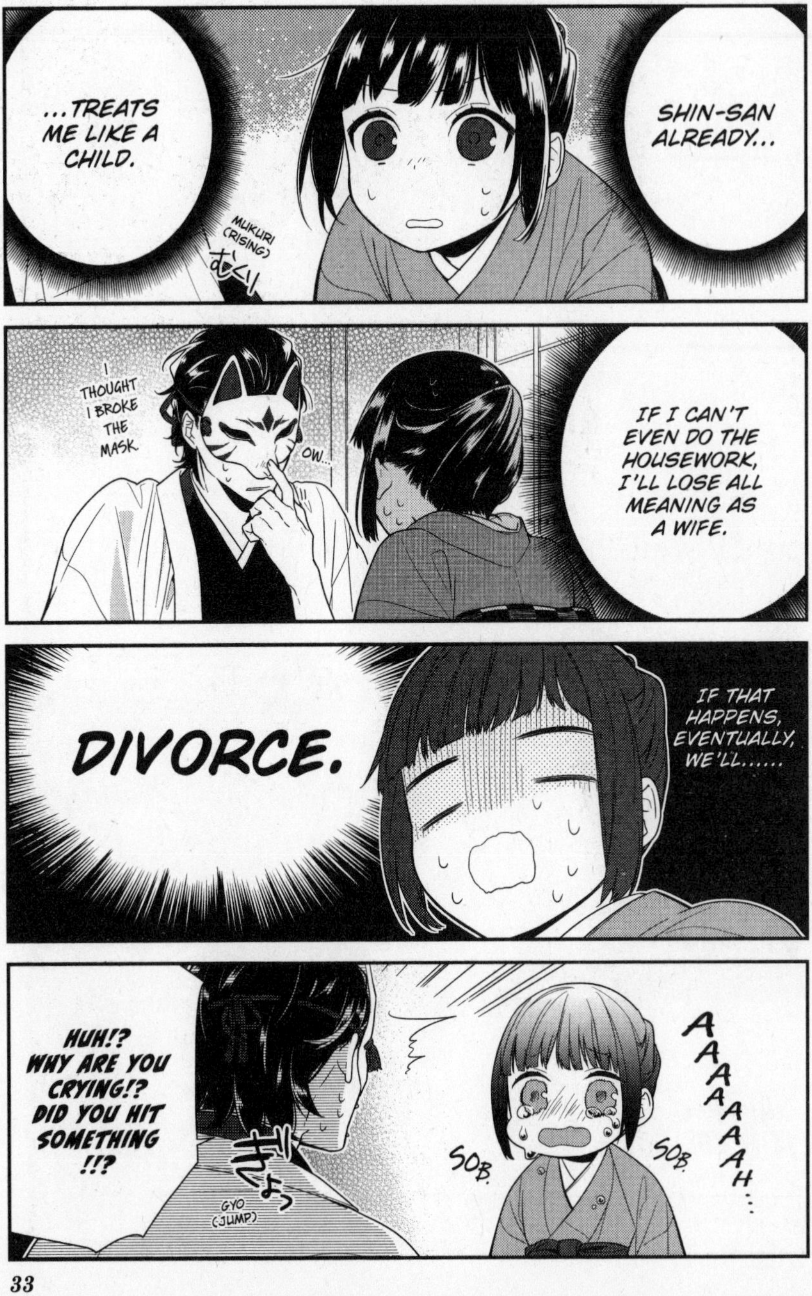
SHIN-SAN ALREADY...
...TREATS ME LIKE A CHILD.
MUKURI (RISING)
むくり
IF I CAN'T EVEN DO THE HOUSEWORK, I'LL LOSE ALL MEANING AS A WIFE.
OW...
I THOUGHT I BROKE THE MASK.
IF THAT HAPPENS, EVENTUALLY, WE'LL......
DIVORCE.
AAAAAAAH...
SOB
SOB
GYO (JUMP)
ぎょっ
HUH!? WHY ARE YOU CRYING!? DID YOU HIT SOMETHING!!?

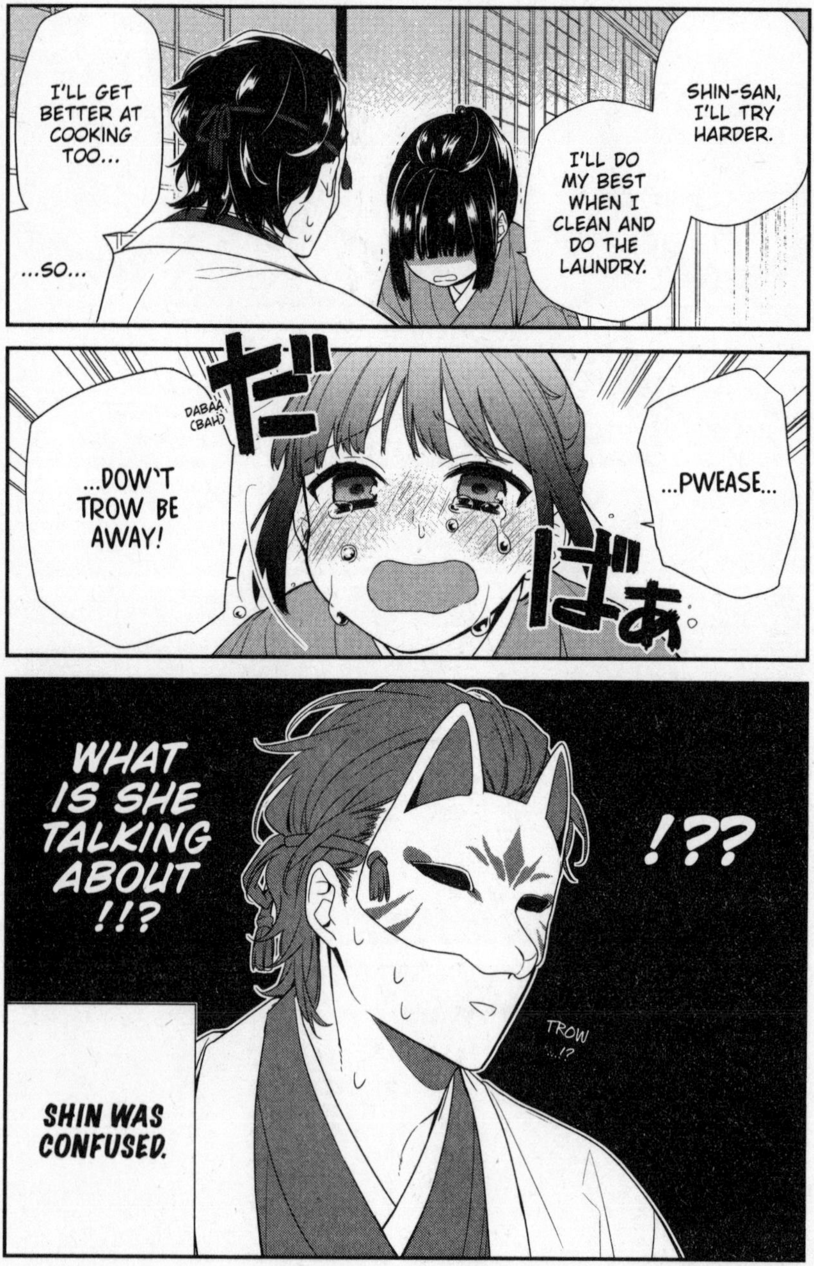
SHIN-SAN, I'LL TRY HARDER.
I'LL DO MY BEST WHEN I CLEAN AND DO THE LAUNDRY.
I'LL GET BETTER AT COOKING TOO...
...SO...
...PWEASE...
だばぁ
DABAA (BAH)
...DOW'T TROW BE AWAY!
!??
WHAT IS SHE TALKING ABOUT!!?
TROW ...!?
SHIN WAS CONFUSED.

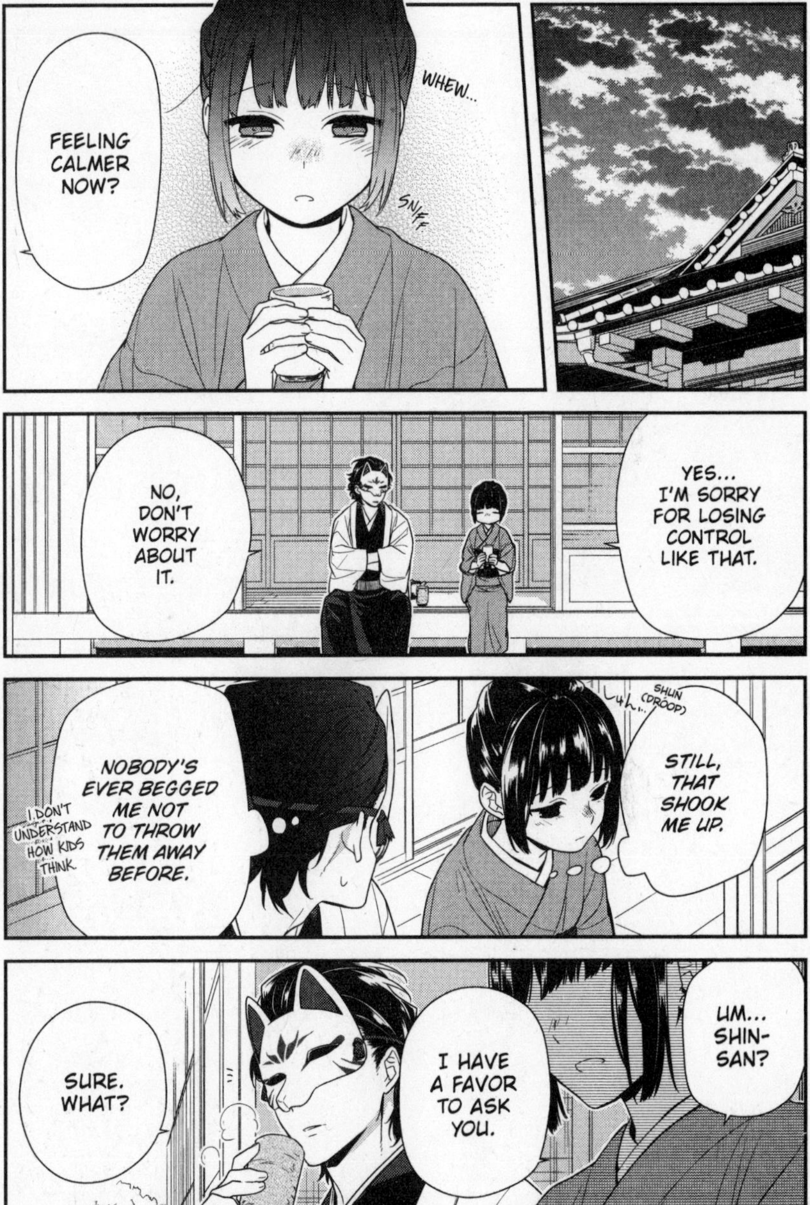
WHEW...
SNIFF
FEELING CALMER NOW?
YES... I'M SORRY FOR LOSING CONTROL LIKE THAT.
NO, DON'T WORRY ABOUT IT.
しゅん...
SHUN (DROOP)
STILL, THAT SHOOK ME UP.
NOBODY'S EVER BEGGED ME NOT TO THROW THEM AWAY BEFORE.
I DON'T UNDERSTAND HOW KIDS THINK.
UM... SHIN-SAN?
I HAVE A FAVOR TO ASK YOU.
SURE. WHAT?

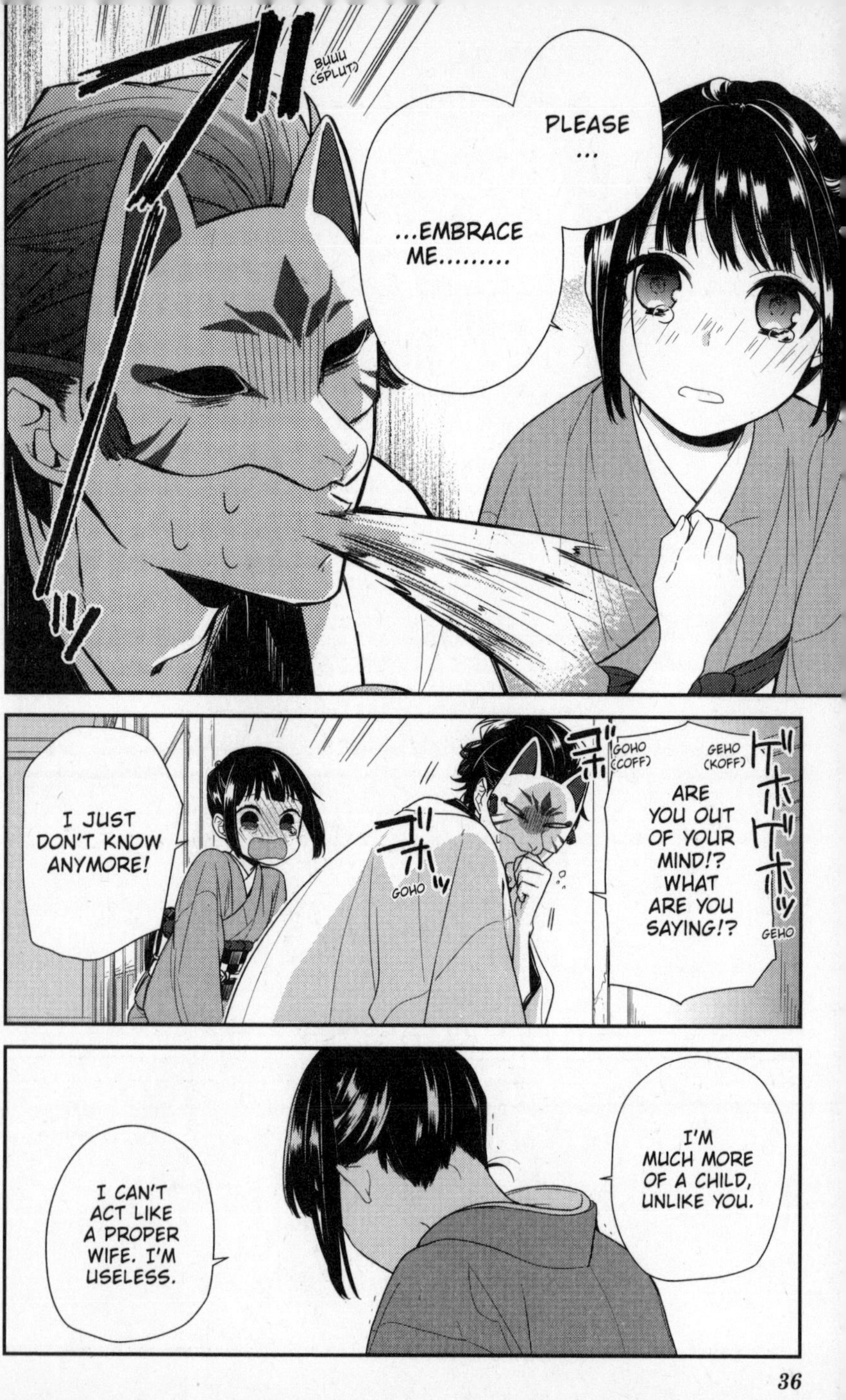
PLEASE
...
...EMBRACE ME.........
BUUU (SPLUT)
GEHO (KOFF)
ゲホゲホッ
GEHO
ARE YOU OUT OF YOUR MIND!? WHAT ARE YOU SAYING!?
ゴボ
GOHO (COFF)
ゴホッ
GOHO
I JUST DON'T KNOW ANYMORE!
I'M MUCH MORE OF A CHILD, UNLIKE YOU.
I CAN'T ACT LIKE A PROPER WIFE. I'M USELESS.

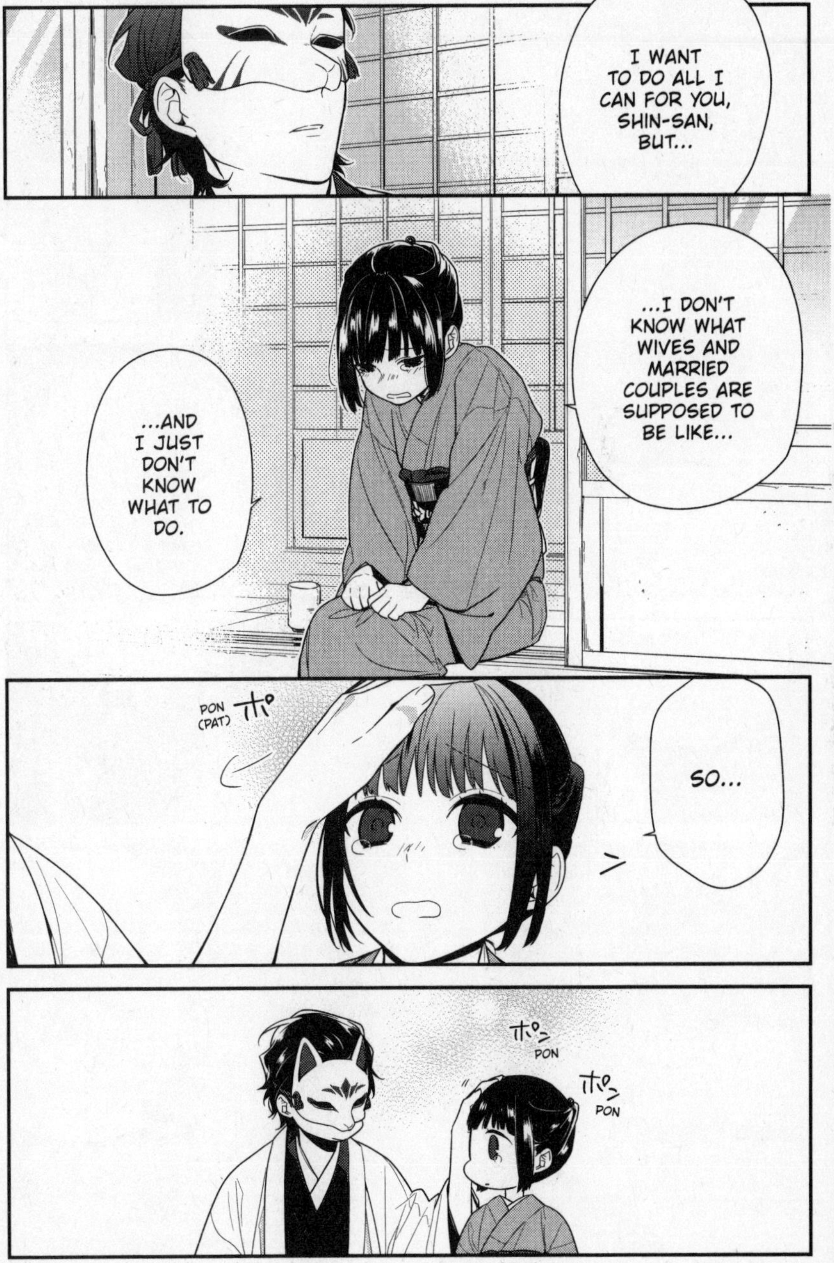
I WANT TO DO ALL I CAN FOR YOU, SHIN-SAN, BUT...
...I DON'T KNOW WHAT WIVES AND MARRIED COUPLES ARE SUPPOSED TO BE LIKE...
...AND I JUST DON'T KNOW WHAT TO DO.
SO...
ポ
PON (PAT)
ポン
PON
ポン
PON

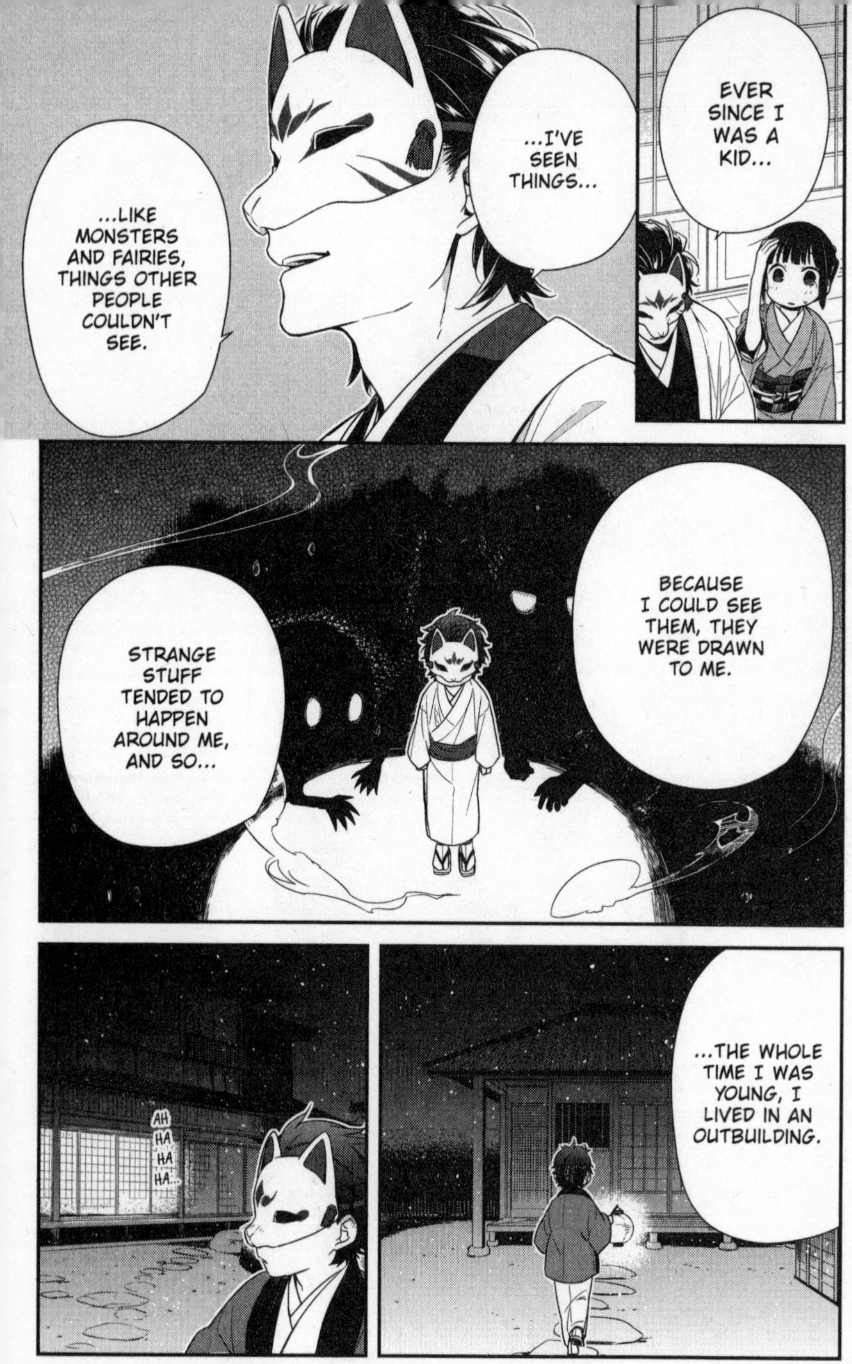
EVER SINCE I WAS A KID...
...I'VE SEEN THINGS...
...LIKE MONSTERS AND FAIRIES, THINGS OTHER PEOPLE COULDN'T SEE.
BECAUSE I COULD SEE THEM, THEY WERE DRAWN TO ME.
STRANGE STUFF TENDED TO HAPPEN AROUND ME, AND SO...
...THE WHOLE TIME I WAS YOUNG, I LIVED IN AN OUTBUILDING.
AH HA HA HA...

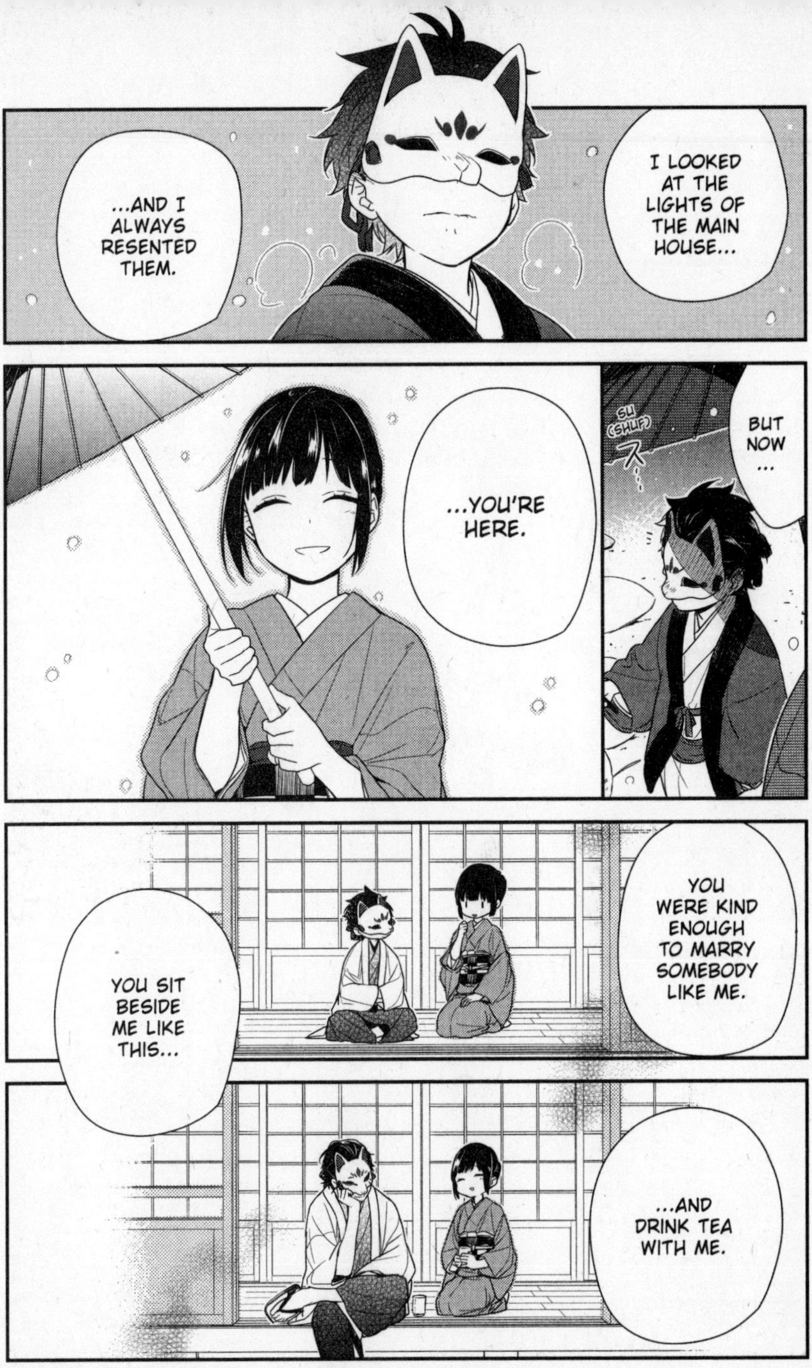
I LOOKED AT THE LIGHTS OF THE MAIN HOUSE...
...AND I ALWAYS RESENTED THEM.
BUT NOW...
SU (SHUF)
ス...
...YOU'RE HERE.
YOU WERE KIND ENOUGH TO MARRY SOMEBODY LIKE ME.
YOU SIT BESIDE ME LIKE THIS...
...AND DRINK TEA WITH ME.

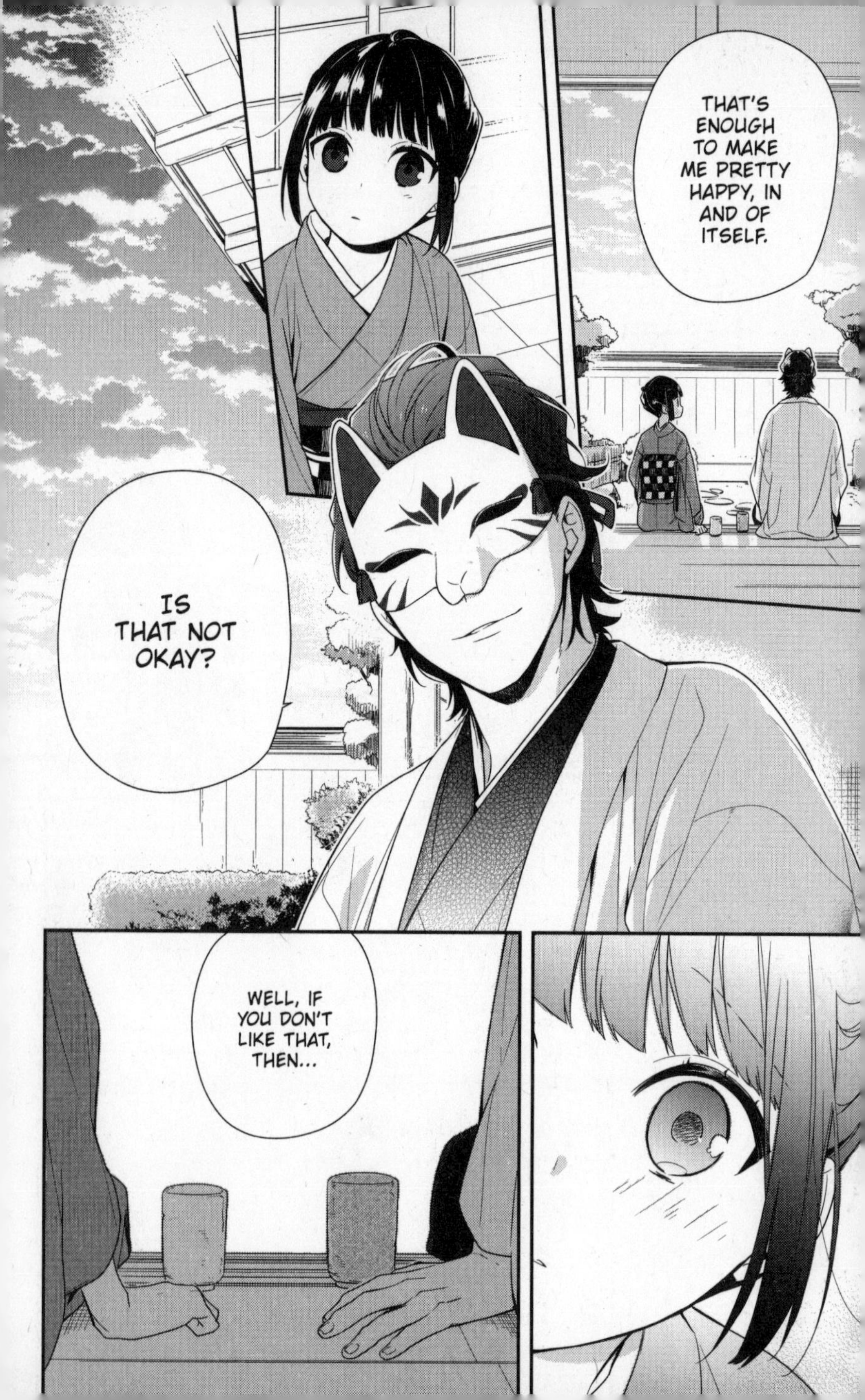
THAT'S ENOUGH TO MAKE ME PRETTY HAPPY, IN AND OF ITSELF.
IS THAT NOT OKAY?
WELL, IF YOU DON'T LIKE THAT, THEN...

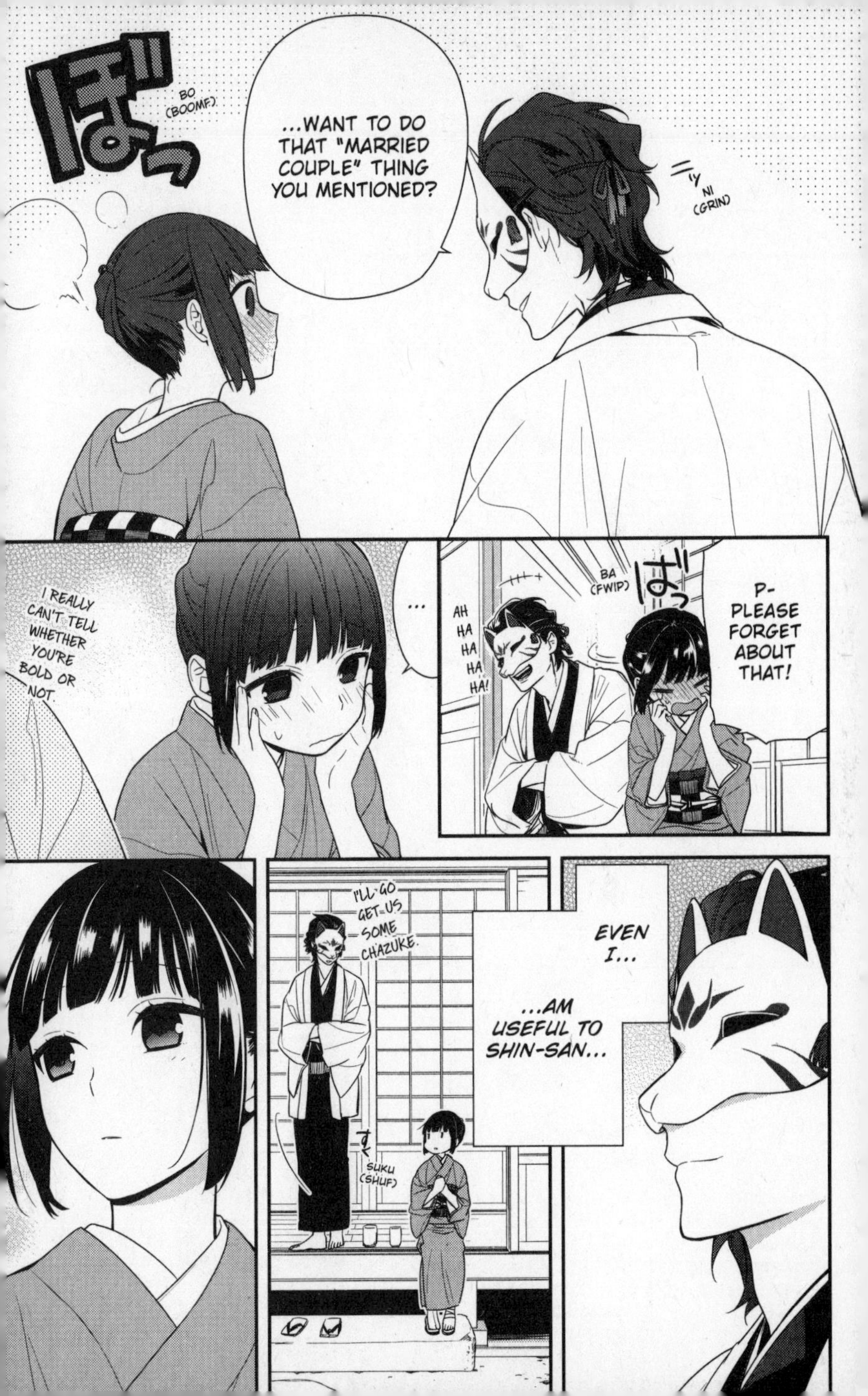
ぼっ
BO (BOOMF)
...WANT TO DO THAT "MARRIED COUPLE" THING YOU MENTIONED?
ニッ
NI (GRIN)
ばっ
BA (FWIP)
P- PLEASE FORGET ABOUT THAT!
AH HA HA HA HA!
...
I REALLY CAN'T TELL WHETHER YOU'RE BOLD OR NOT.
EVEN I...
...AM USEFUL TO SHIN-SAN...
I'LL GO GET US SOME CHAZUKE.
すく
SUKU (SHUF)

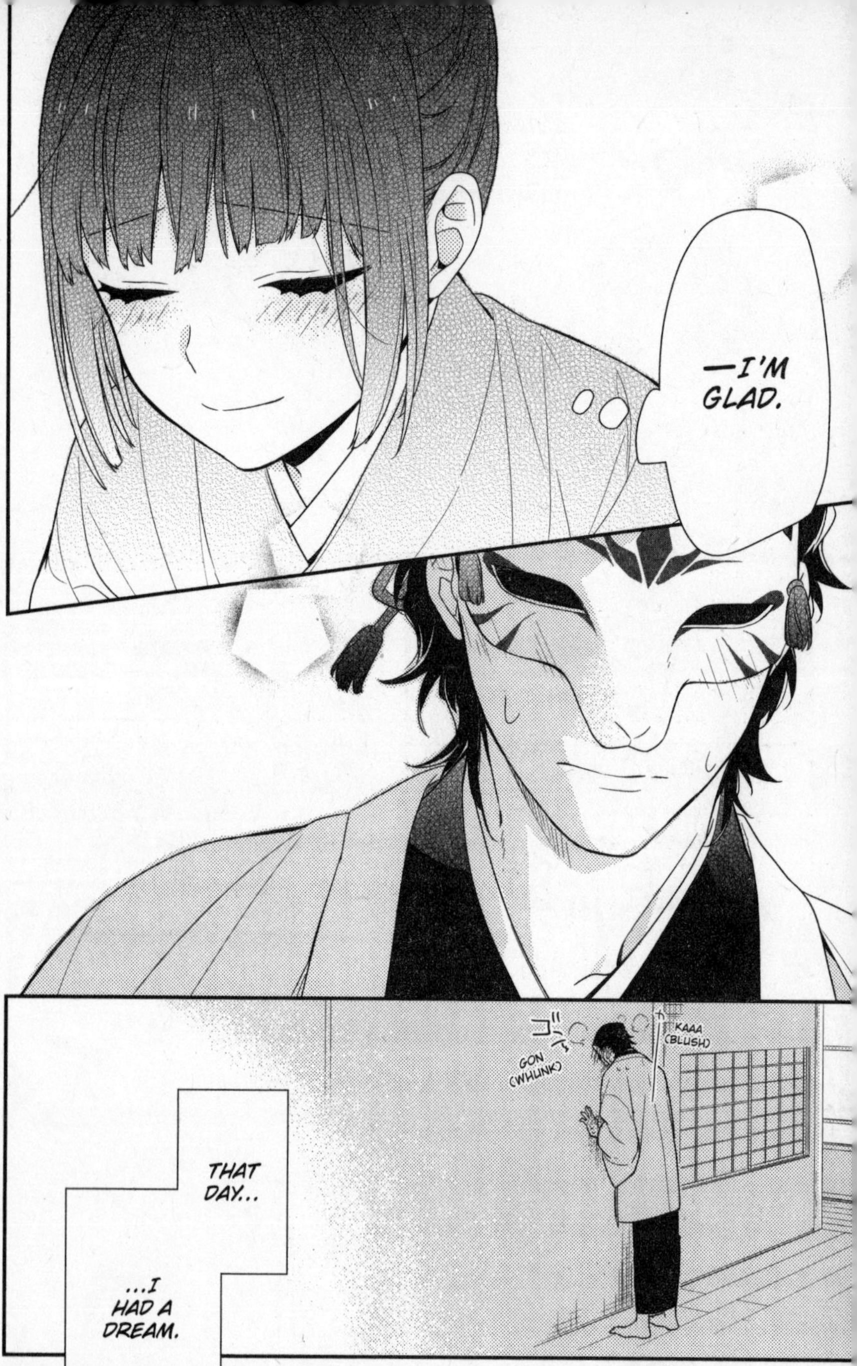
—I'M GLAD.
GON (WHUNK)
KAAA (BLUSH)
THAT DAY...
...I HAD A DREAM.

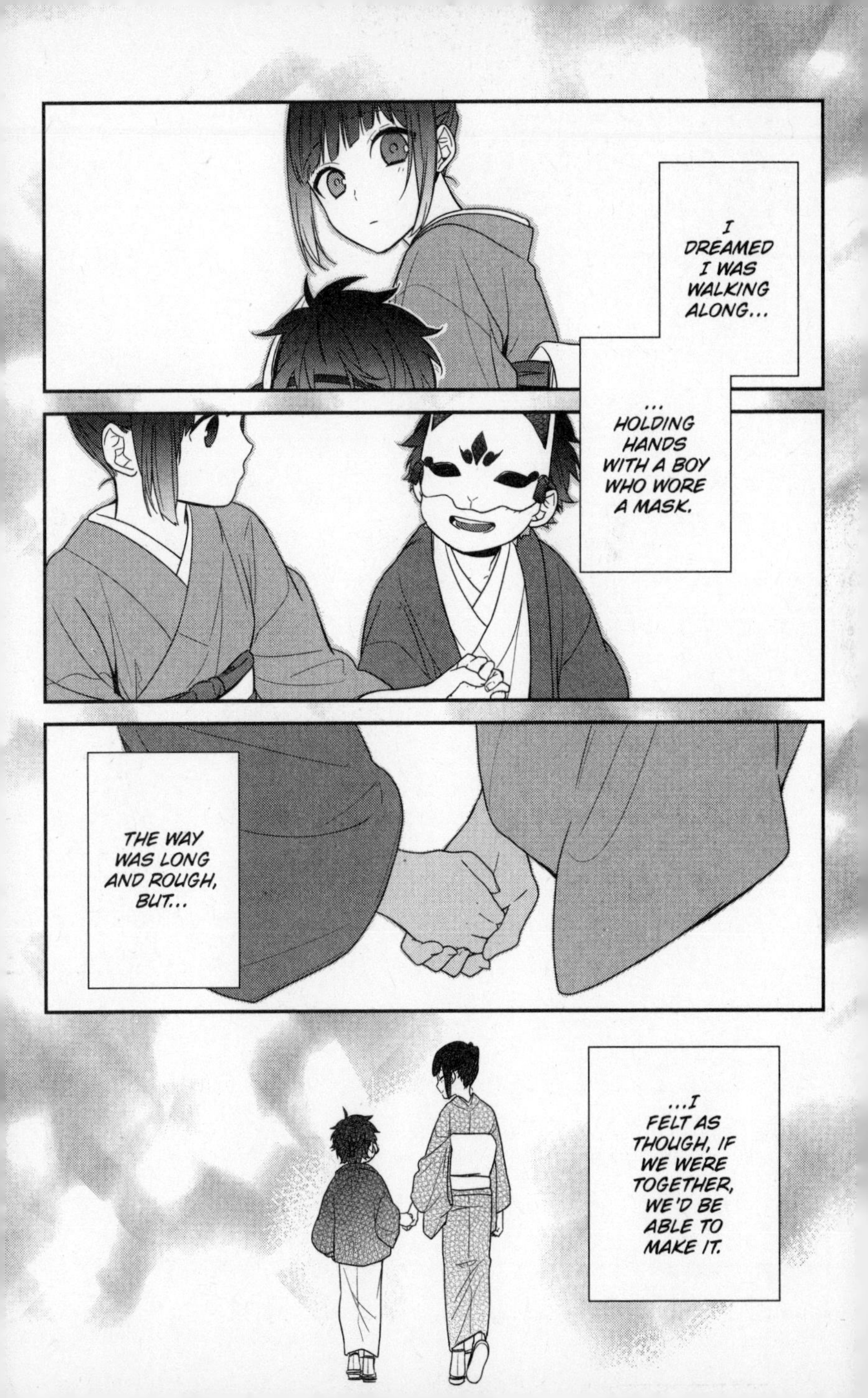
I DREAMED I WAS WALKING ALONG...
...HOLDING HANDS WITH A BOY WHO WORE A MASK.
THE WAY WAS LONG AND ROUGH, BUT...
...I FELT AS THOUGH, IF WE WERE TOGETHER, WE'D BE ABLE TO MAKE IT.

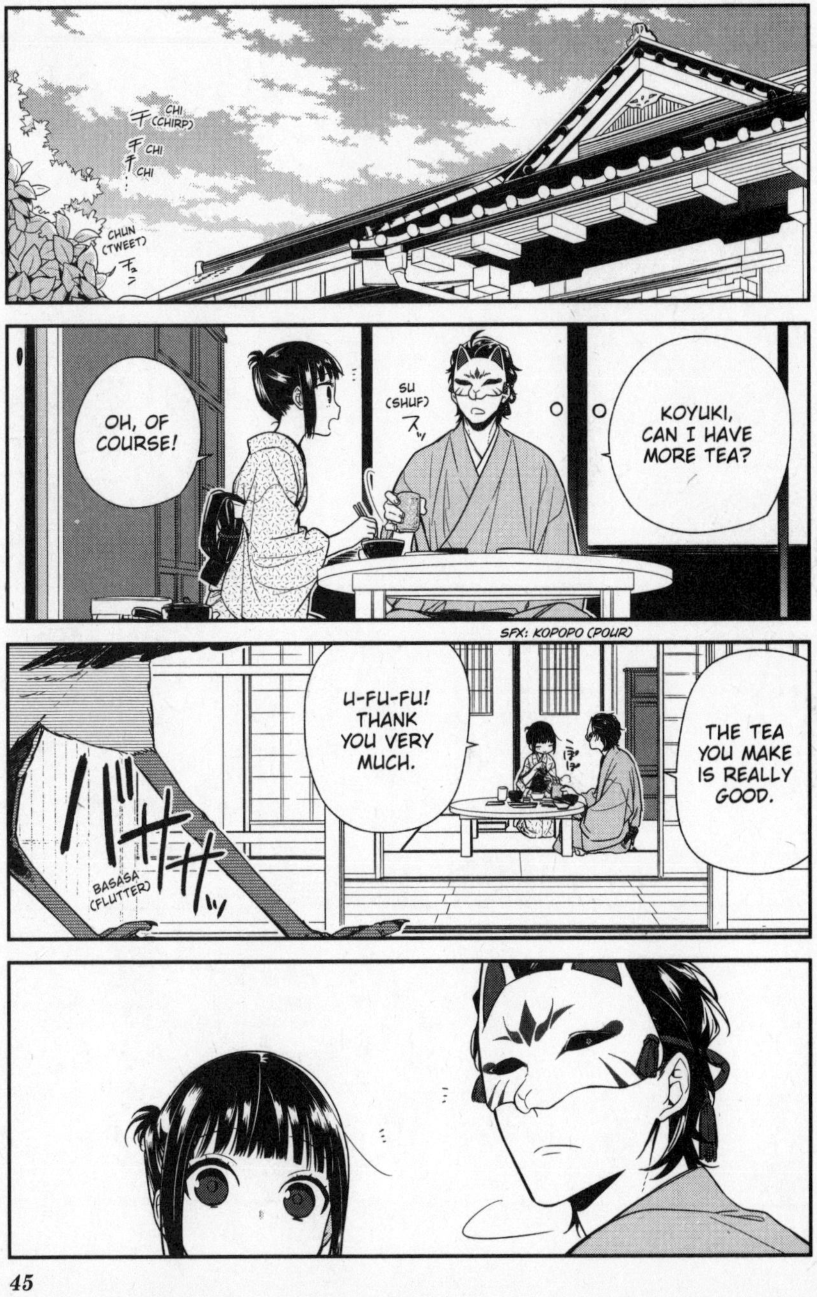
CHI (CHIRP)
CHI
CHI
CHUN (TWEET)
KOYUKI, CAN I HAVE MORE TEA?
SU (SHUF)
OH, OF COURSE!
SFX: KOPOPO (POUR)
THE TEA YOU MAKE IS REALLY GOOD.
U-FU-FU! THANK YOU VERY MUCH.
BASASA (FLUTTER)

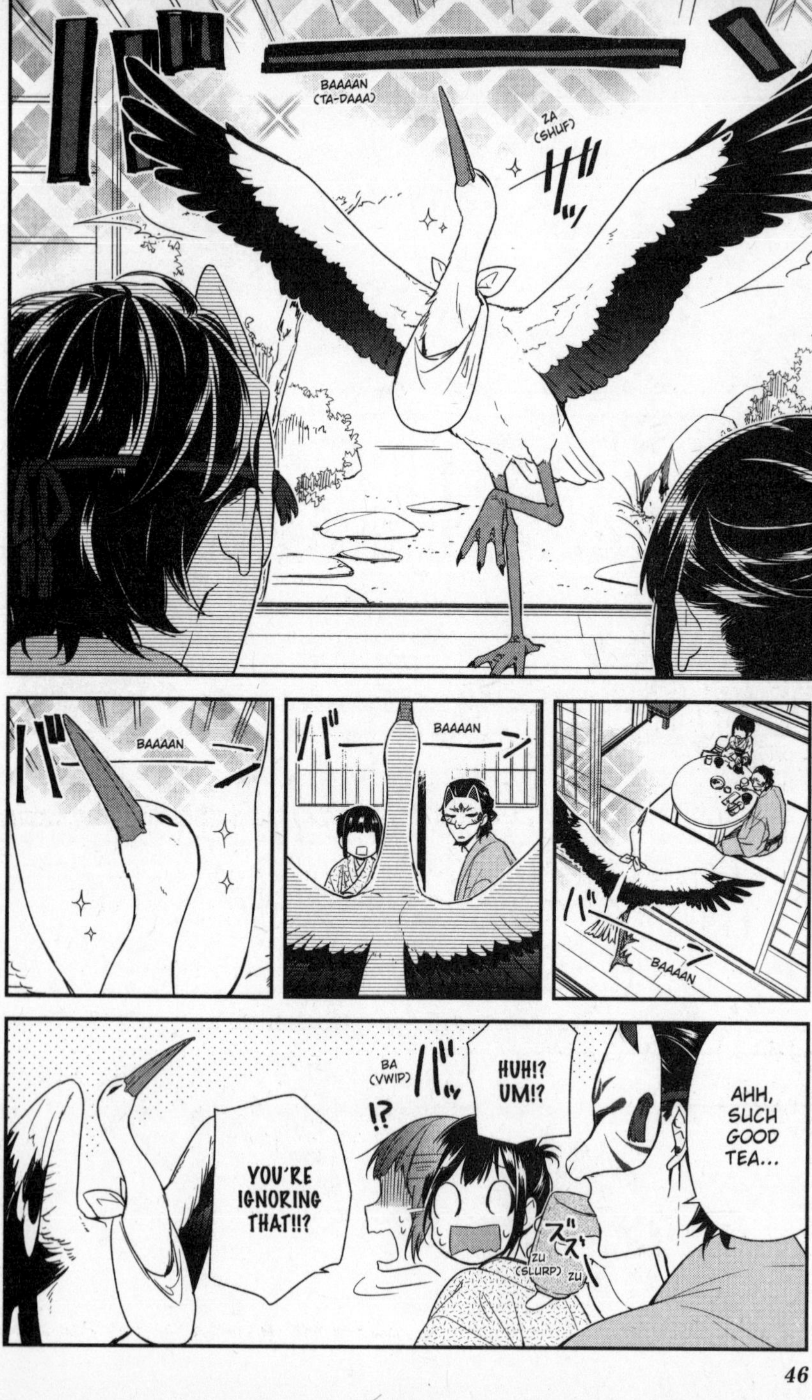
BAAAAN (TA-DAAA)
ZA (SHUF)
BAAAAN
BAAAAN
BAAAAN
AHH, SUCH GOOD TEA...
HUH!? UM!?
BA (VWIP)
!?
ZU (SLURP) ZU
YOU'RE IGNORING THAT!!?

Chapter 3

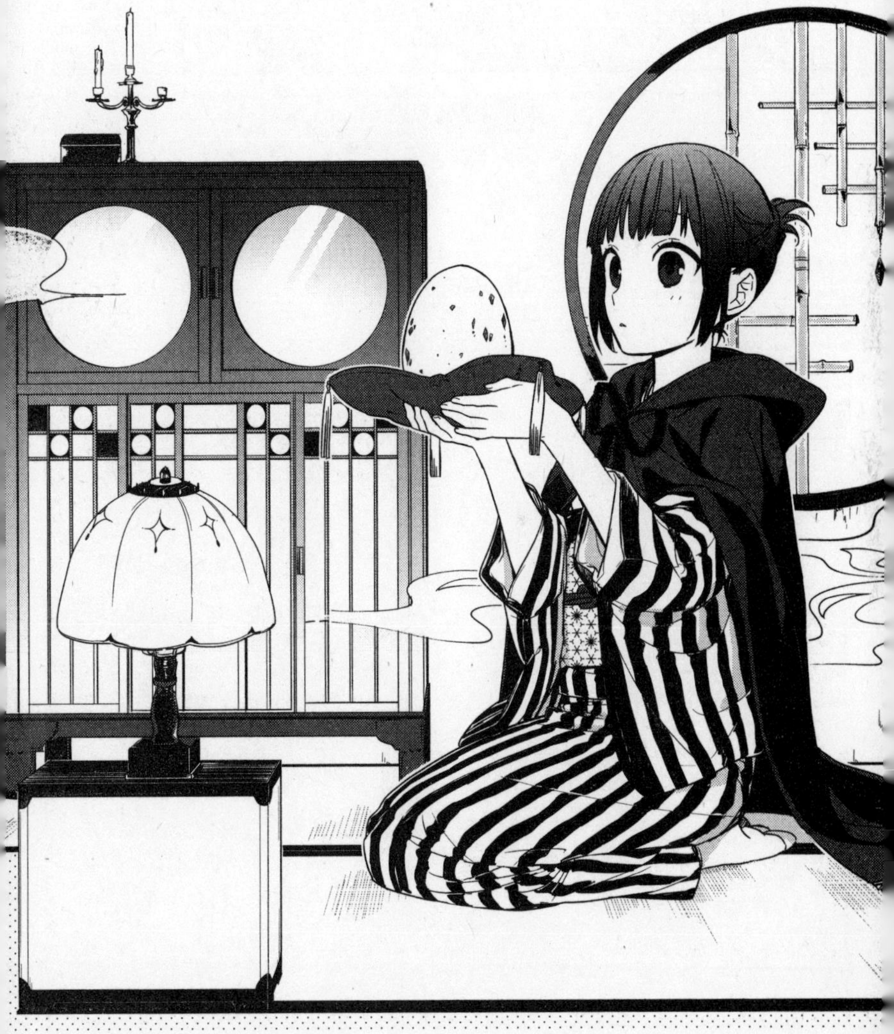

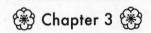

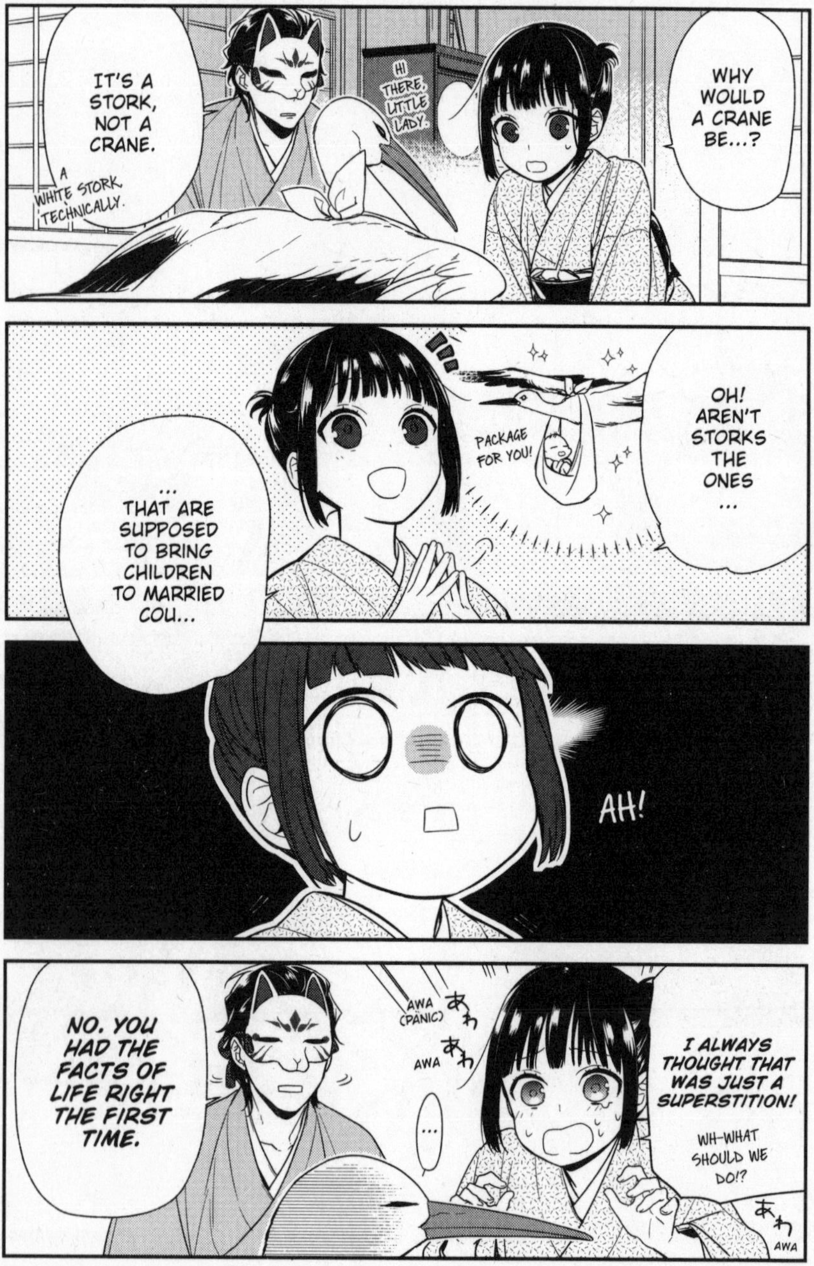
WHY WOULD A CRANE BE...?
HI THERE, LITTLE LADY.
IT'S A STORK, NOT A CRANE.
A WHITE STORK, TECHNICALLY.
OH! AREN'T STORKS THE ONES ...
PACKAGE FOR YOU!
... THAT ARE SUPPOSED TO BRING CHILDREN TO MARRIED COU...
AH!
I ALWAYS THOUGHT THAT WAS JUST A SUPERSTITION!
WH-WHAT SHOULD WE DO!?
あわ AWA
あわ AWA
...
あわ AWA (PANIC)
NO. YOU HAD THE FACTS OF LIFE RIGHT THE FIRST TIME.

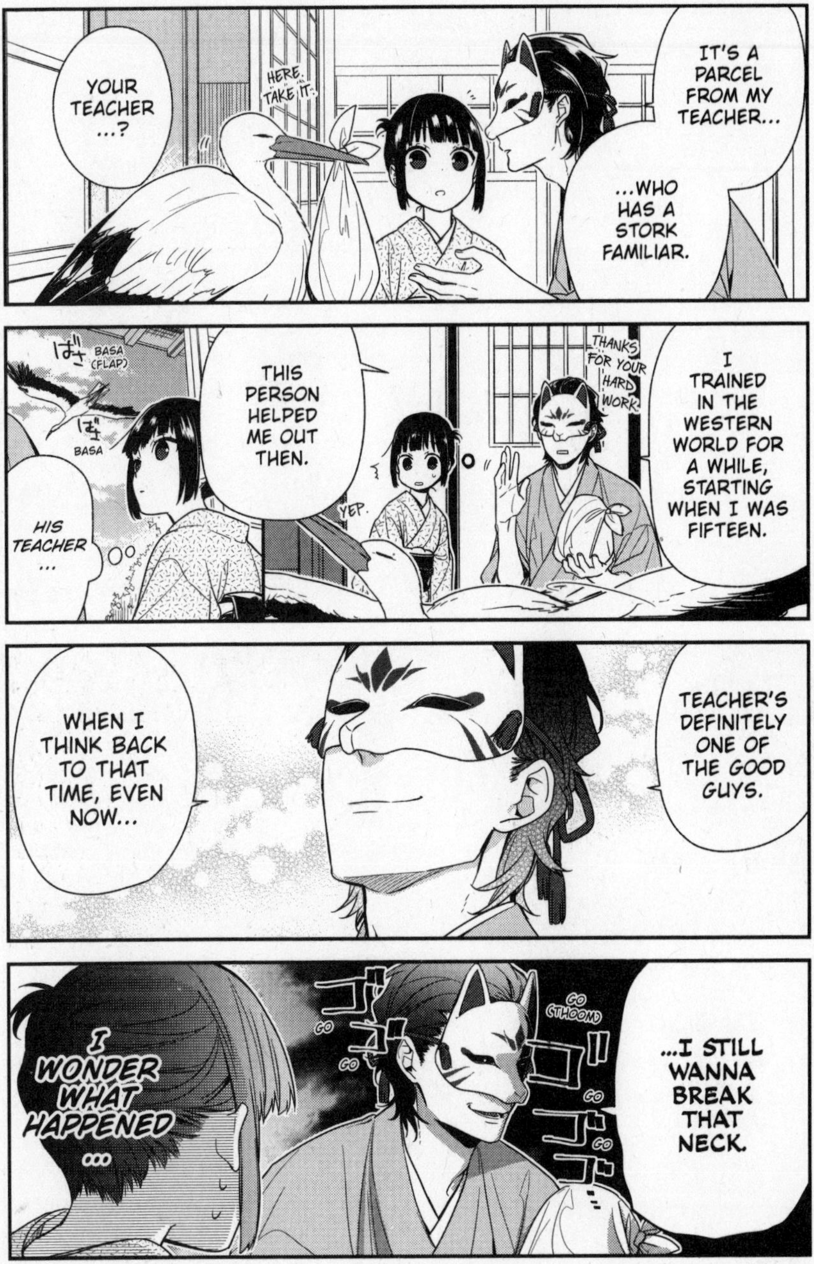
IT'S A PARCEL FROM MY TEACHER...
...WHO HAS A STORK FAMILIAR.
HERE. TAKE IT.
YOUR TEACHER ...?
I TRAINED IN THE WESTERN WORLD FOR A WHILE, STARTING WHEN I WAS FIFTEEN.
THANKS FOR YOUR HARD WORK.
THIS PERSON HELPED ME OUT THEN.
YEP.
ばさ BASA (FLAP)
ばさ BASA
HIS TEACHER ...
TEACHER'S DEFINITELY ONE OF THE GOOD GUYS.
WHEN I THINK BACK TO THAT TIME, EVEN NOW...
...I STILL WANNA BREAK THAT NECK.
GO (THOOM)
GO GO GO GO
I WONDER WHAT HAPPENED ...

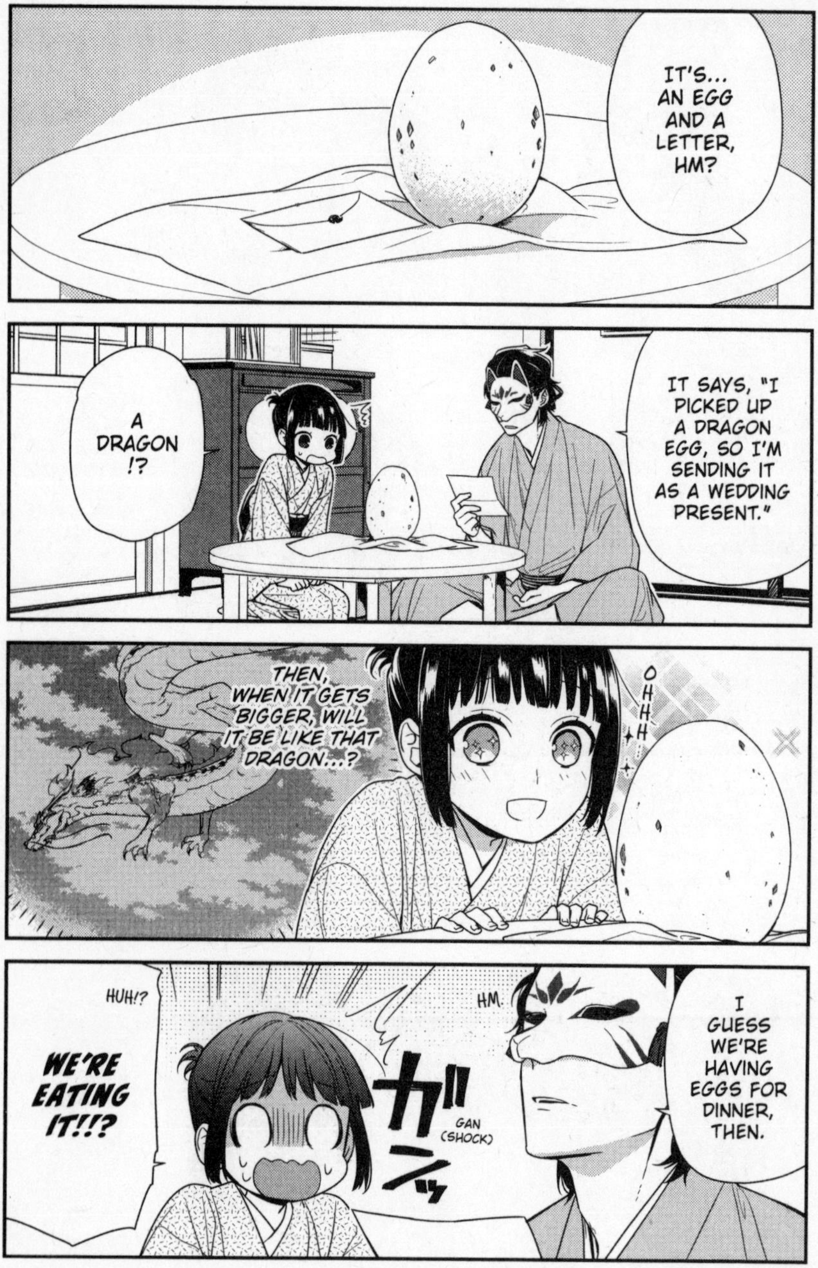
IT'S... AN EGG AND A LETTER, HM?
IT SAYS, "I PICKED UP A DRAGON EGG, SO I'M SENDING IT AS A WEDDING PRESENT."
A DRAGON !?
OHHH...
THEN, WHEN IT GETS BIGGER, WILL IT BE LIKE THAT DRAGON...?
I GUESS WE'RE HAVING EGGS FOR DINNER, THEN.
HM.
GAN (SHOCK)
HUH!?
WE'RE EATING IT!!?

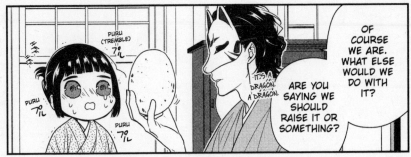

OF COURSE WE ARE. WHAT ELSE WOULD WE DO WITH IT?
ARE YOU SAYING WE SHOULD RAISE IT OR SOMETHING?
IT'S A DRAGON. A DRAGON.
PURU (TREMBLE) プル
PURU プル
PURU プル
BUT... BUT... WE COULD FLY!
BUN ぶん
FUYO ふよ
WHEEEE!
FUYO (FLOAT) ふよ
BUN (SHAKE) ぶん
THIS IS A LAND DRAGON EGG, SO IT'LL BE FLIGHTLESS.
WH- WHEN IT GETS BIGGER, IT CAN CARRY THINGS!
YOU'RE VERY STRONG, AREN'T YOU?
HIYAAH!
KYARUN (TWINKLE) きゃるん
THIS TYPE DOESN'T GET VERY BIG.
HNNNNGH...
ん
SHUN (DROOP) しゅん
IT KINDA FEELS LIKE I'M PICKING ON HER.
GUILT...

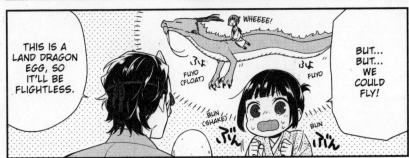

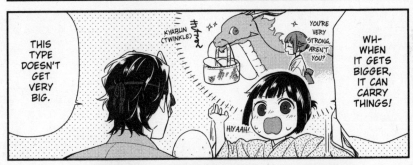

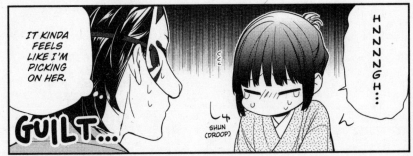

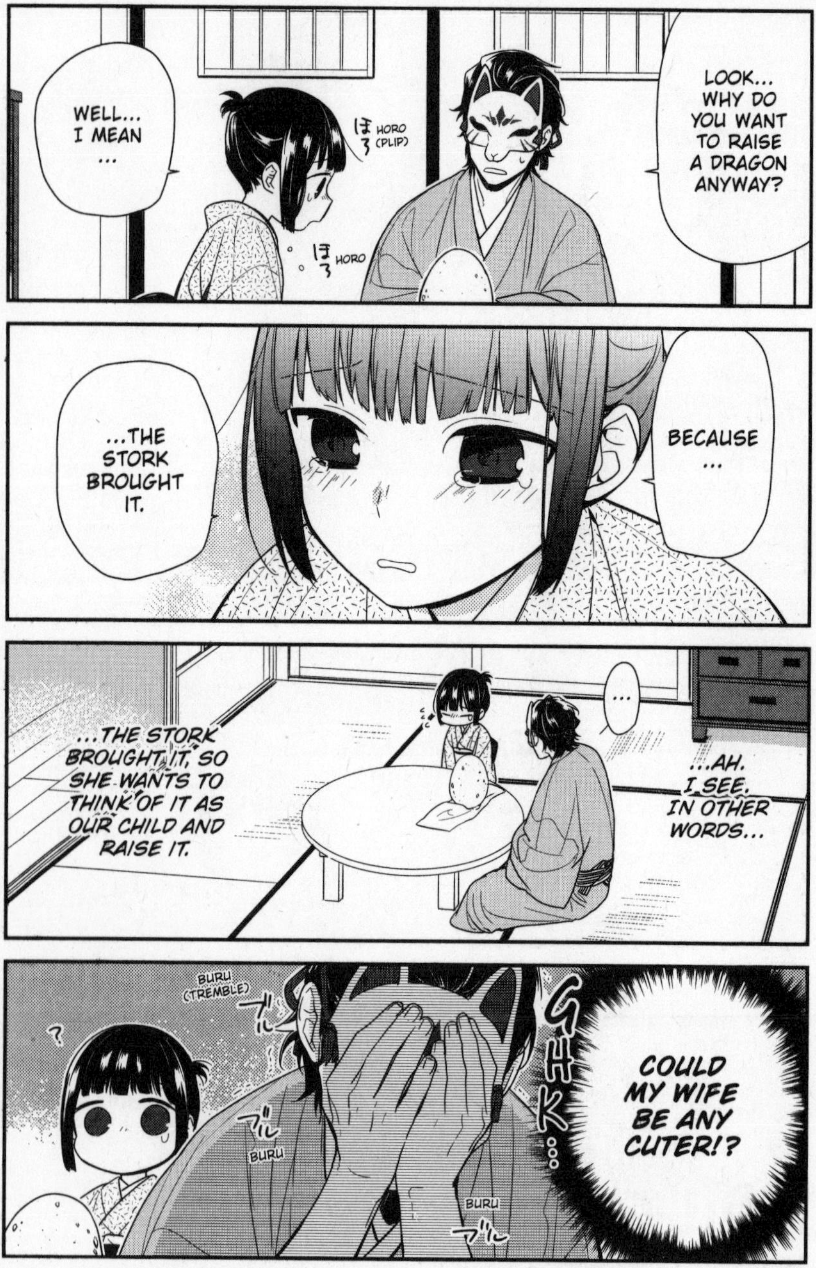
LOOK... WHY DO YOU WANT TO RAISE A DRAGON ANYWAY?
ほろ HORO (PLIP)
ほろ HORO
WELL... I MEAN ...
BECAUSE ...
...THE STORK BROUGHT IT.
...
...AH. I SEE. IN OTHER WORDS...
...THE STORK BROUGHT IT, SO SHE WANTS TO THINK OF IT AS OUR CHILD AND RAISE IT.
COULD MY WIFE BE ANY CUTER!?
GHK...
ブル BURU (TREMBLE)
ブル BURU
ブル BURU
?

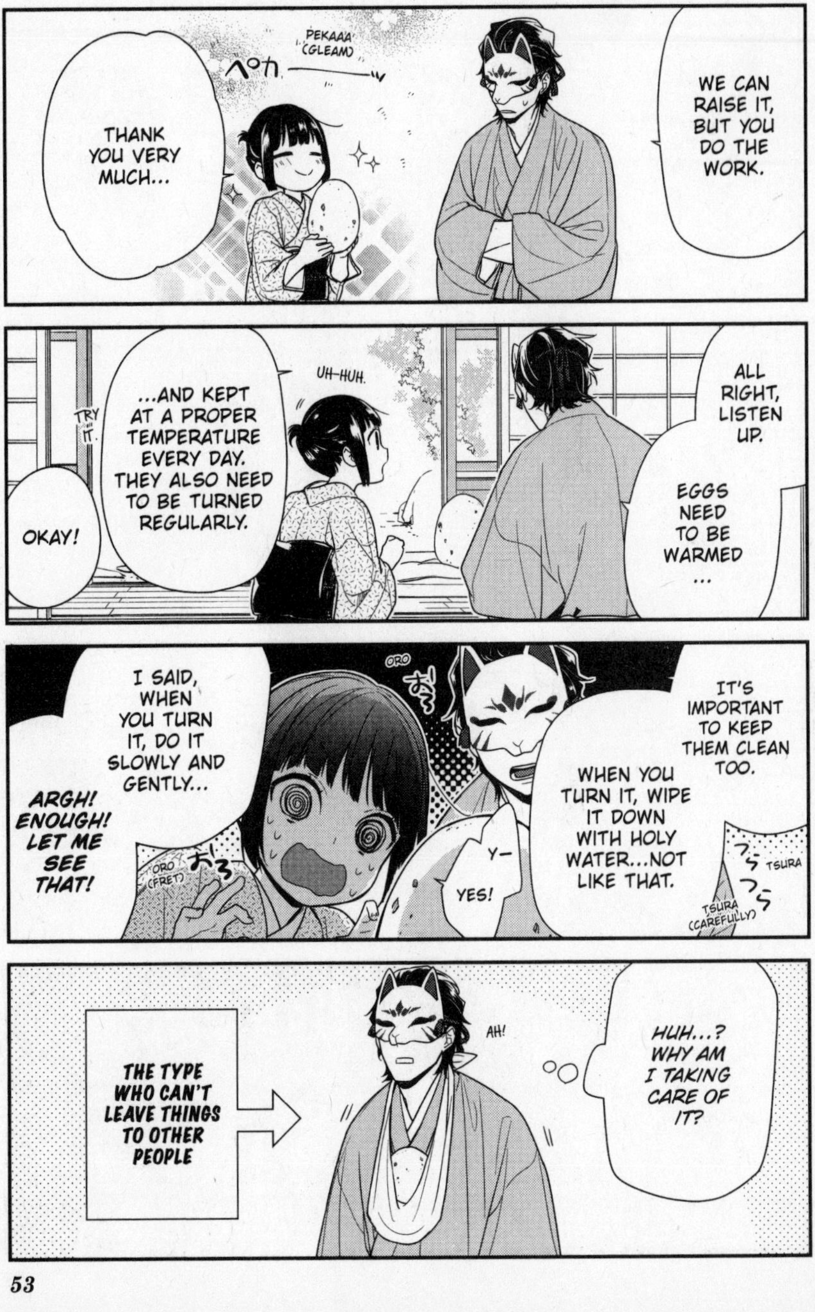
WE CAN RAISE IT, BUT YOU DO THE WORK.
PEKAAA (GLEAM)
THANK YOU VERY MUCH...
ALL RIGHT, LISTEN UP.
EGGS NEED TO BE WARMED ...
UH-HUH.
...AND KEPT AT A PROPER TEMPERATURE EVERY DAY. THEY ALSO NEED TO BE TURNED REGULARLY.
TRY IT.
OKAY!
IT'S IMPORTANT TO KEEP THEM CLEAN TOO.
TSURA TSURA (CAREFULLY)
WHEN YOU TURN IT, WIPE IT DOWN WITH HOLY WATER...NOT LIKE THAT.
Y— YES!
ORO
I SAID, WHEN YOU TURN IT, DO IT SLOWLY AND GENTLY...
ORO (FRET)
ARGH! ENOUGH! LET ME SEE THAT!
HUH...? WHY AM I TAKING CARE OF IT?
AH!
THE TYPE WHO CAN'T LEAVE THINGS TO OTHER PEOPLE

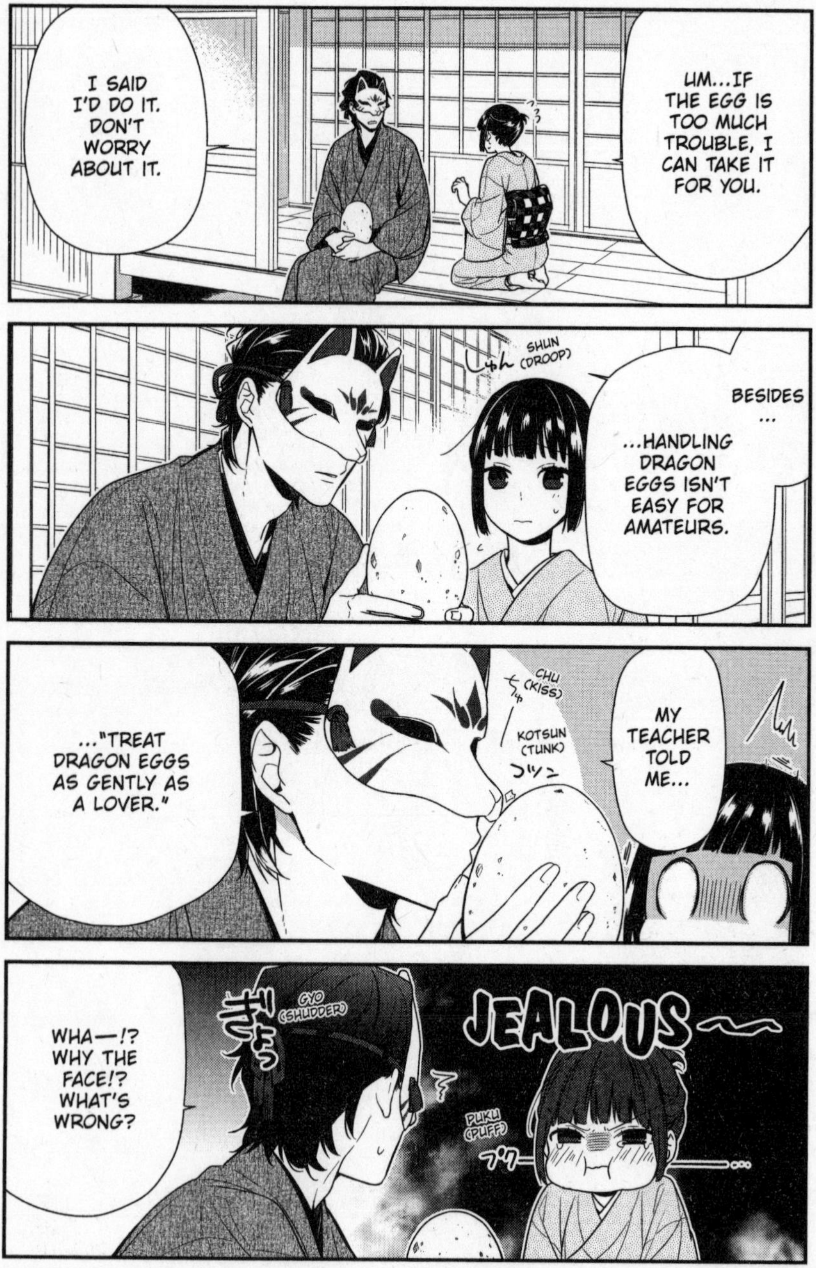
UM...IF THE EGG IS TOO MUCH TROUBLE, I CAN TAKE IT FOR YOU.
I SAID I'D DO IT. DON'T WORRY ABOUT IT.
SHUN (DROOP)
BESIDES...
...HANDLING DRAGON EGGS ISN'T EASY FOR AMATEURS.
MY TEACHER TOLD ME...
CHU (KISS)
KOTSUN (TUNK)
..."TREAT DRAGON EGGS AS GENTLY AS A LOVER."
JEALOUS
PUKU (PUFF)
GYO (SHUDDER)
WHA—!? WHY THE FACE!? WHAT'S WRONG?

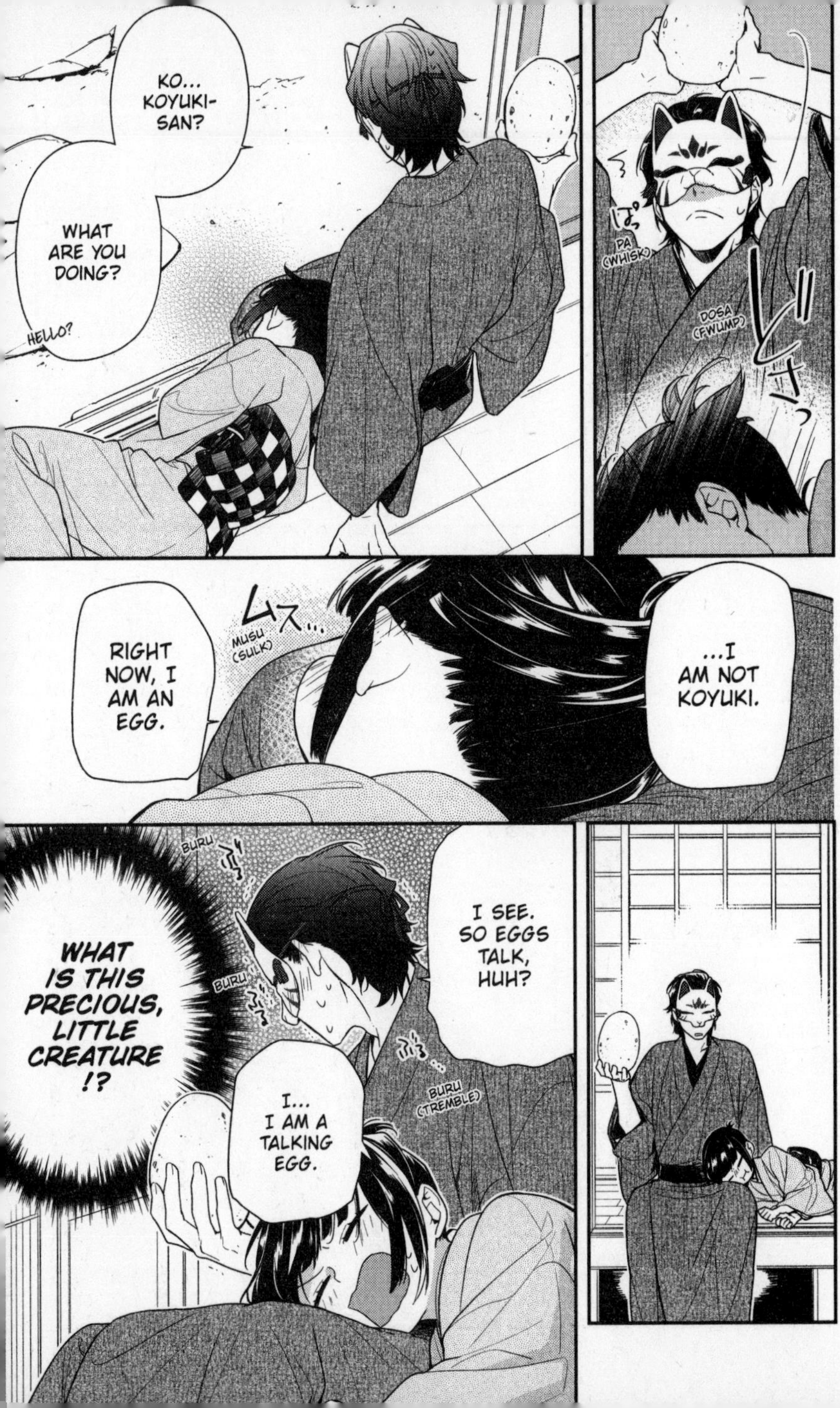
PA (WHISK)
DOSA (FWUMP)
KO... KOYUKI-SAN?
WHAT ARE YOU DOING?
HELLO?
...I AM NOT KOYUKI.
MUSU (SULK)
RIGHT NOW, I AM AN EGG.
I SEE. SO EGGS TALK, HUH?
BURU
BURU
BURU (TREMBLE)
I... I AM A TALKING EGG.
WHAT IS THIS PRECIOUS, LITTLE CREATURE!?

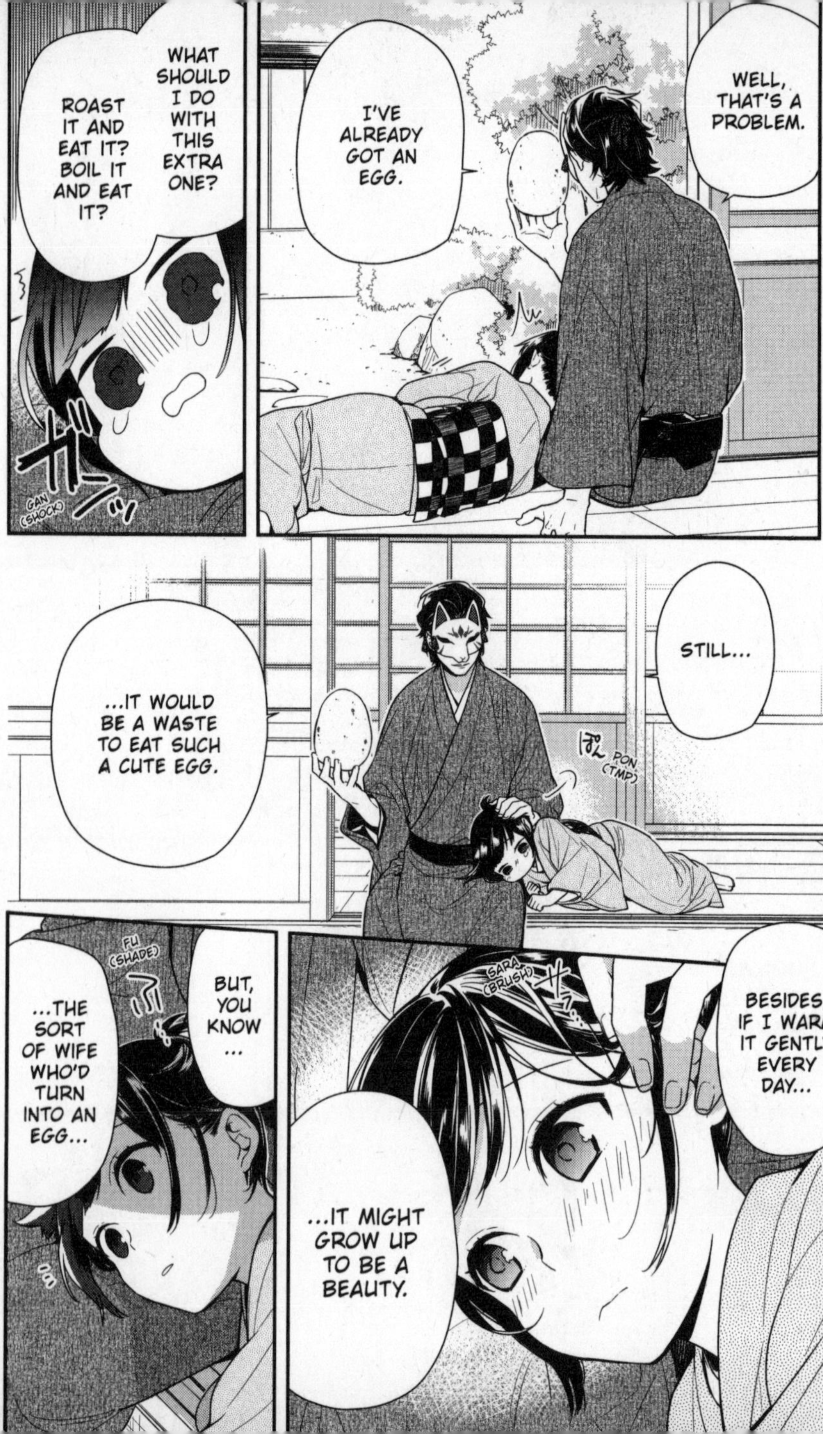
WELL, THAT'S A PROBLEM.
I'VE ALREADY GOT AN EGG.
WHAT SHOULD I DO WITH THIS EXTRA ONE?
ROAST IT AND EAT IT? BOIL IT AND EAT IT?
GAN (SHOCK)
STILL...
...IT WOULD BE A WASTE TO EAT SUCH A CUTE EGG.
ぽん PON (TMP)
BESIDES, IF I WARM IT GENTLY EVERY DAY...
SARA (BRUSH)
...IT MIGHT GROW UP TO BE A BEAUTY.
BUT, YOU KNOW...
FU (SHADE)
...THE SORT OF WIFE WHO'D TURN INTO AN EGG...

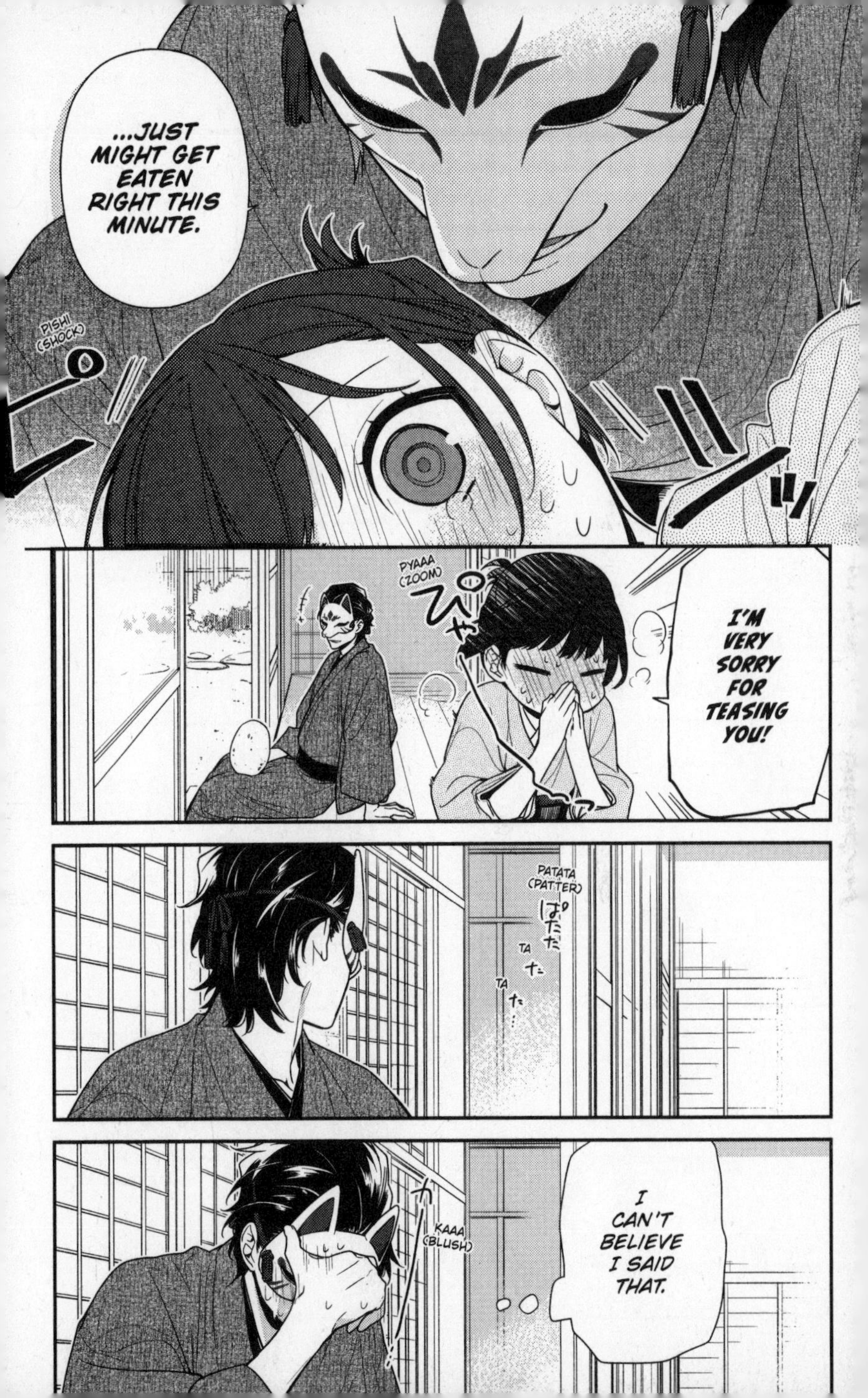
...JUST MIGHT GET EATEN RIGHT THIS MINUTE.
PISHI (SHOCK)
I'M VERY SORRY FOR TEASING YOU!
PYAAA (ZOOM)
PATATA (PATTER)
TA
TA
I CAN'T BELIEVE I SAID THAT.
KAAA (BLUSH)

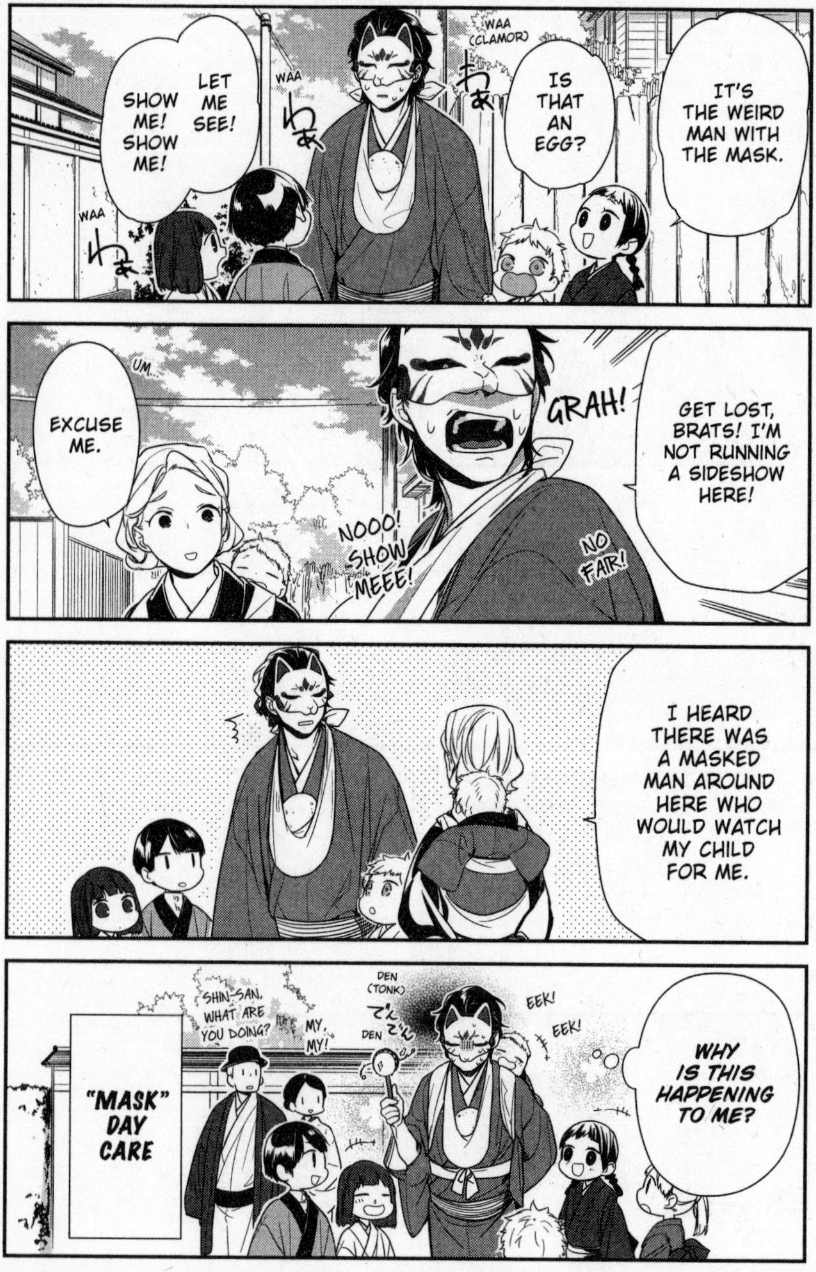
IT'S THE WEIRD MAN WITH THE MASK.
WAA (CLAMOR)
わぁ
IS THAT AN EGG?
WAA
わぁ
LET ME SEE!
SHOW ME! SHOW ME!
WAA
わぁ
GET LOST, BRATS! I'M NOT RUNNING A SIDESHOW HERE!
NO FAIR!
GRAH!
NOOO! SHOW MEEE!
UM...
EXCUSE ME.
I HEARD THERE WAS A MASKED MAN AROUND HERE WHO WOULD WATCH MY CHILD FOR ME.
WHY IS THIS HAPPENING TO ME?
EEK!
EEK!
DEN (TONK)
でんでん
DEN
MY, MY!
SHIN-SAN, WHAT ARE YOU DOING?
"MASK" DAY CARE

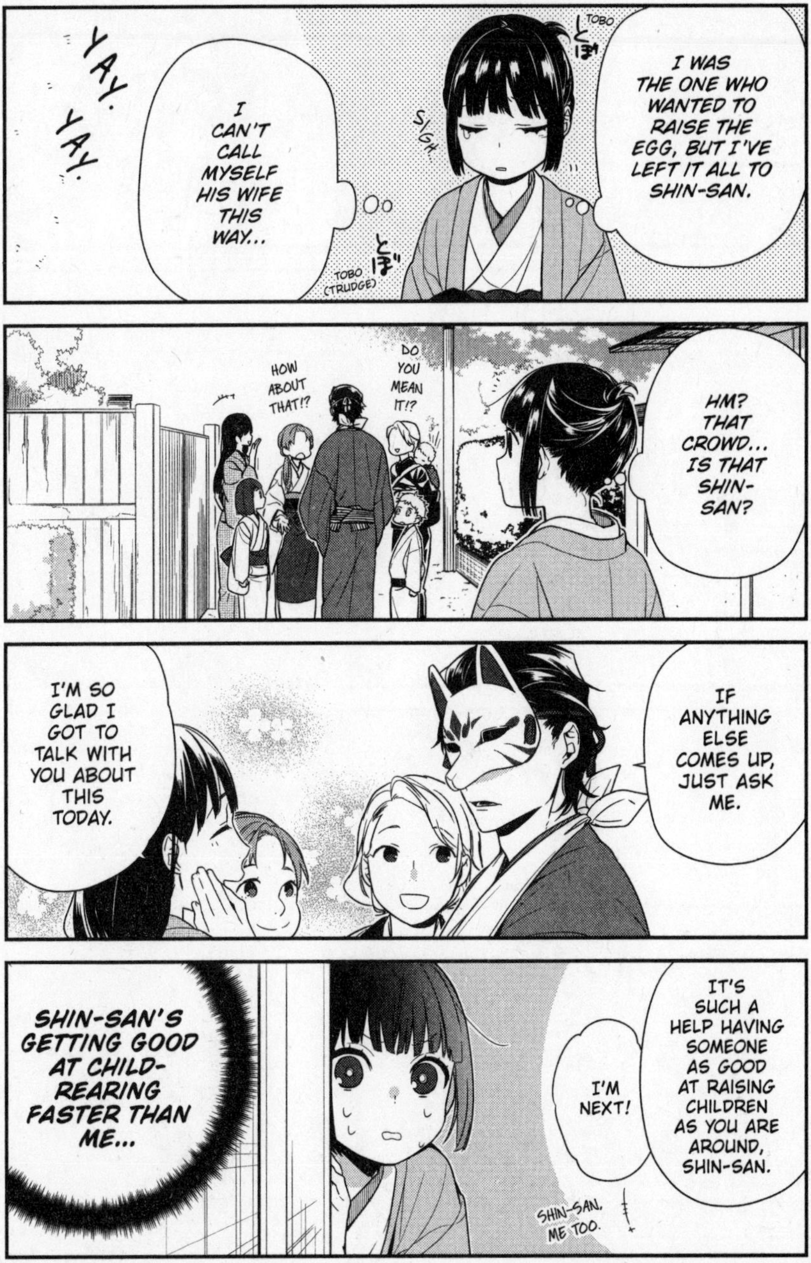
TOBO とぼ
I WAS THE ONE WHO WANTED TO RAISE THE EGG, BUT I'VE LEFT IT ALL TO SHIN-SAN.
SIGH
TOBO とぼ (TRUDGE)
I CAN'T CALL MYSELF HIS WIFE THIS WAY...
YAY. YAY.
HM? THAT CROWD... IS THAT SHIN-SAN?
DO YOU MEAN IT!?
HOW ABOUT THAT!?
IF ANYTHING ELSE COMES UP, JUST ASK ME.
I'M SO GLAD I GOT TO TALK WITH YOU ABOUT THIS TODAY.
IT'S SUCH A HELP HAVING SOMEONE AS GOOD AT RAISING CHILDREN AS YOU ARE AROUND, SHIN-SAN.
I'M NEXT!
SHIN-SAN, ME TOO.
SHIN-SAN'S GETTING GOOD AT CHILD-REARING FASTER THAN ME...

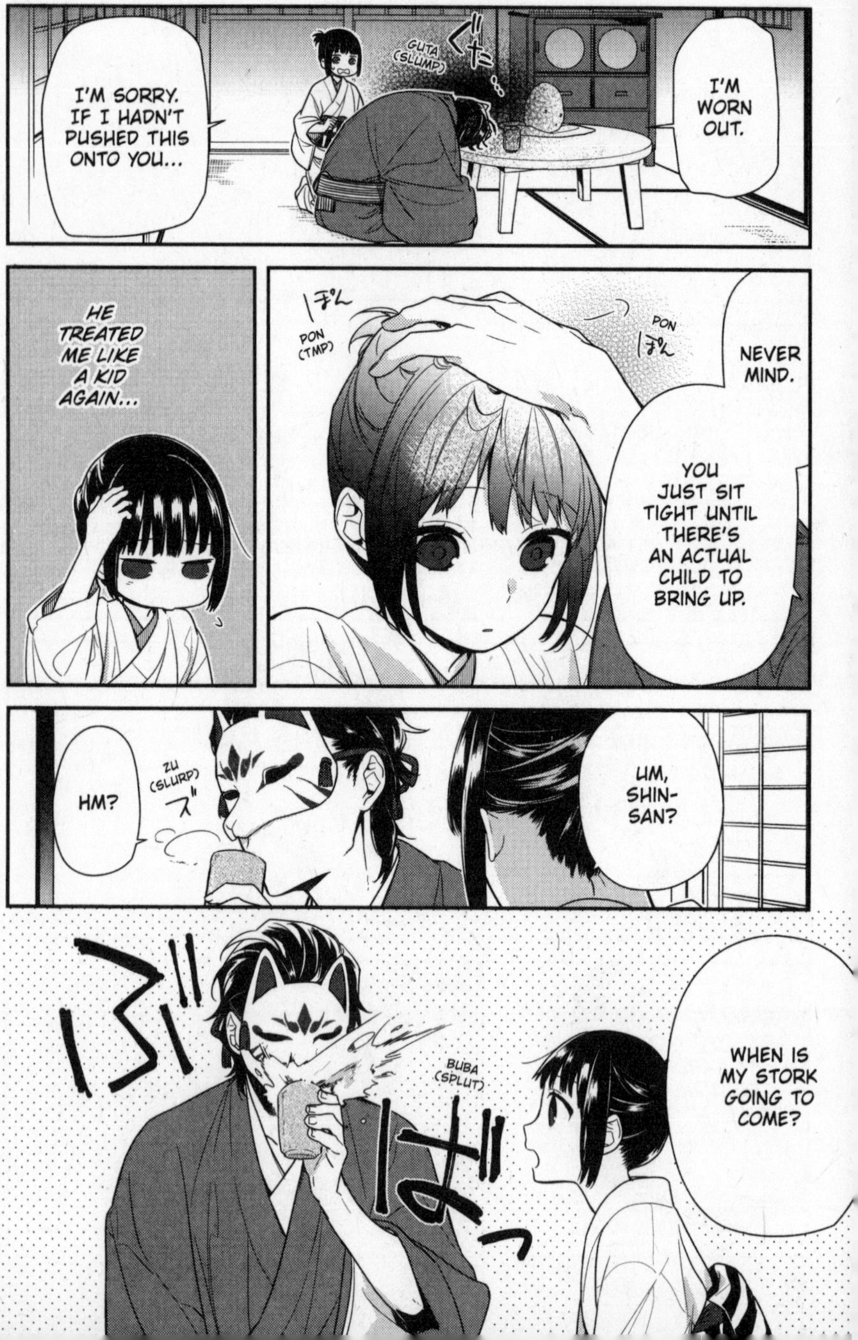
I'M WORN OUT.
GUTA (SLUMP)
I'M SORRY. IF I HADN'T PUSHED THIS ONTO YOU...
PON
NEVER MIND.
YOU JUST SIT TIGHT UNTIL THERE'S AN ACTUAL CHILD TO BRING UP.
PON (TMP)
HE TREATED ME LIKE A KID AGAIN...
UM, SHIN-SAN?
ZU (SLURP)
HM?
WHEN IS MY STORK GOING TO COME?
BUBA (SPLUT)

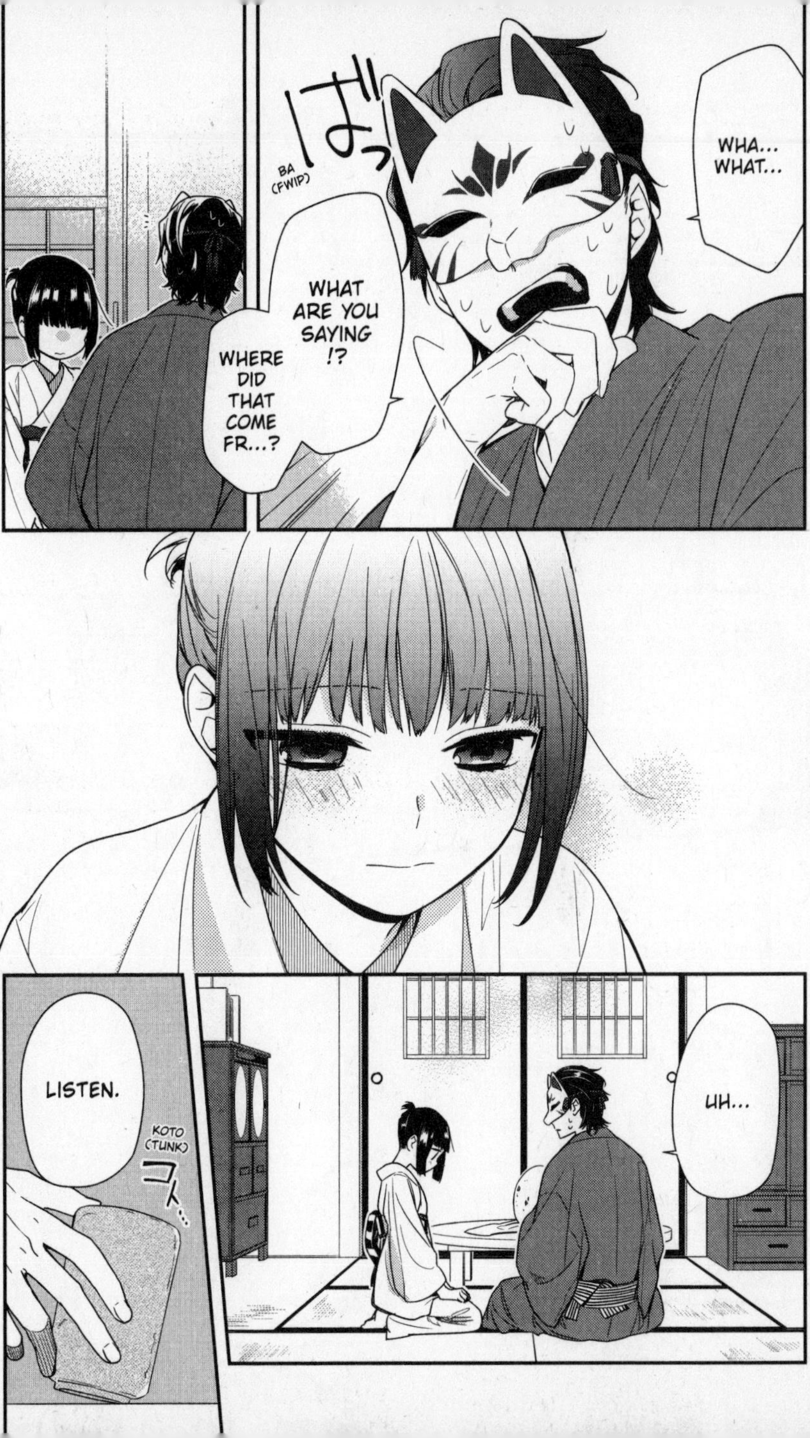
WHA... WHAT...
ばっ
BA (FWIP)
WHAT ARE YOU SAYING !?
WHERE DID THAT COME FR...?
UH...
LISTEN.
KOTO (TUNK)
コト…

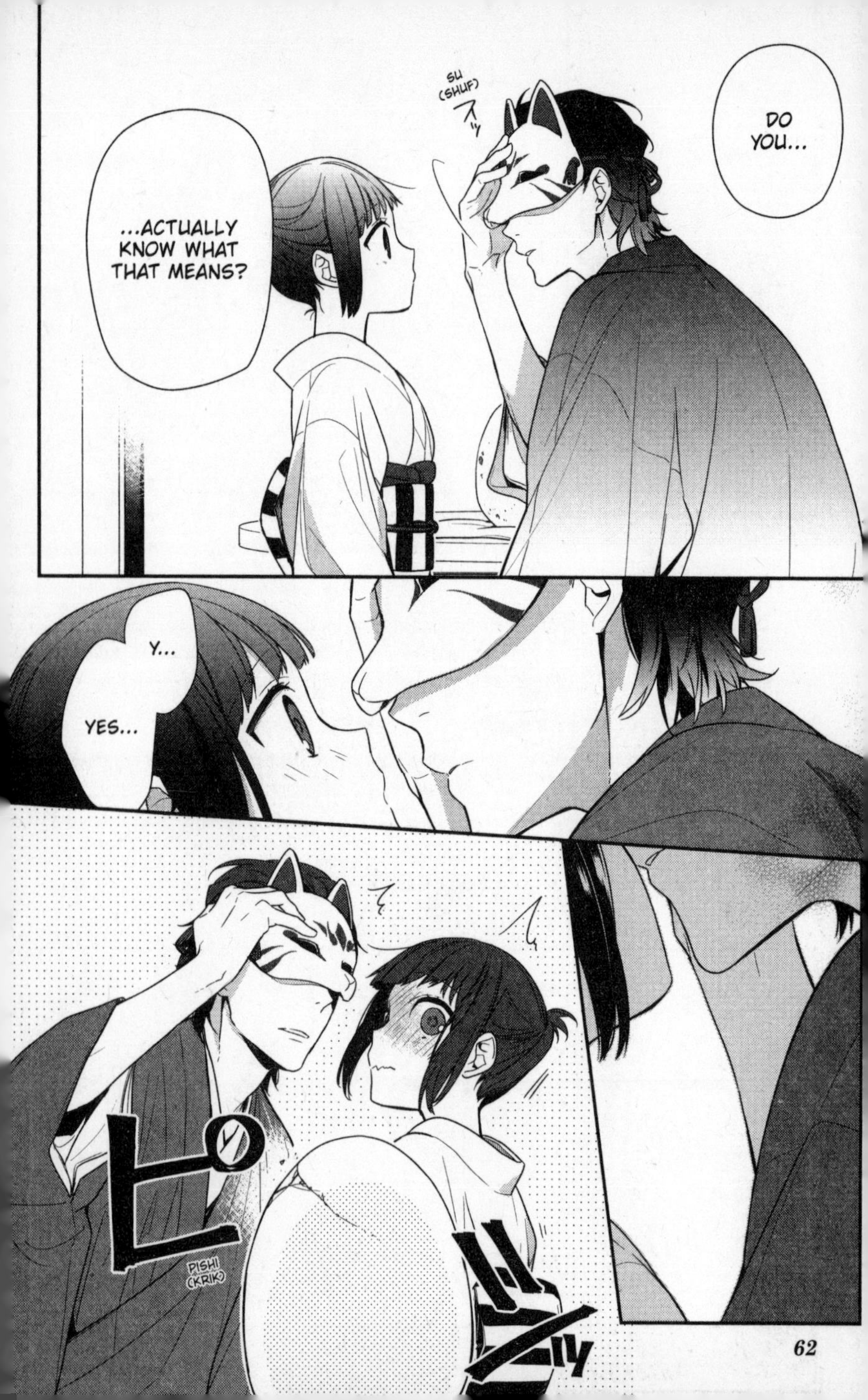
DO YOU...
SU (SHUF)
...ACTUALLY KNOW WHAT THAT MEANS?
Y...
YES...
PISHI (KRIK)

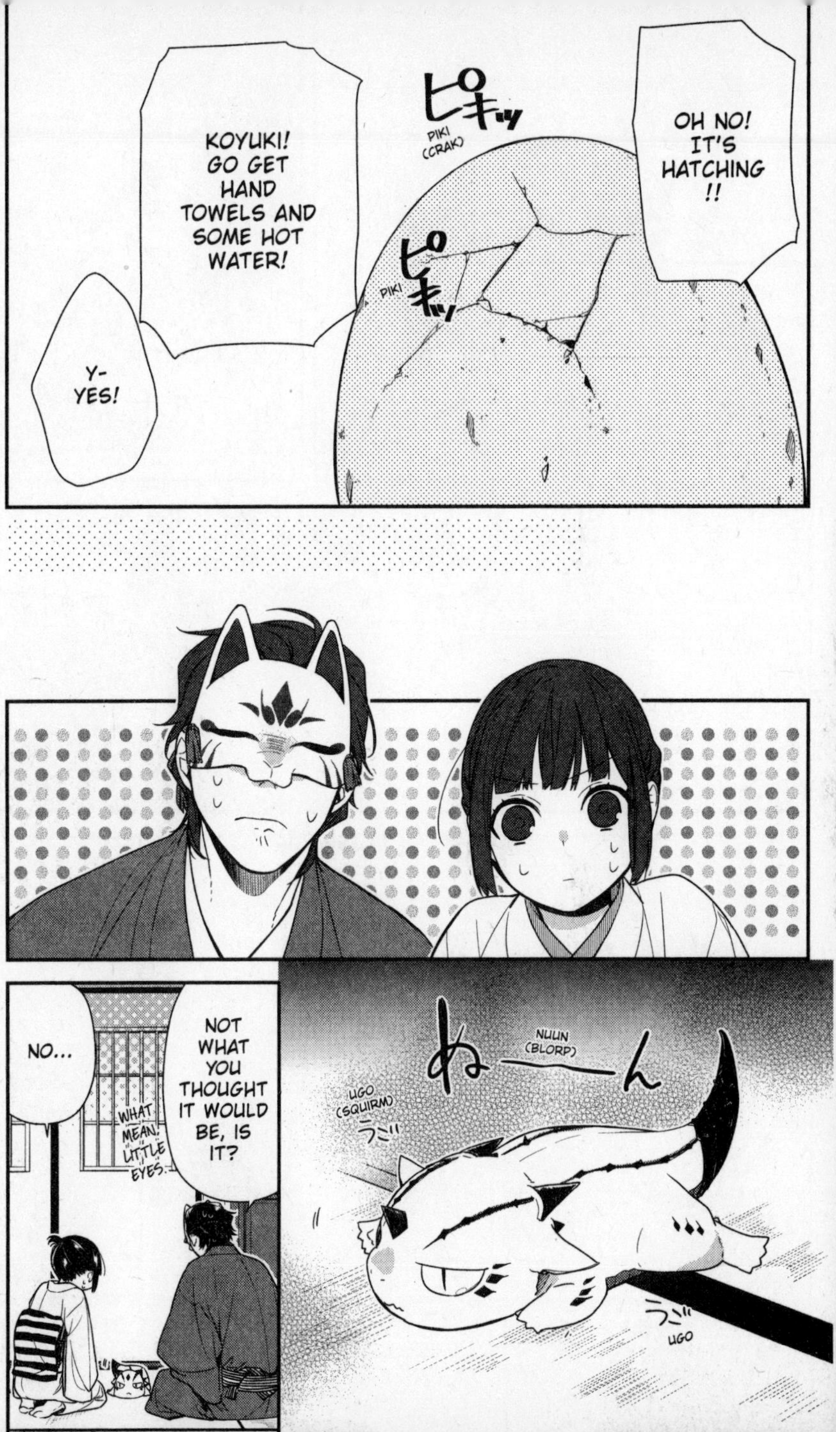
OH NO! IT'S HATCHING !!
PIKI (CRAK)
KOYUKI! GO GET HAND TOWELS AND SOME HOT WATER!
PIKI
Y-YES!
NUUN (BLORP)
UGO (SQUIRM)
UGO
NOT WHAT YOU THOUGHT IT WOULD BE, IS IT?
NO...
WHAT MEAN LITTLE EYES.

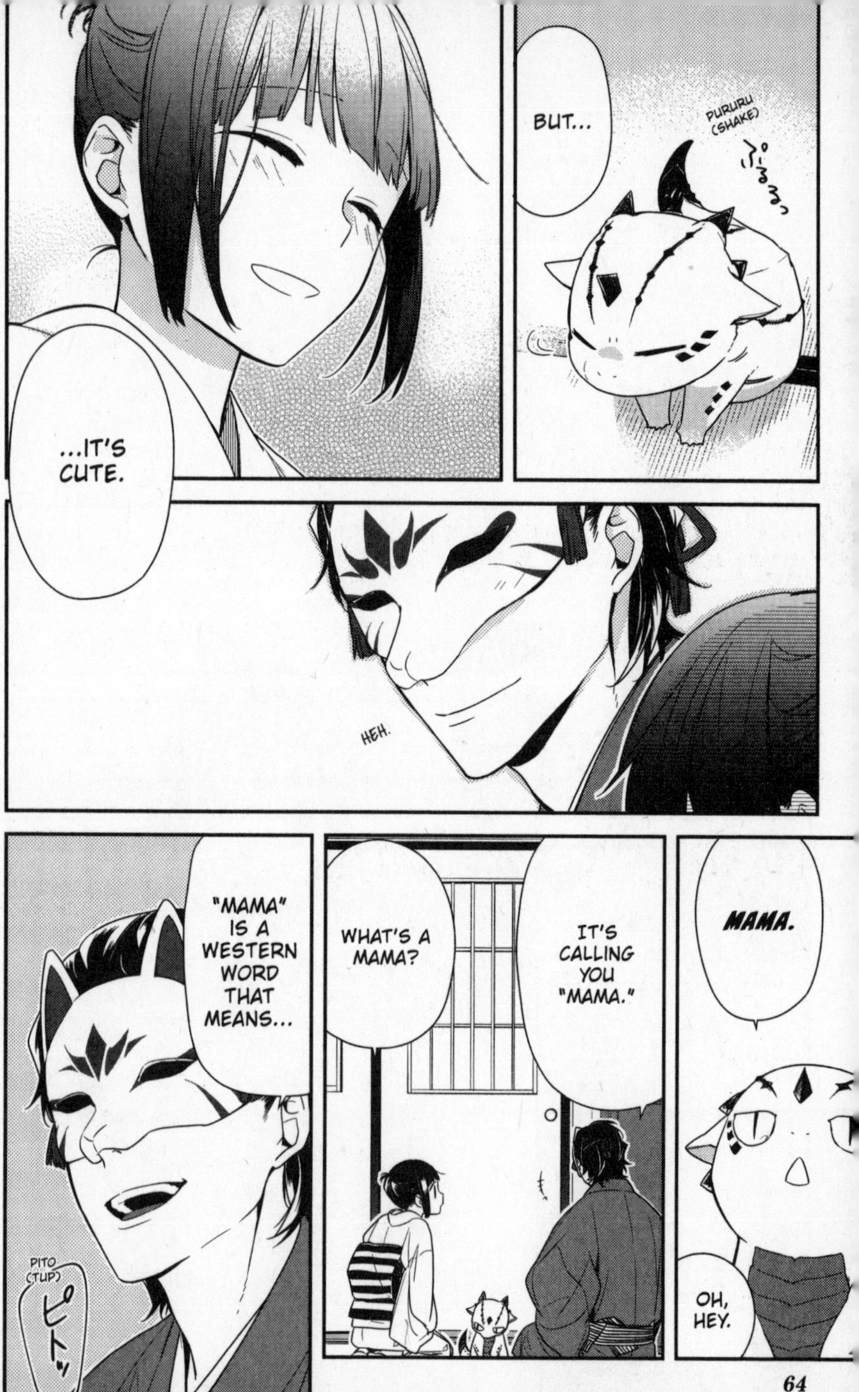
BUT...
PURURU (SHAKE)
ぷるるっ
...IT'S CUTE.
HEH.
MAMA.
OH, HEY.
IT'S CALLING YOU "MAMA."
WHAT'S A MAMA?
"MAMA" IS A WESTERN WORD THAT MEANS...
PITO (TUP)
ピトッ

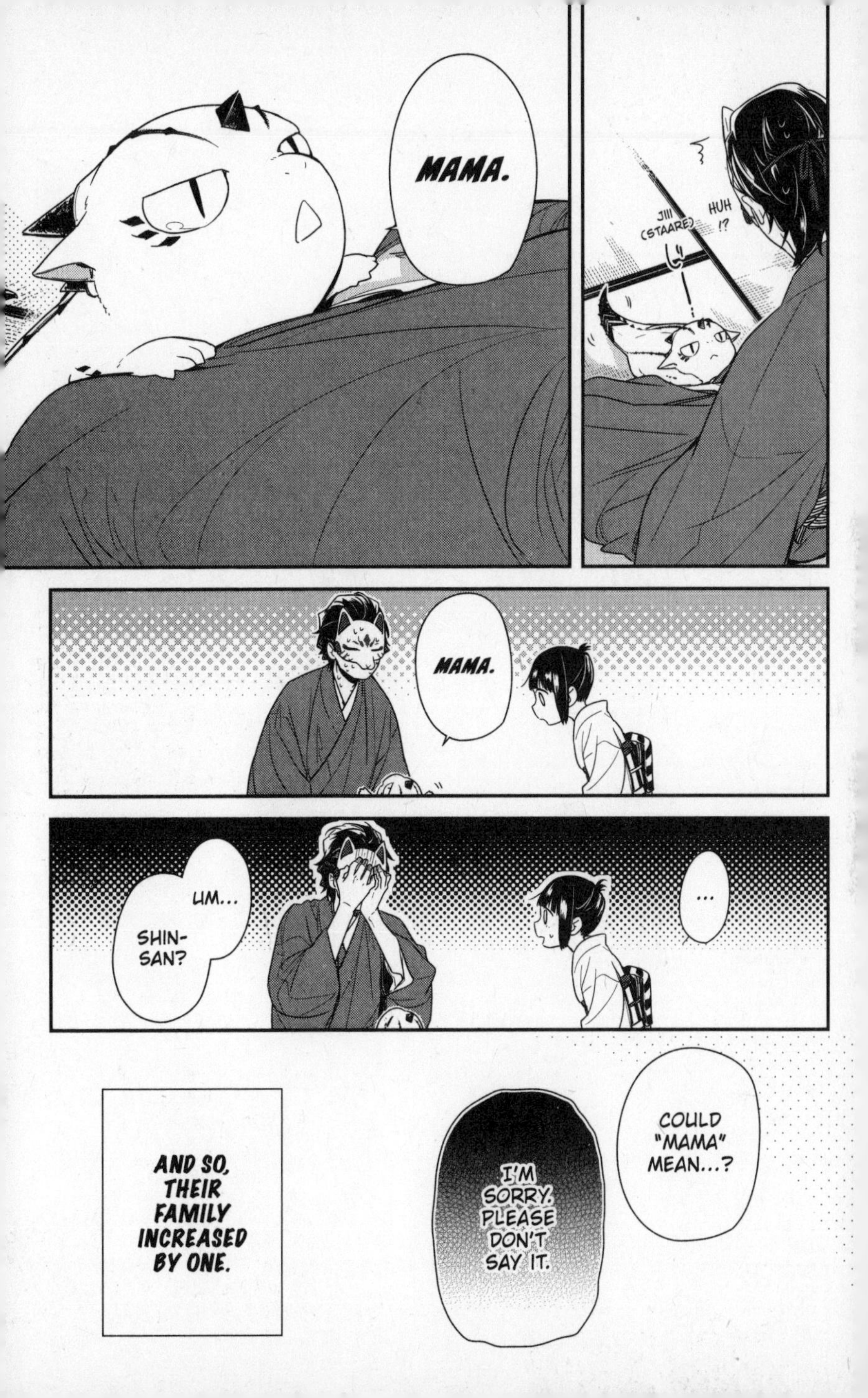
HUH !?
JIII (STAARE)
MAMA.
MAMA.
...
UM... SHIN-SAN?
COULD "MAMA" MEAN...?
I'M SORRY. PLEASE DON'T SAY IT.
AND SO, THEIR FAMILY INCREASED BY ONE.

Ne Ne Ne

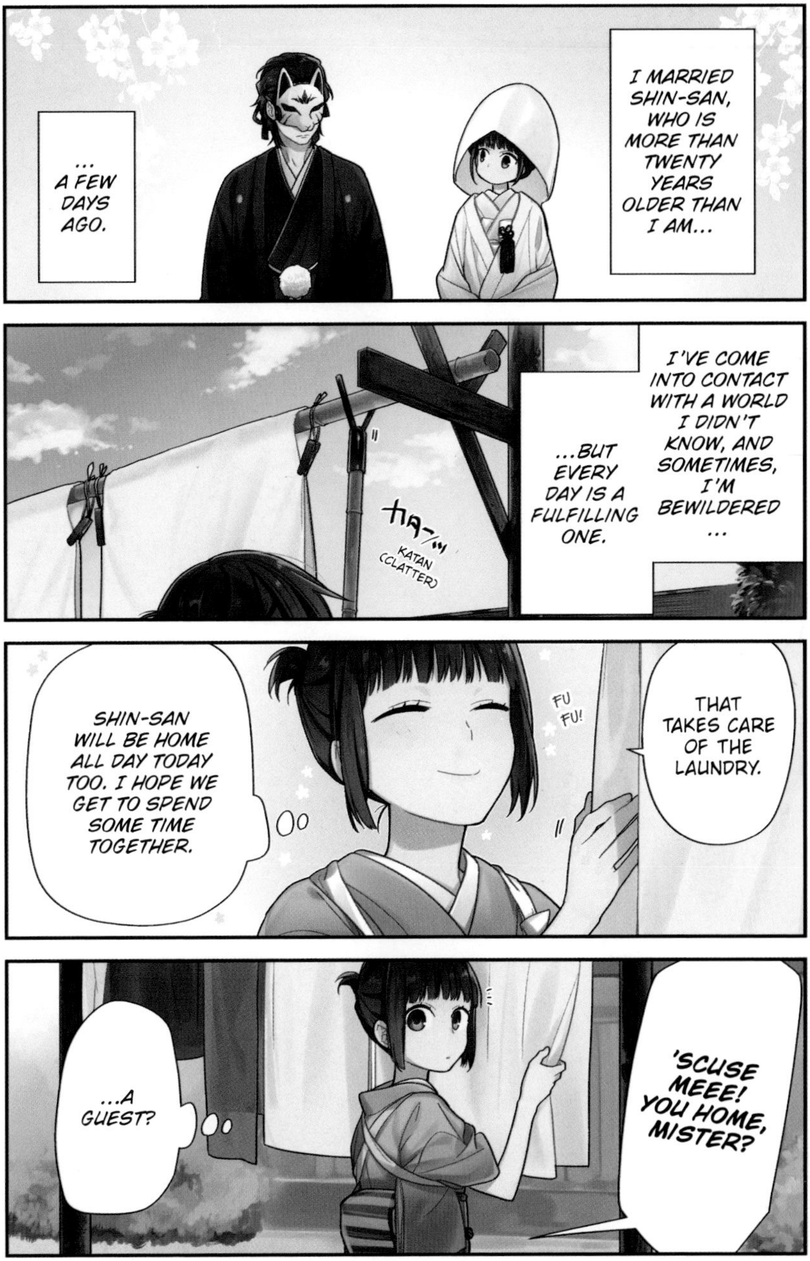
I MARRIED SHIN-SAN, WHO IS MORE THAN TWENTY YEARS OLDER THAN I AM...
... A FEW DAYS AGO.
I'VE COME INTO CONTACT WITH A WORLD I DIDN'T KNOW, AND SOMETIMES, I'M BEWILDERED ...
...BUT EVERY DAY IS A FULFILLING ONE.
KATAN (CLATTER)
THAT TAKES CARE OF THE LAUNDRY.
FU FU!
SHIN-SAN WILL BE HOME ALL DAY TODAY TOO. I HOPE WE GET TO SPEND SOME TIME TOGETHER.
'SCUSE MEEE! YOU HOME, MISTER?
...A GUEST?

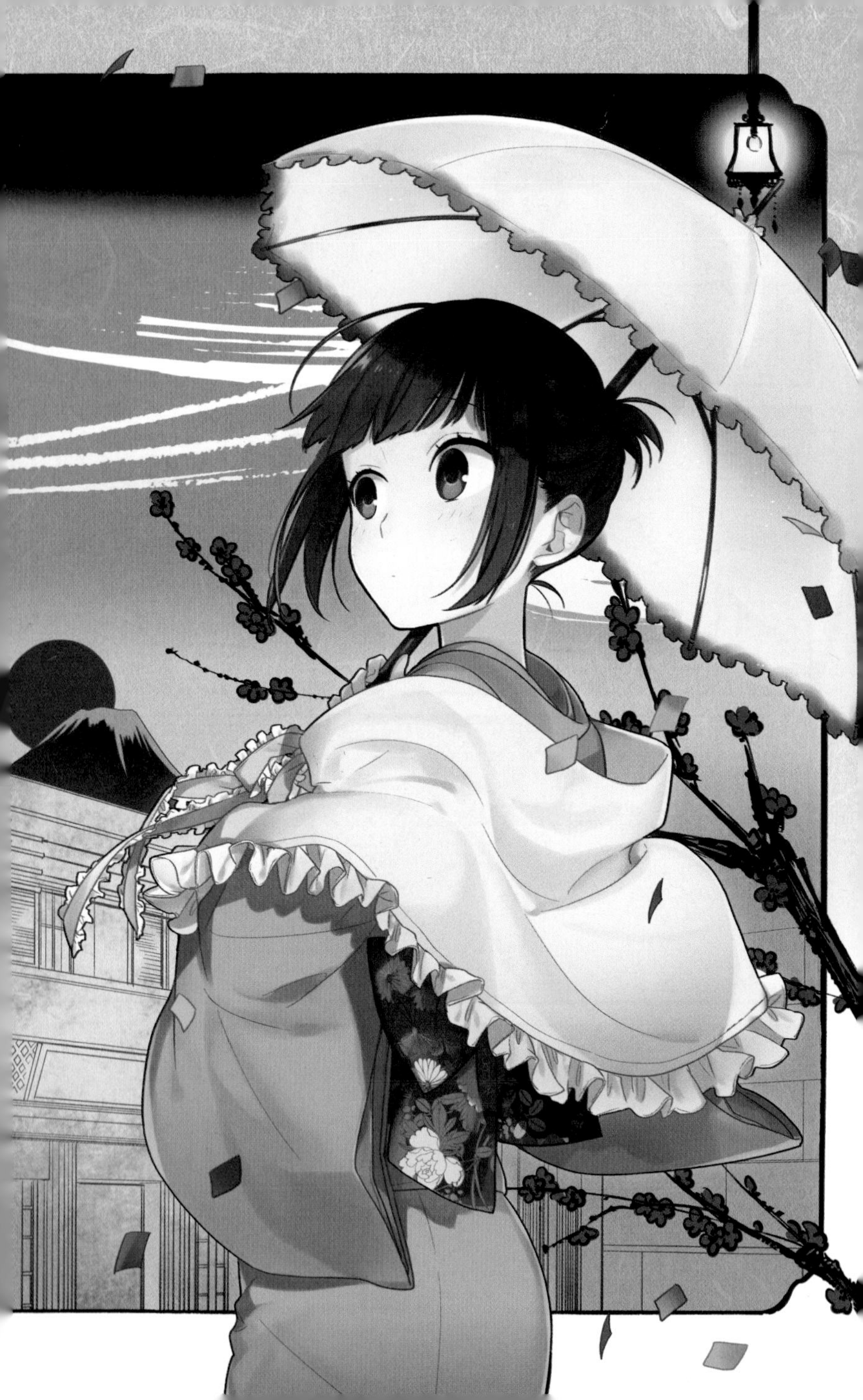

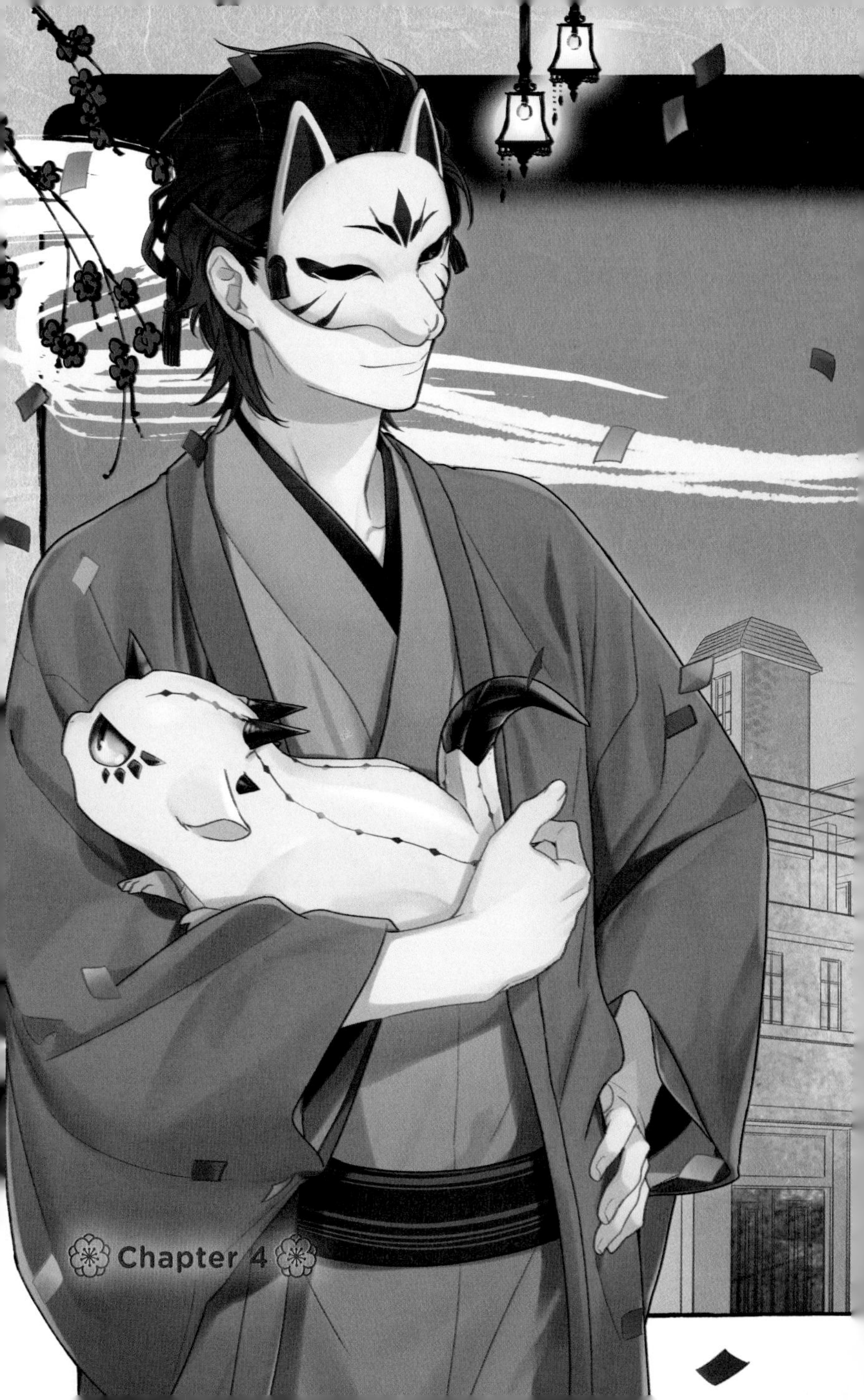
Chapter 4

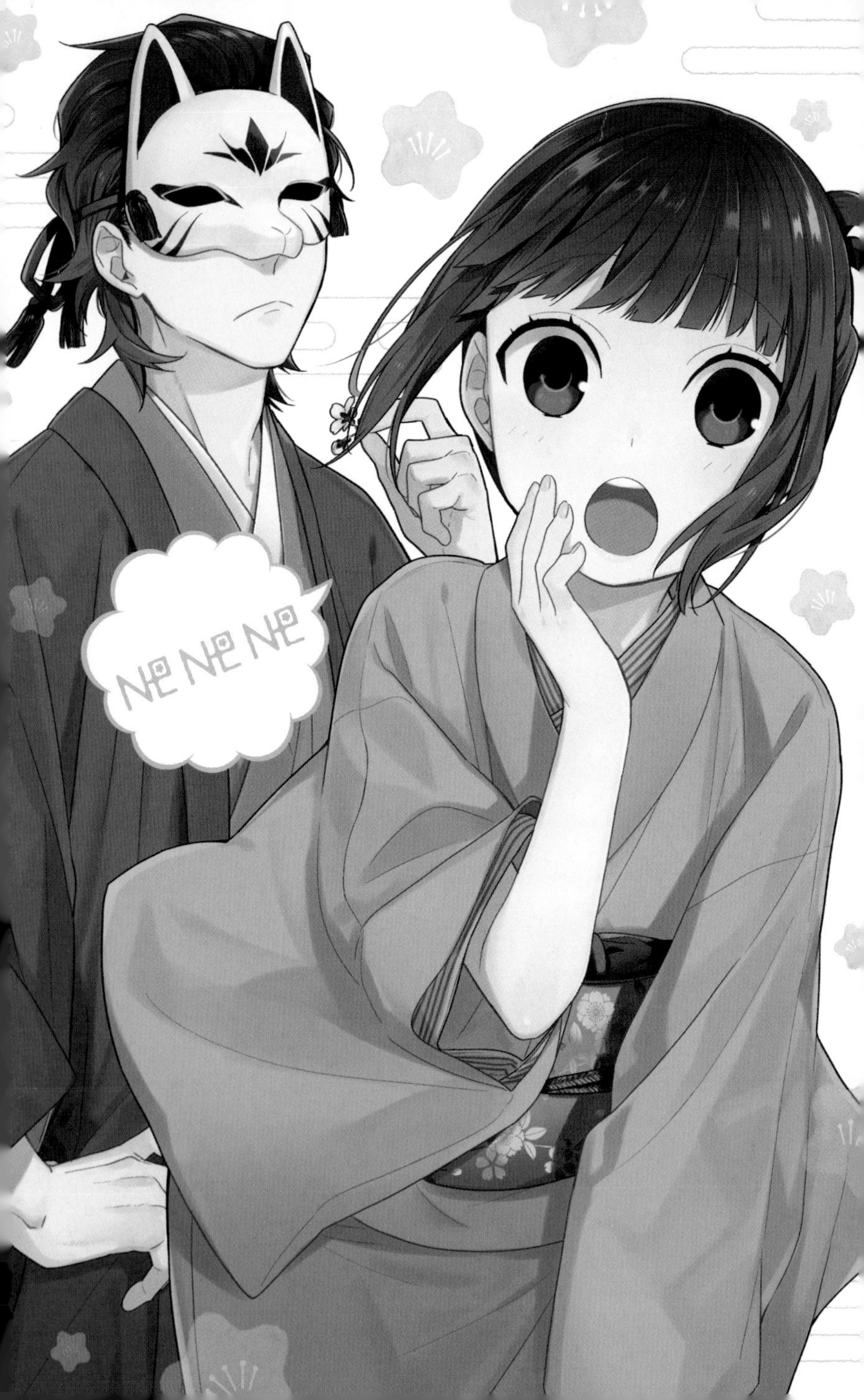
NE NE NE

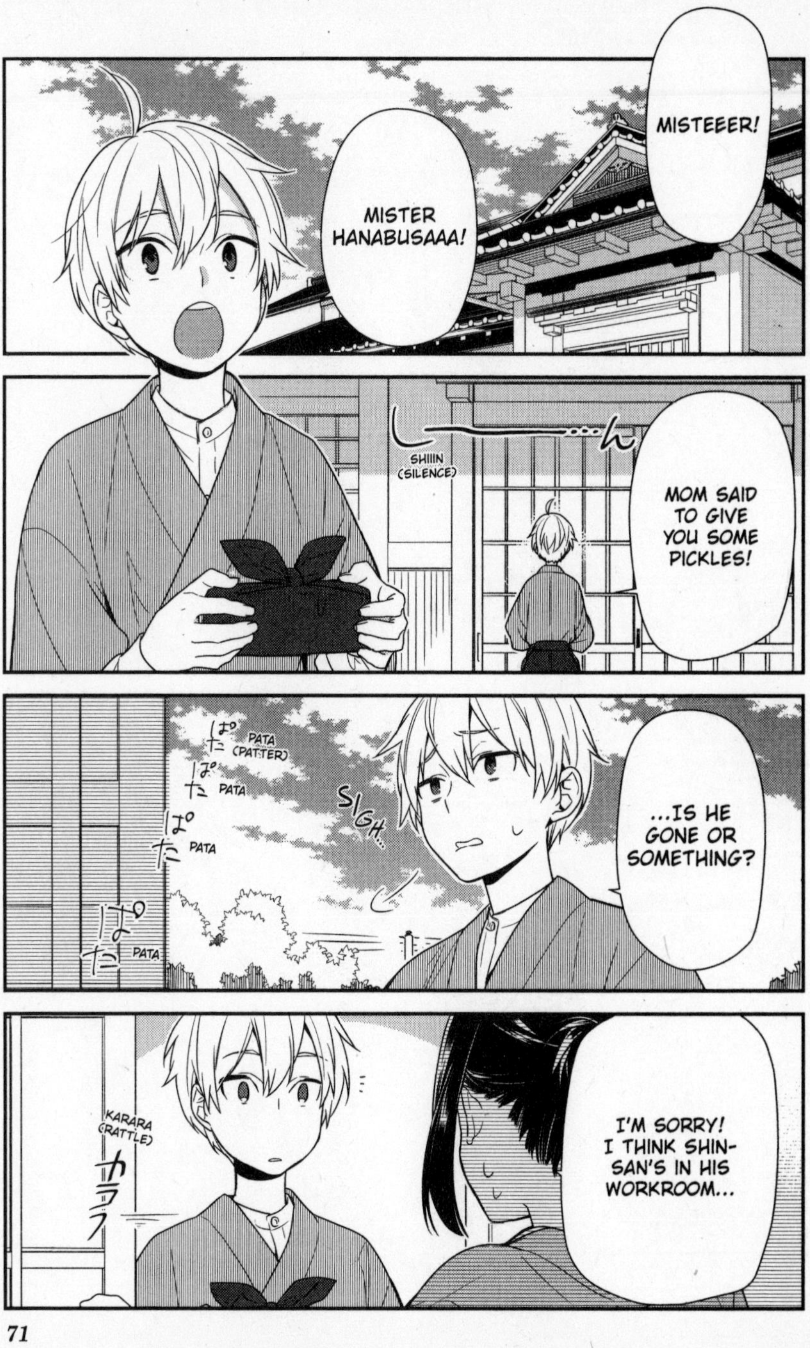
MISTEEER!
MISTER HANABUSAAA!
MOM SAID TO GIVE YOU SOME PICKLES!
SHIIN (SILENCE)
...IS HE GONE OR SOMETHING?
SIGH...
PATA (PATTER)
PATA
PATA
PATA
I'M SORRY! I THINK SHIN-SAN'S IN HIS WORKROOM...
KARARA (RATTLE)

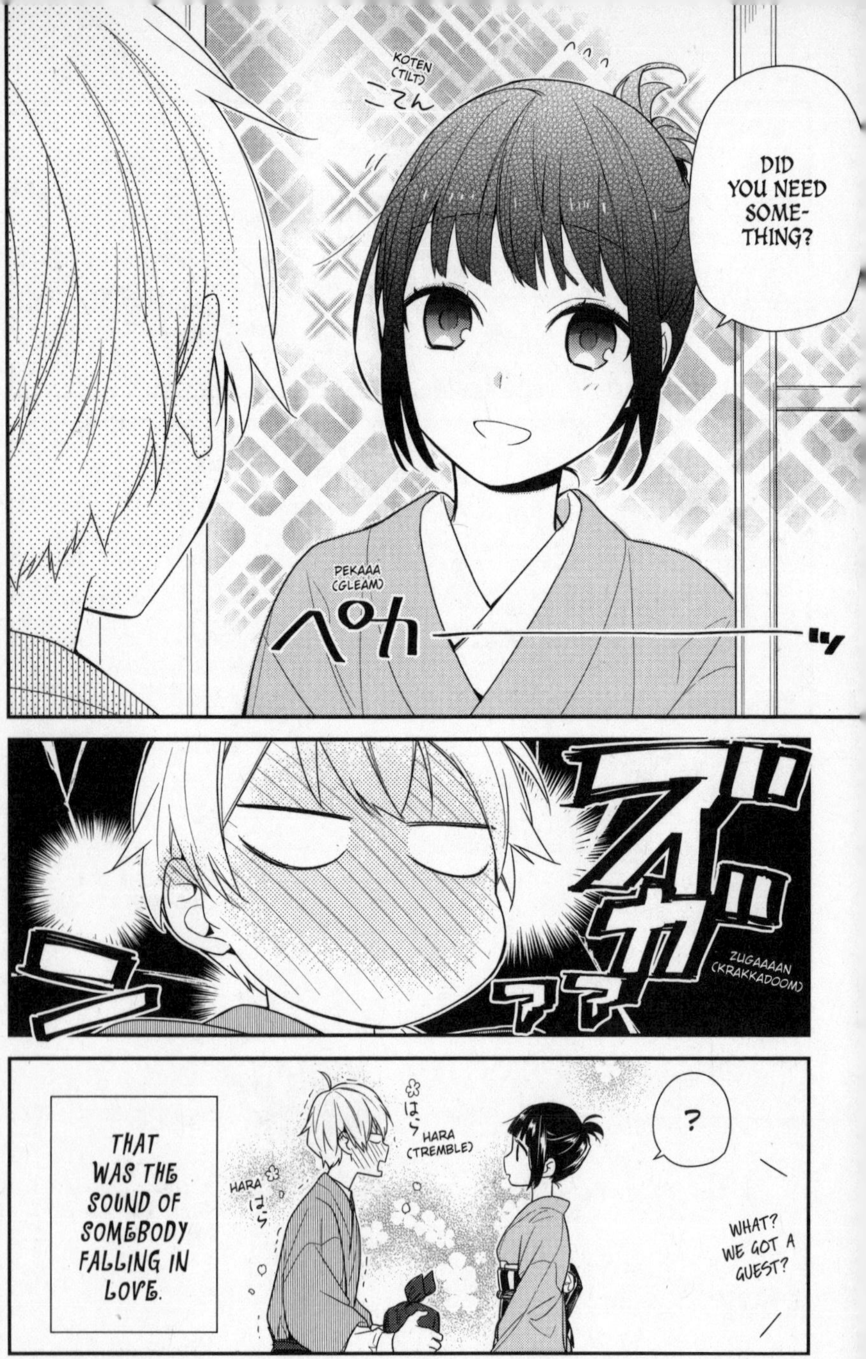
DID YOU NEED SOMETHING?
KOTEN (TILT)
こてん
PEKAAA (GLEAM)
ZUGAAAAN (KRAKKADOOM)
?
WHAT? WE GOT A GUEST?
HARA (TREMBLE)
はら
HARA
はら
THAT WAS THE SOUND OF SOMEBODY FALLING IN LOVE.

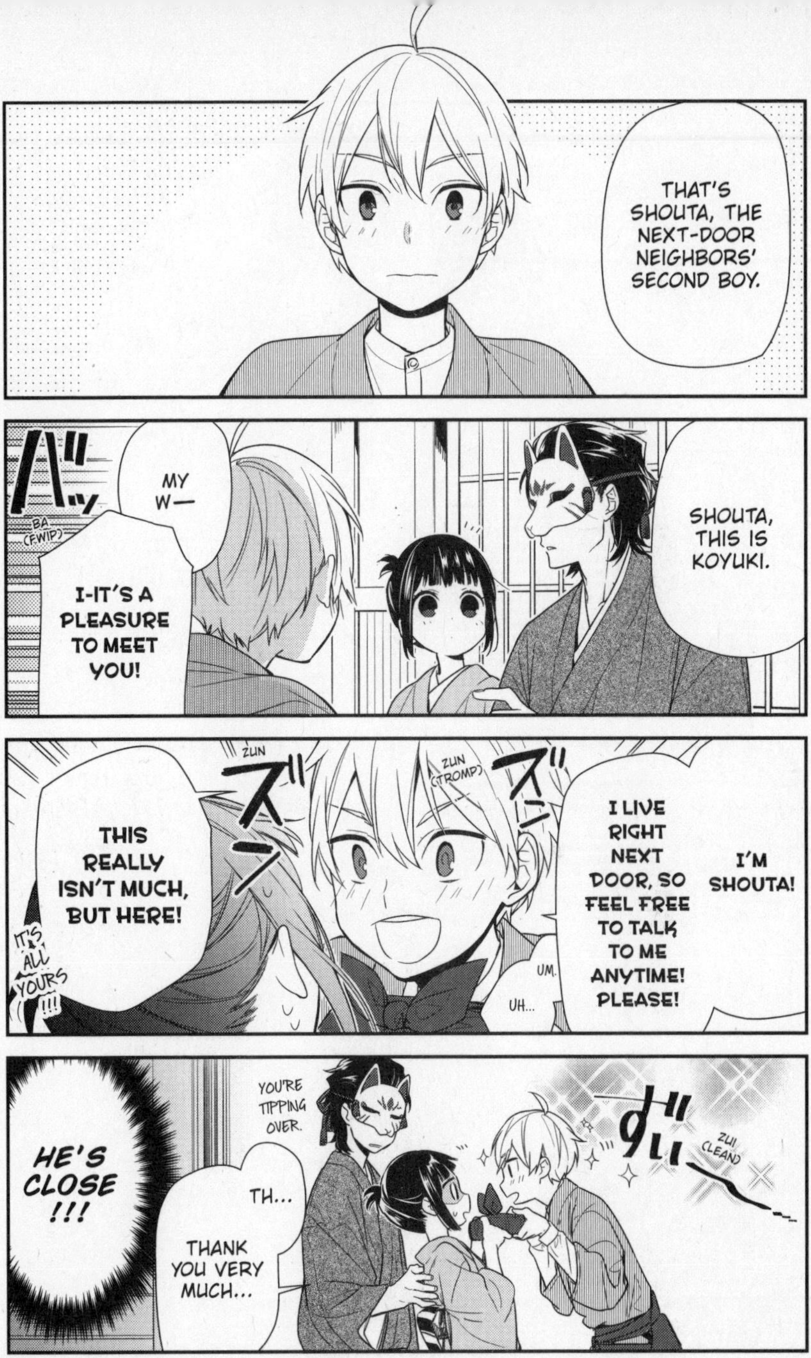
THAT'S SHOUTA, THE NEXT-DOOR NEIGHBORS' SECOND BOY.
SHOUTA, THIS IS KOYUKI.
MY W—
BA (FWIP)
I-IT'S A PLEASURE TO MEET YOU!
I'M SHOUTA!
I LIVE RIGHT NEXT DOOR, SO FEEL FREE TO TALK TO ME ANYTIME! PLEASE!
ZUN (TROMP)
UM.
UH...
ZUN
THIS REALLY ISN'T MUCH, BUT HERE!
IT'S ALL YOURS!!!
ZUI (CLEAN)
YOU'RE TIPPING OVER.
TH...
THANK YOU VERY MUCH...
HE'S CLOSE!!!

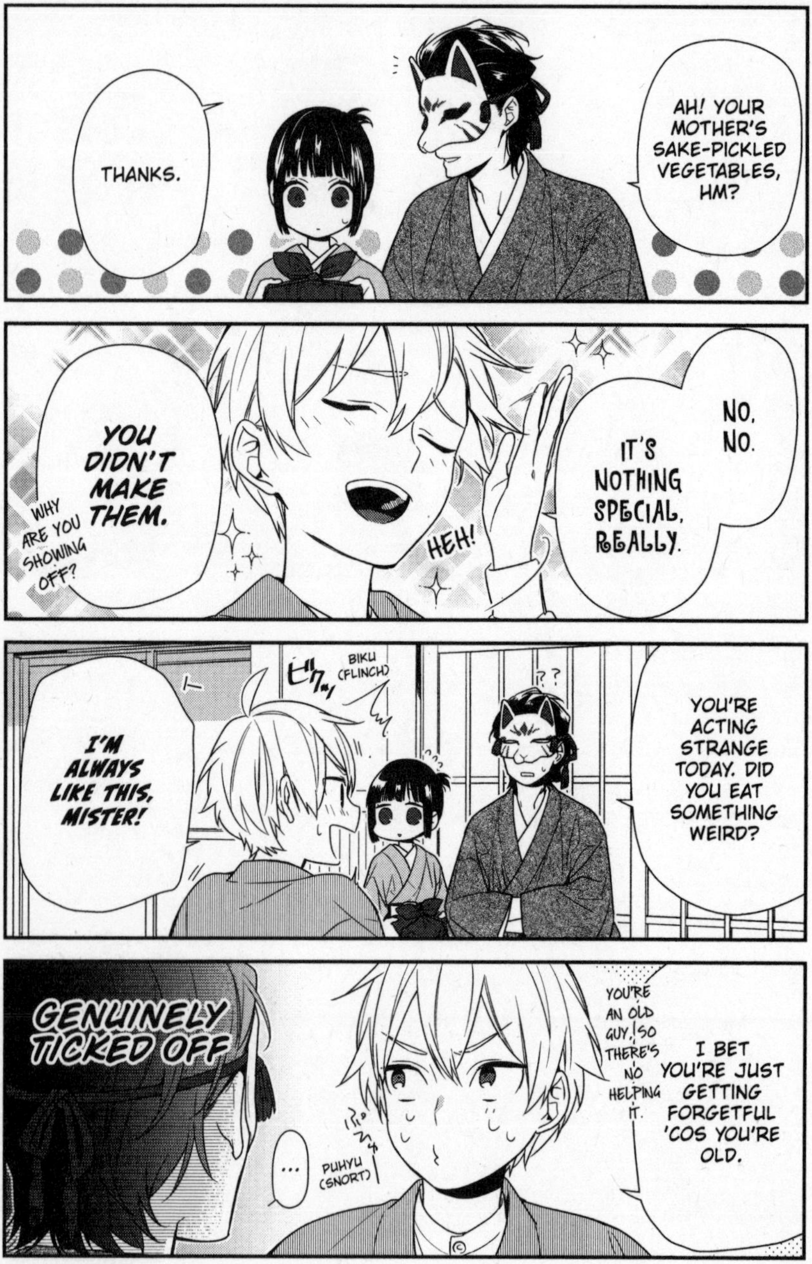
AH! YOUR MOTHER'S SAKE-PICKLED VEGETABLES, HM?
THANKS.
NO. NO.
IT'S NOTHING SPECIAL, REALLY.
HEH!
YOU DIDN'T MAKE THEM.
WHY ARE YOU SHOWING OFF?
YOU'RE ACTING STRANGE TODAY. DID YOU EAT SOMETHING WEIRD?
BIKU (FLINCH)
I'M ALWAYS LIKE THIS, MISTER!
I BET YOU'RE JUST GETTING FORGETFUL 'COS YOU'RE OLD.
YOU'RE AN OLD GUY, SO THERE'S NO HELPING IT.
PUHYU (SNORT)
...
GENUINELY TICKED OFF

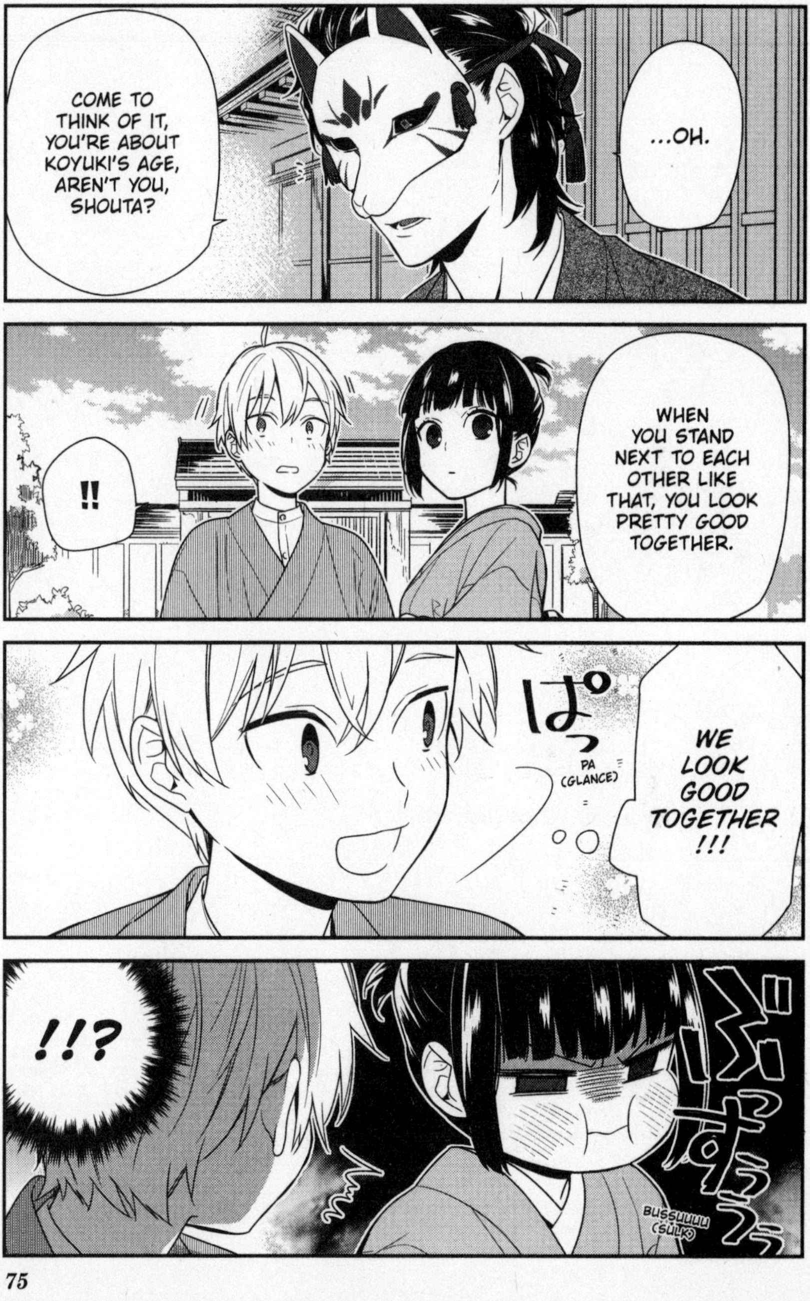
...OH.
COME TO THINK OF IT, YOU'RE ABOUT KOYUKI'S AGE, AREN'T YOU, SHOUTA?
WHEN YOU STAND NEXT TO EACH OTHER LIKE THAT, YOU LOOK PRETTY GOOD TOGETHER.
!!
WE LOOK GOOD TOGETHER !!!
ぱっ
PA (GLANCE)
BUSSUUUU (SULK)
!!?

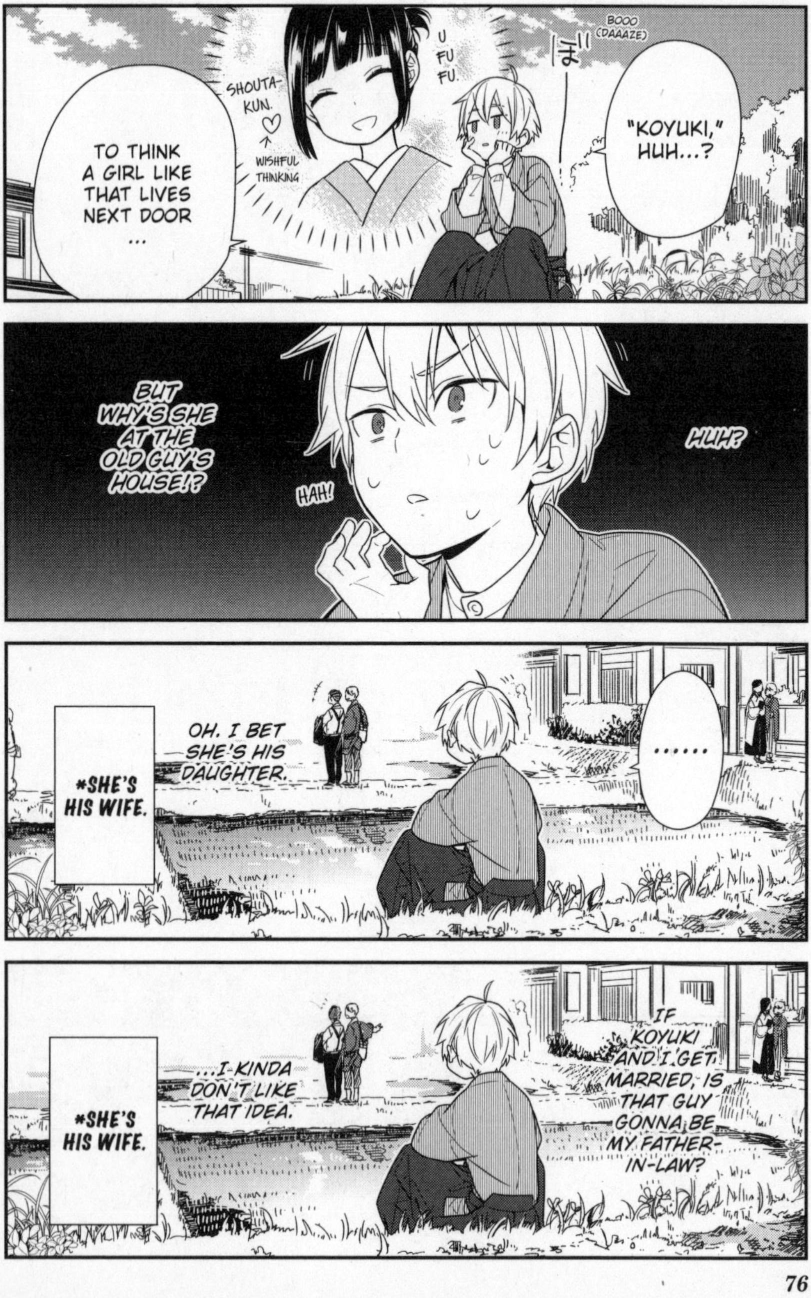
BOOO (DAAAZE)
ぼ
"KOYUKI," HUH...?
U FU FU.
SHOUTA-KUN. ♡
WISHFUL THINKING
TO THINK A GIRL LIKE THAT LIVES NEXT DOOR ...
HUH?
HAH!
BUT WHY'S SHE AT THE OLD GUY'S HOUSE!?
......
OH. I BET SHE'S HIS DAUGHTER.
*SHE'S HIS WIFE.
IF KOYUKI AND I GET MARRIED, IS THAT GUY GONNA BE MY FATHER-IN-LAW?
...I KINDA DON'T LIKE THAT IDEA.
*SHE'S HIS WIFE.

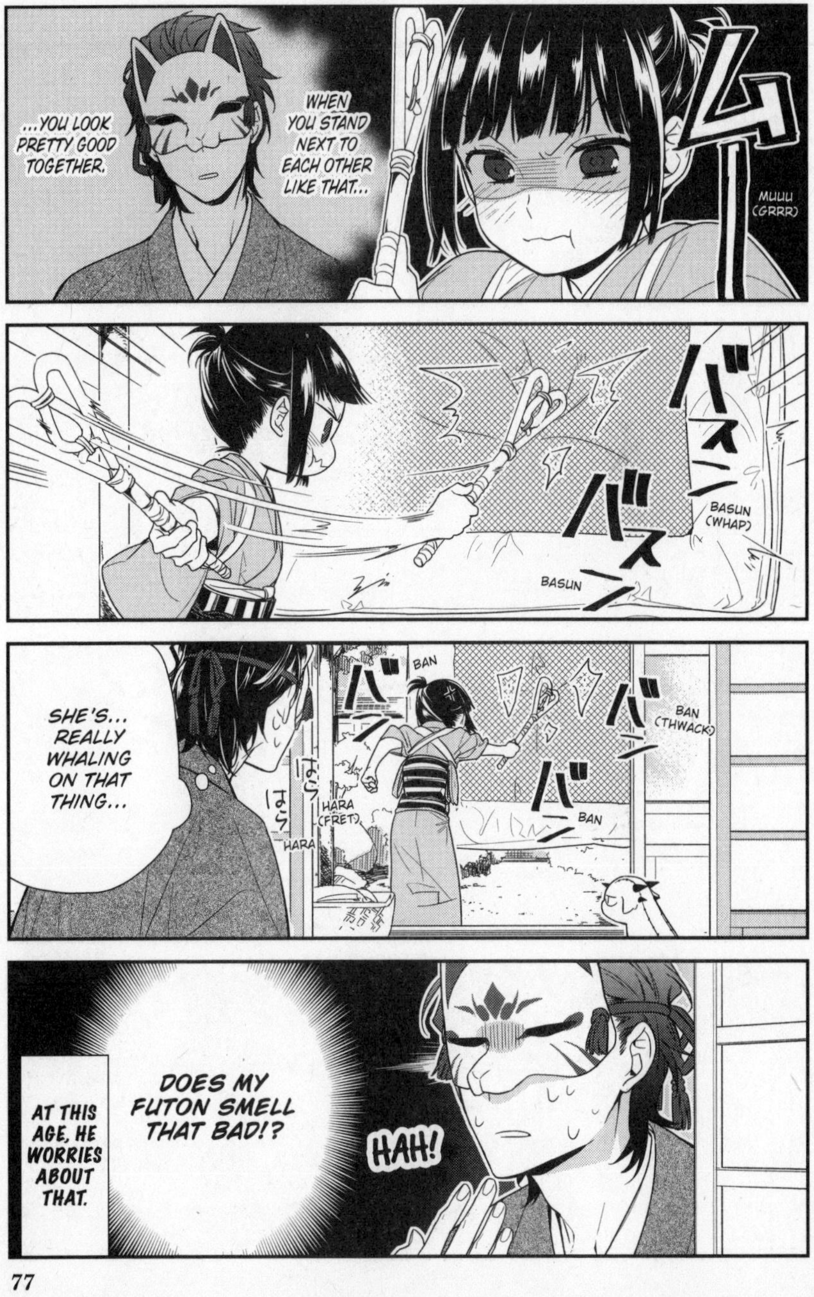

MUUU (GRRR)
WHEN YOU STAND NEXT TO EACH OTHER LIKE THAT...
...YOU LOOK PRETTY GOOD TOGETHER.
BASUN (WHAP)
BASUN
BAN (THWACK)
BAN
BAN
HARA (FRET)
HARA
SHE'S... REALLY WHALING ON THAT THING...
HAH!
DOES MY FUTON SMELL THAT BAD!?
AT THIS AGE, HE WORRIES ABOUT THAT.

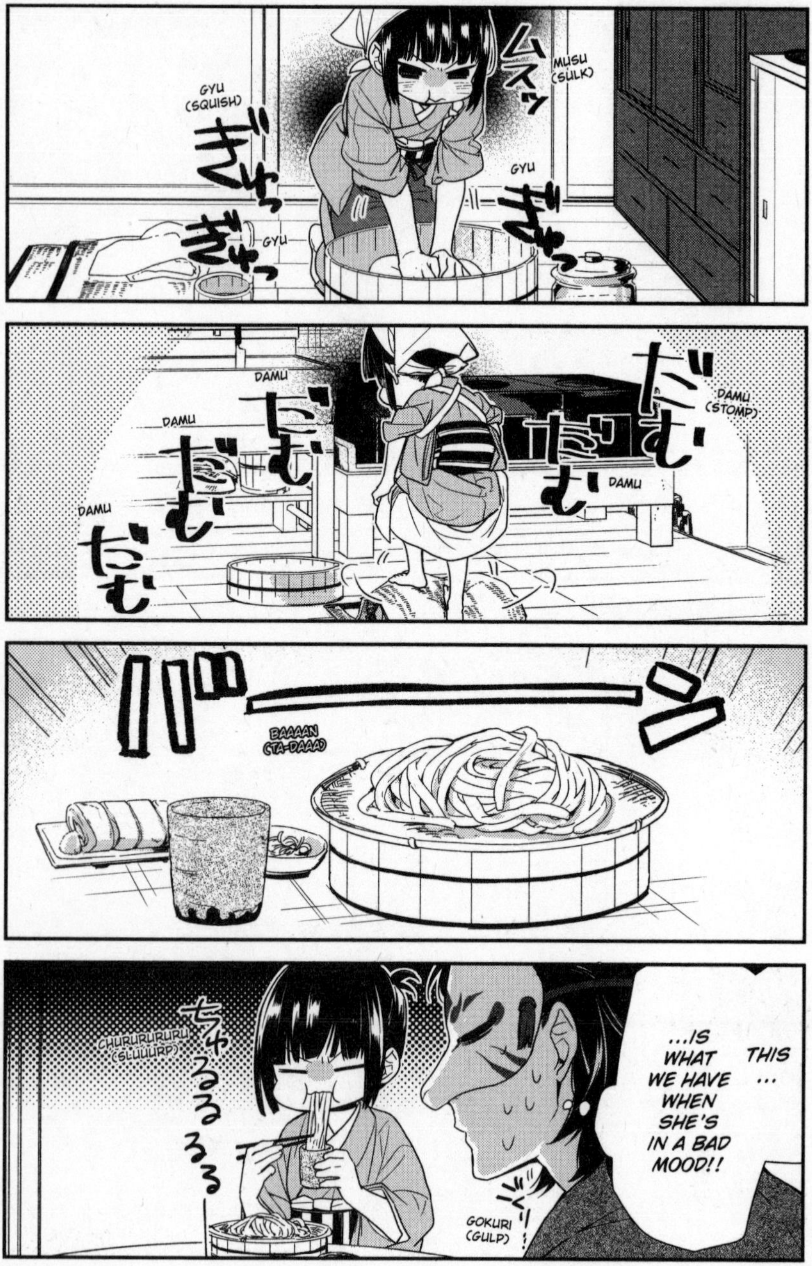
ムスッ
MUSU (SULK)
ぎゅっ
GYU
ぎゅっ
GYU (SQUISH)
ぎゅっ
GYU
だむ
DAMU (STOMP)
だむ
DAMU
だむ
DAMU
だむ
DAMU
だむ
DAMU
バーーーン
BAAAAN (TA-DAAA)
THIS ...
...IS WHAT WE HAVE WHEN SHE'S IN A BAD MOOD!!
ゴクリ
GOKURI (GULP)
ちゅるるるる
CHURURURURU (SLUUURP)

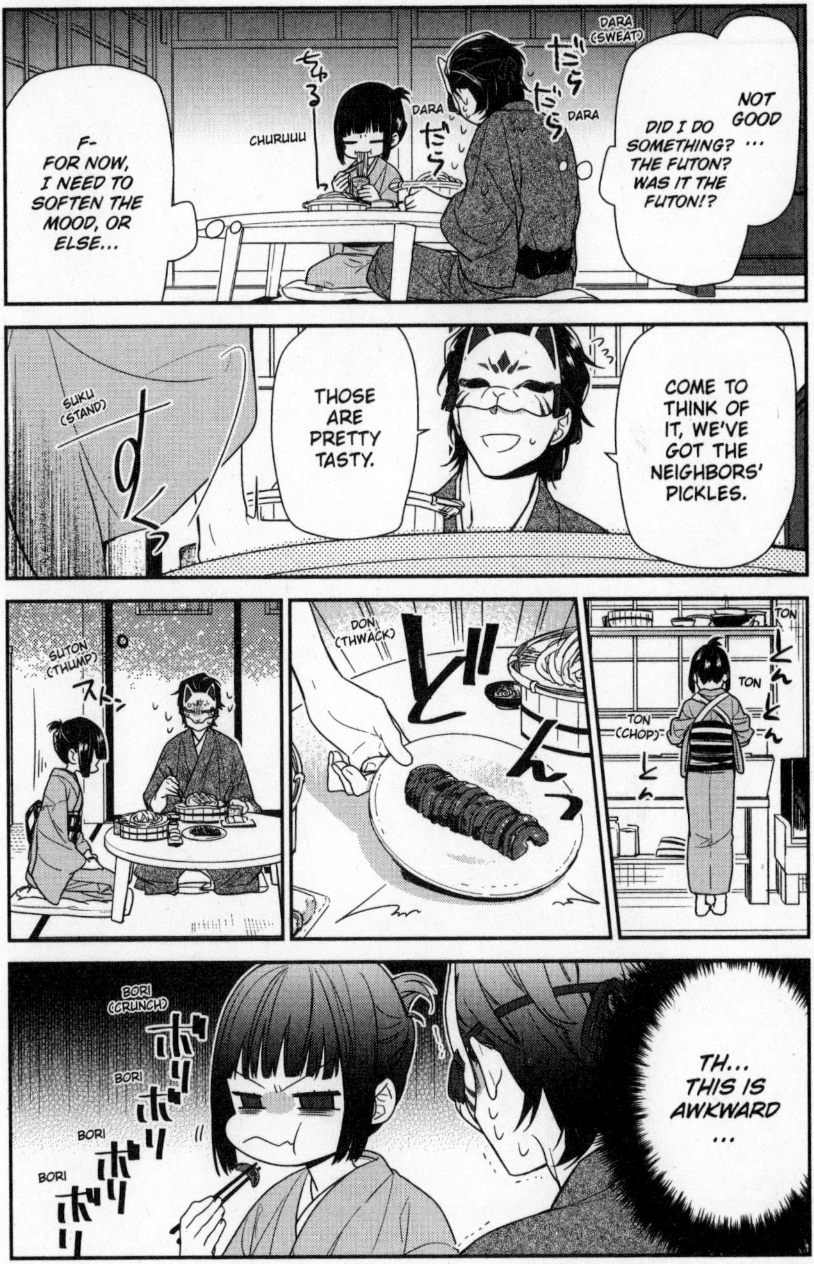

NOT GOOD ...
DID I DO SOMETHING? THE FUTON? WAS IT THE FUTON!?
DARA (SWEAT)
DARA
DARA
CHURUUU
F- FOR NOW, I NEED TO SOFTEN THE MOOD, OR ELSE...
COME TO THINK OF IT, WE'VE GOT THE NEIGHBORS' PICKLES.
THOSE ARE PRETTY TASTY.
SUKU (STAND)
TON
TON
TON (CHOP)
DON (THWACK)
SUTON (THUMP)
TH... THIS IS AWKWARD ...
BORI (CRUNCH)
BORI
BORI
BORI

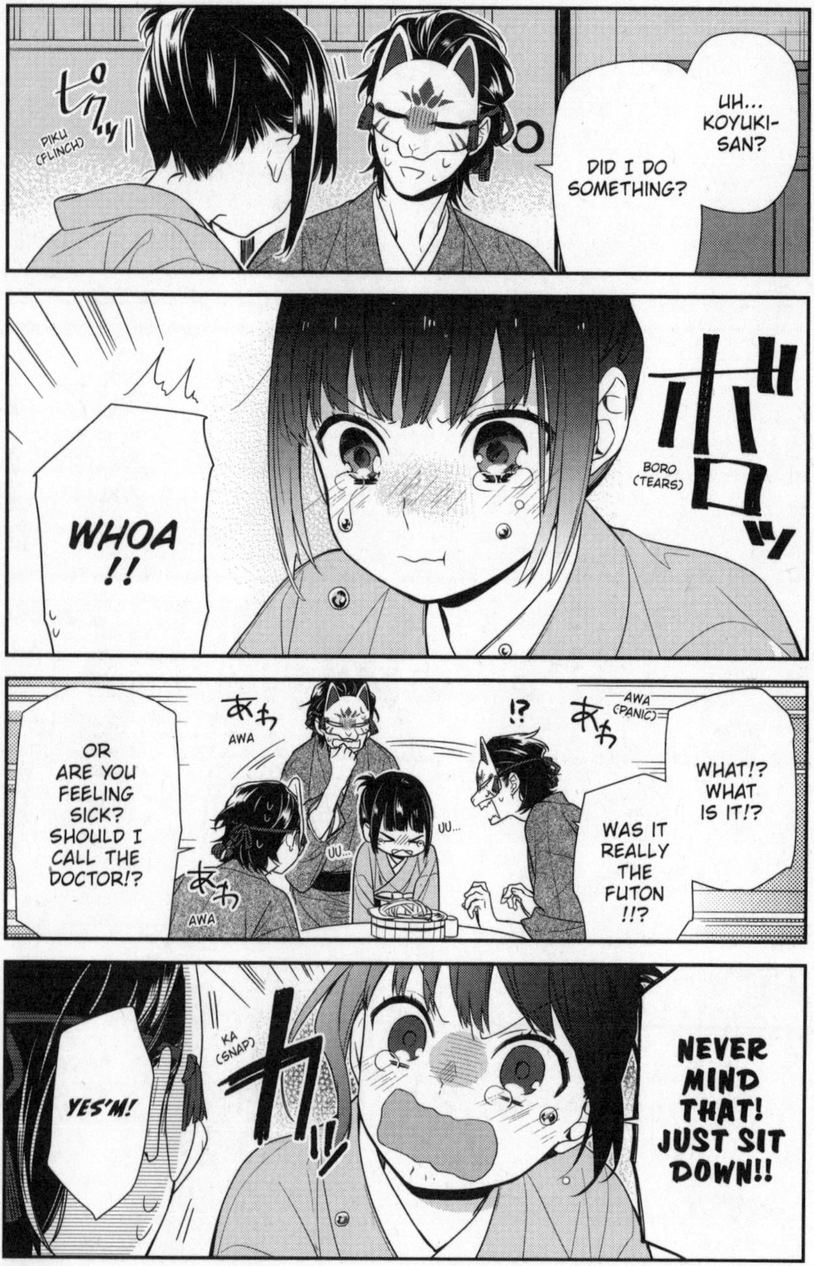
UH... KOYUKI-SAN?
DID I DO SOMETHING?
ピクッ
PIKU (FLINCH)
ボロッ
BORO (TEARS)
WHOA!!
WHAT!? WHAT IS IT!?
WAS IT REALLY THE FUTON!!?
あわ
AWA (PANIC)
!?
あわ
AWA
UU...
UU...
OR ARE YOU FEELING SICK? SHOULD I CALL THE DOCTOR!?
あわ
AWA
NEVER MIND THAT! JUST SIT DOWN!!
カッ
KA (SNAP)
YES'M!

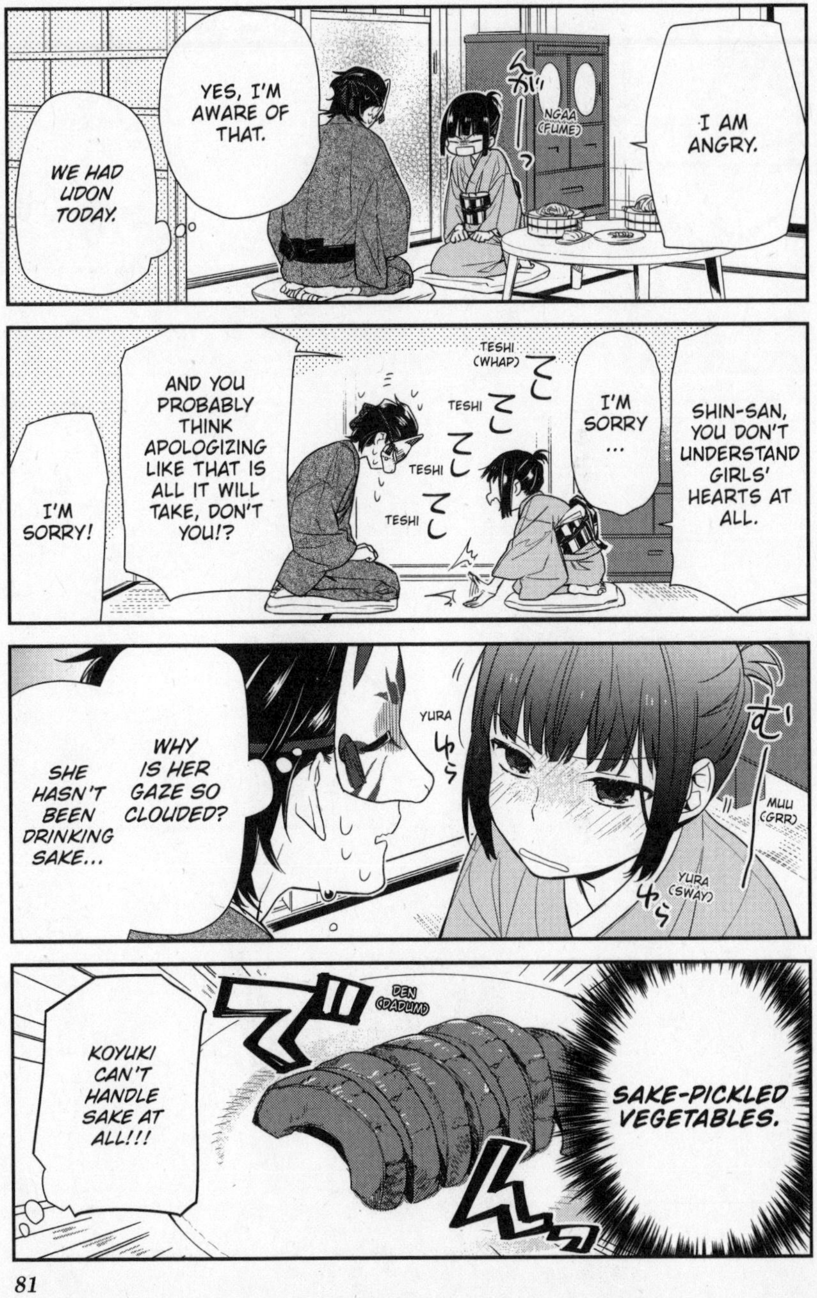
I AM ANGRY.
NGAA (FUME)
YES, I'M AWARE OF THAT.
WE HAD UDON TODAY.
SHIN-SAN, YOU DON'T UNDERSTAND GIRLS' HEARTS AT ALL.
I'M SORRY ...
TESHI (WHAP)
TESHI
TESHI
TESHI
AND YOU PROBABLY THINK APOLOGIZING LIKE THAT IS ALL IT WILL TAKE, DON'T YOU!?
I'M SORRY!
MUU (GRR)
YURA (SWAY)
YURA
WHY IS HER GAZE SO CLOUDED?
SHE HASN'T BEEN DRINKING SAKE...
SAKE-PICKLED VEGETABLES.
DEN (DADUM)
KOYUKI CAN'T HANDLE SAKE AT ALL!!!

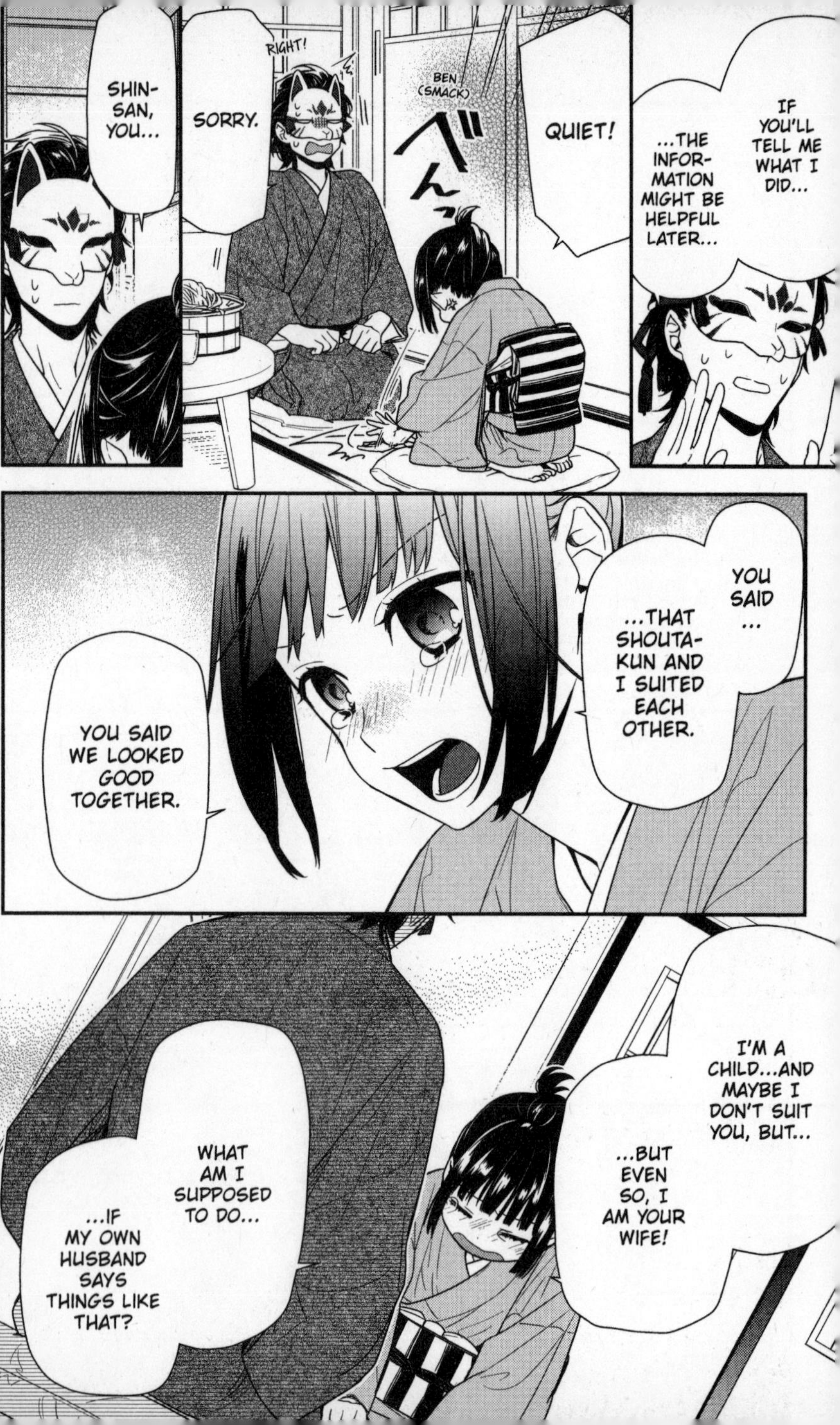
IF YOU'LL TELL ME WHAT I DID...
...THE INFORMATION MIGHT BE HELPFUL LATER...
QUIET!
BEN (SMACK)
べんっ
RIGHT!
SORRY.
SHIN-SAN, YOU...
YOU SAID...
...THAT SHOUTA-KUN AND I SUITED EACH OTHER.
YOU SAID WE LOOKED GOOD TOGETHER.
I'M A CHILD...AND MAYBE I DON'T SUIT YOU, BUT...
...BUT EVEN SO, I AM YOUR WIFE!
WHAT AM I SUPPOSED TO DO...
...IF MY OWN HUSBAND SAYS THINGS LIKE THAT?

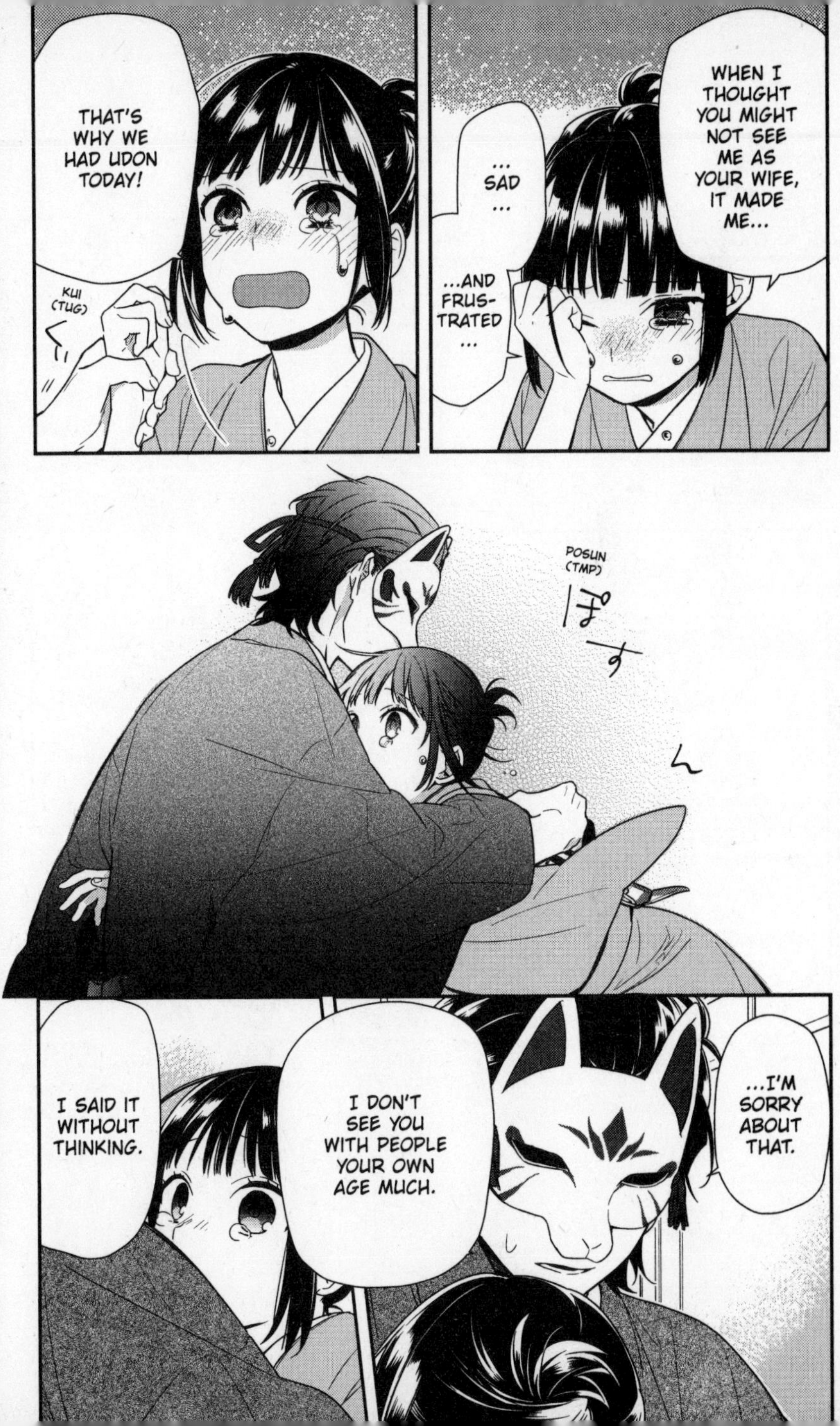
WHEN I THOUGHT YOU MIGHT NOT SEE ME AS YOUR WIFE, IT MADE ME...
... SAD ...
...AND FRUS-TRATED ...
THAT'S WHY WE HAD UDON TODAY!
KUI (TUG)
POSUN (TMP)
ぽす
ん
...I'M SORRY ABOUT THAT.
I DON'T SEE YOU WITH PEOPLE YOUR OWN AGE MUCH.
I SAID IT WITHOUT THINKING.

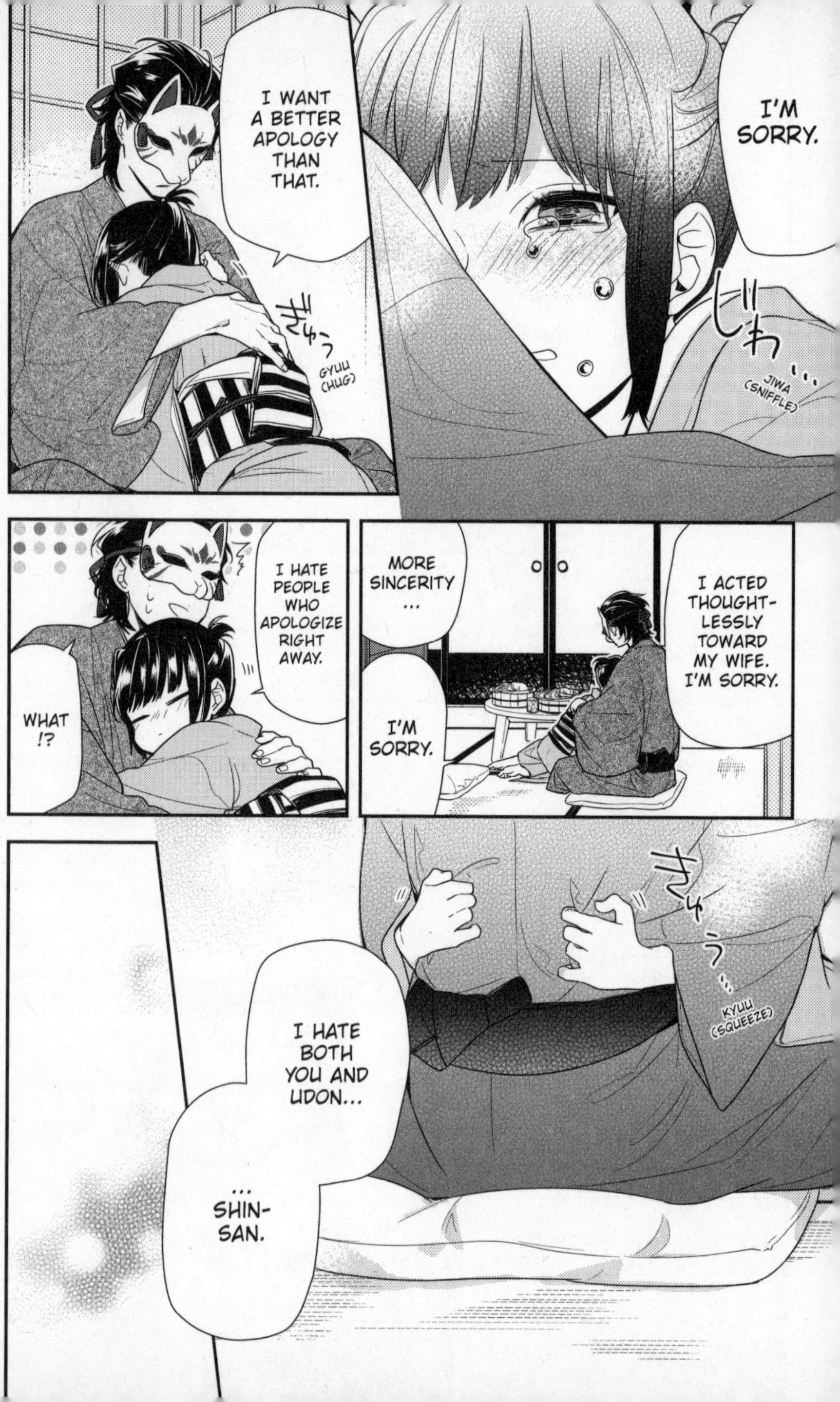
I'M SORRY.
じわ…
JIWA (SNIFFLE)
I WANT A BETTER APOLOGY THAN THAT.
ぎゅう
GYUU (HUG)
I ACTED THOUGHT-LESSLY TOWARD MY WIFE. I'M SORRY.
MORE SINCERITY...
I'M SORRY.
I HATE PEOPLE WHO APOLOGIZE RIGHT AWAY.
WHAT!?
きゅう…
KYUU (SQUEEZE)
I HATE BOTH YOU AND UDON...
...SHIN-SAN.

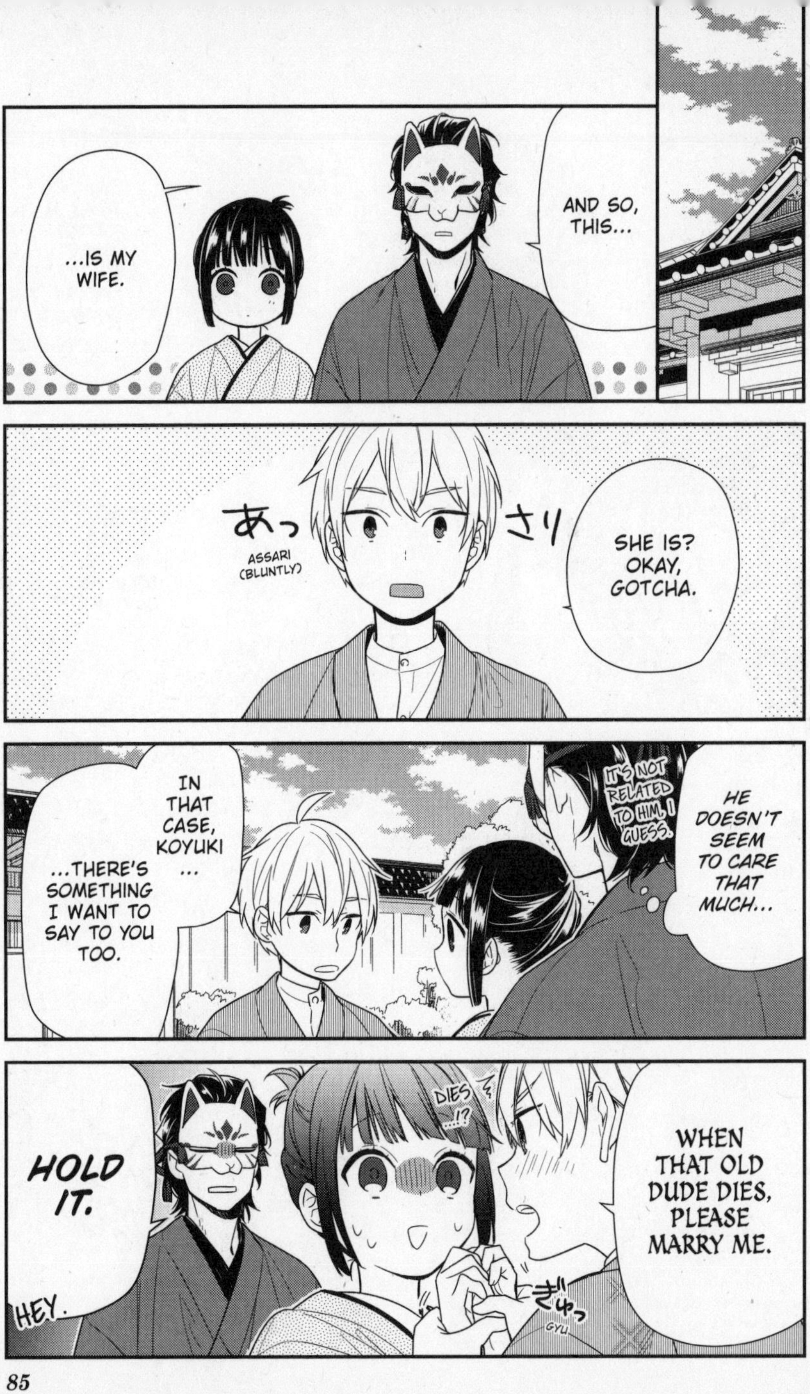
AND SO, THIS...
...IS MY WIFE.
SHE IS? OKAY, GOTCHA.
あっさり
ASSARI (BLUNTLY)
HE DOESN'T SEEM TO CARE THAT MUCH...
IT'S NOT RELATED TO HIM, I GUESS.
IN THAT CASE, KOYUKI...
...THERE'S SOMETHING I WANT TO SAY TO YOU TOO.
WHEN THAT OLD DUDE DIES, PLEASE MARRY ME.
ぎゅっ
GYU
DIES...!?
HOLD IT.
HEY.

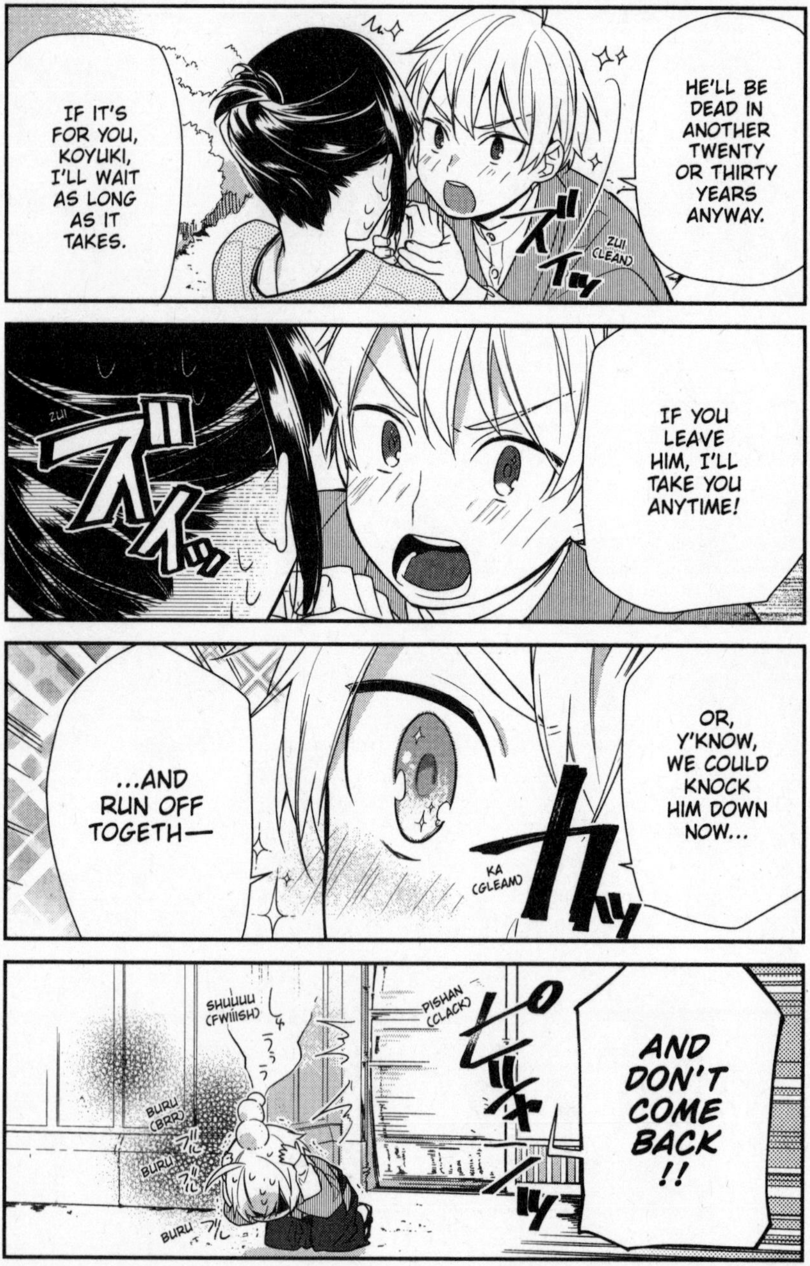
HE'LL BE DEAD IN ANOTHER TWENTY OR THIRTY YEARS ANYWAY.
ZUI (CLEAN)
IF IT'S FOR YOU, KOYUKI, I'LL WAIT AS LONG AS IT TAKES.
IF YOU LEAVE HIM, I'LL TAKE YOU ANYTIME!
ZUI
OR, Y'KNOW, WE COULD KNOCK HIM DOWN NOW...
KA (GLEAM)
...AND RUN OFF TOGETH—
AND DON'T COME BACK!!
PISHAN (CLACK)
SHUUUU (FWIIISH)
BURU (BRR)
BURU
BURU

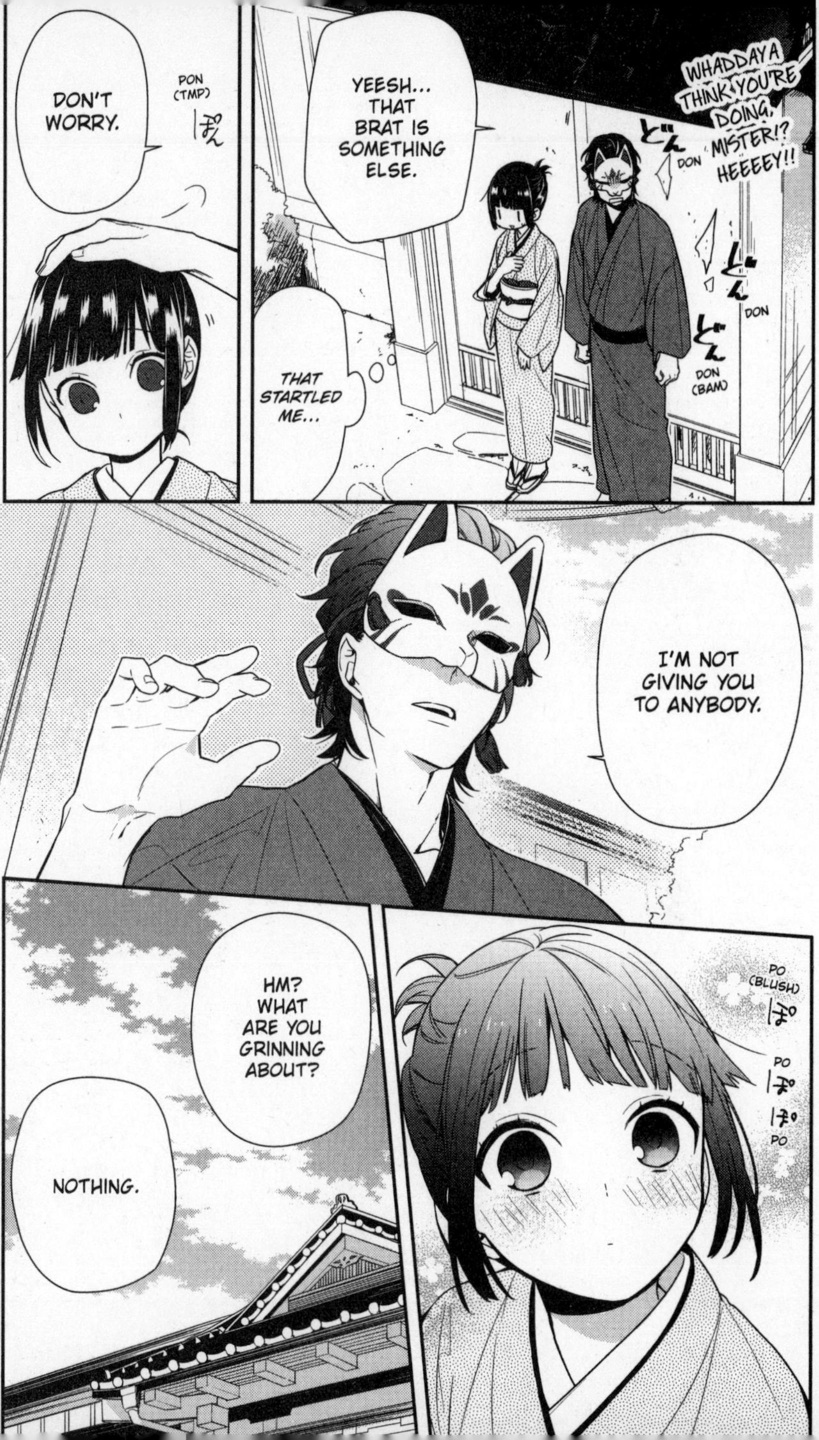
WHADDAYA THINK YOU'RE DOING, MISTER!? HEEEEY!!
どん
DON
どん
DON
どん
DON (BAM)
YEESH... THAT BRAT IS SOMETHING ELSE.
THAT STARTLED ME...
PON (TMP)
ぽん
DON'T WORRY.
I'M NOT GIVING YOU TO ANYBODY.
PO (BLUSH)
ぽ
PO
ぽ
ぽ
PO
HM? WHAT ARE YOU GRINNING ABOUT?
NOTHING.

Ne Ne Ne

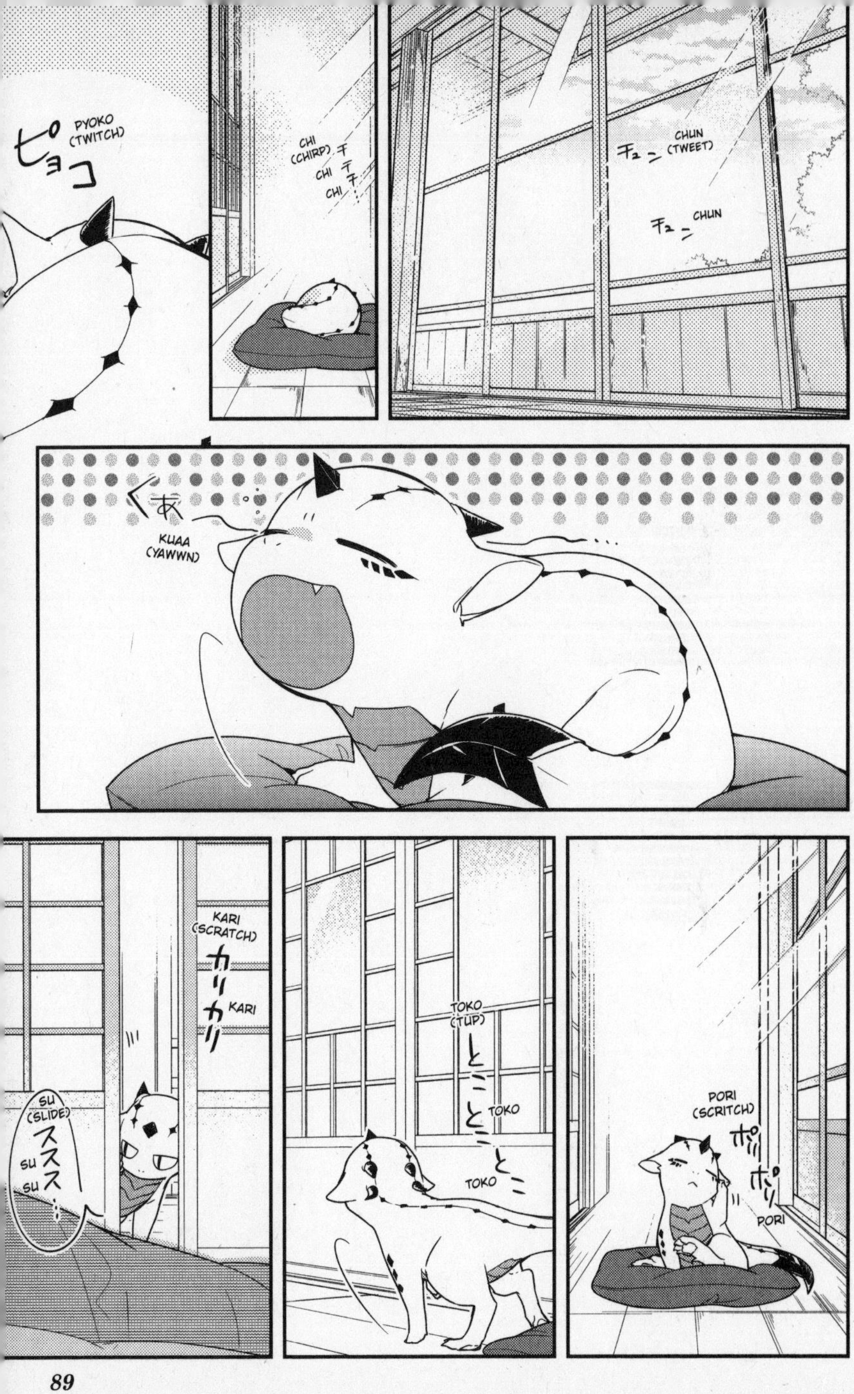
チュン CHUN (TWEET)
チュン CHUN
CHI (CHIRP) チ
CHI チ
CHI チ…
ピョコ PYOKO (TWITCH)
くあ… KUAA (YAWWN)
ポリ PORI (SCRITCH)
ポリ PORI
TOKO (TUP) とこ
とこ TOKO
TOKO
KARI (SCRATCH) カリ
カリ KARI
SU (SLIDE) ススス…
SU
SU

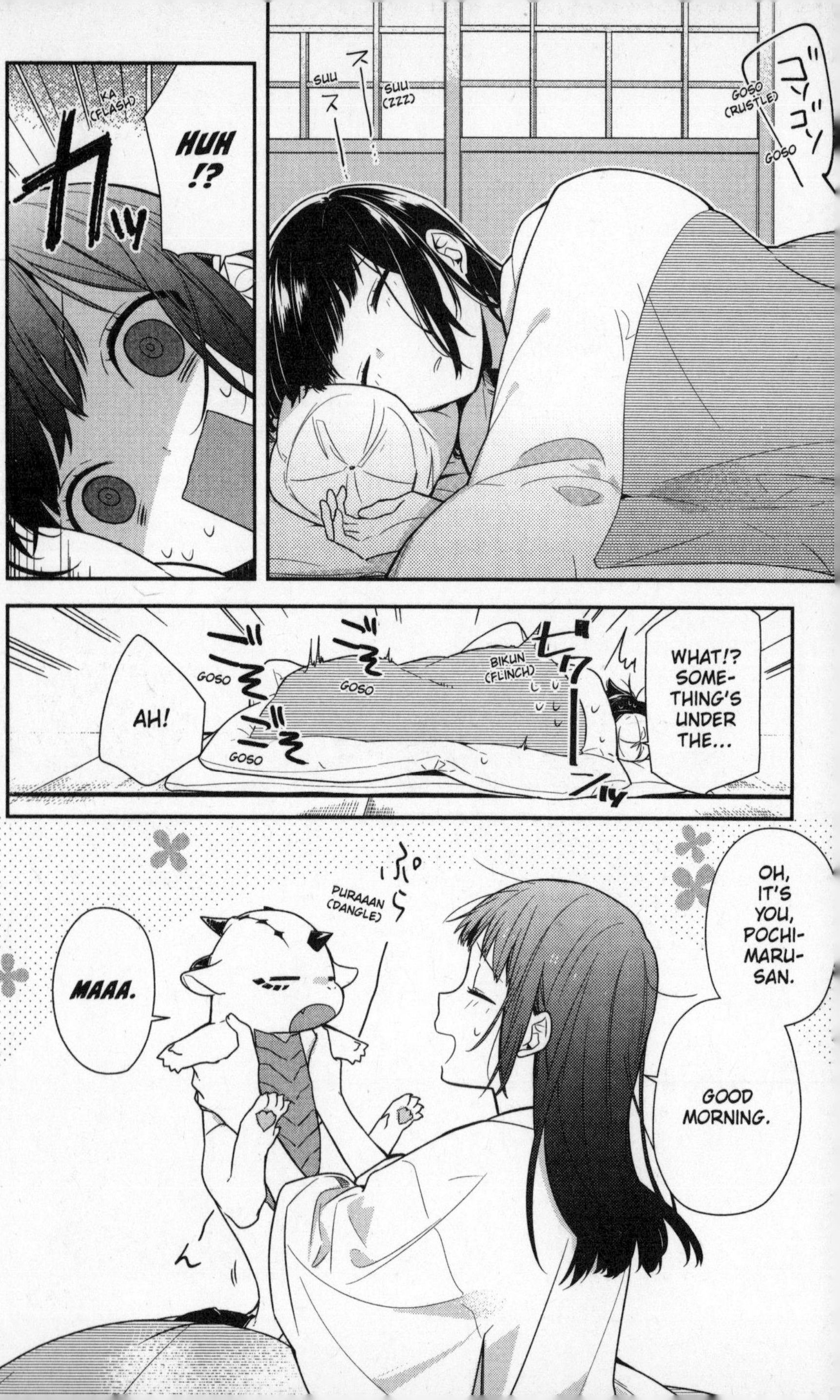
GOSO (RUSTLE)
GOSO
SUU (ZZZ)
SUU
KA (FLASH)
HUH !?
WHAT!? SOME-THING'S UNDER THE...
BIKUN (FLINCH)
GOSO
GOSO
GOSO
AH!
OH, IT'S YOU, POCHI-MARU-SAN.
GOOD MORNING.
PURAAAN (DANGLE)
MAAA.

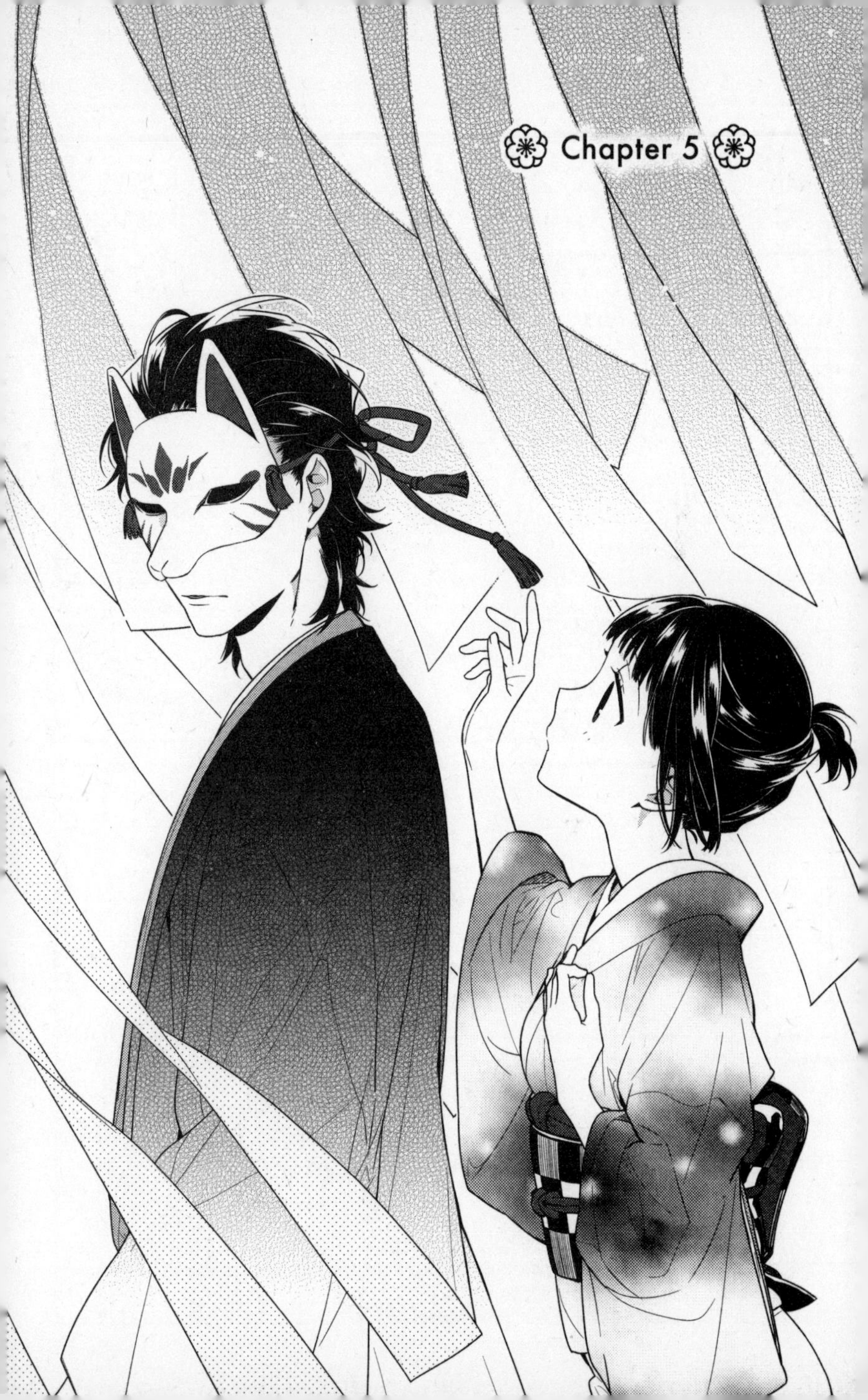
Chapter 5

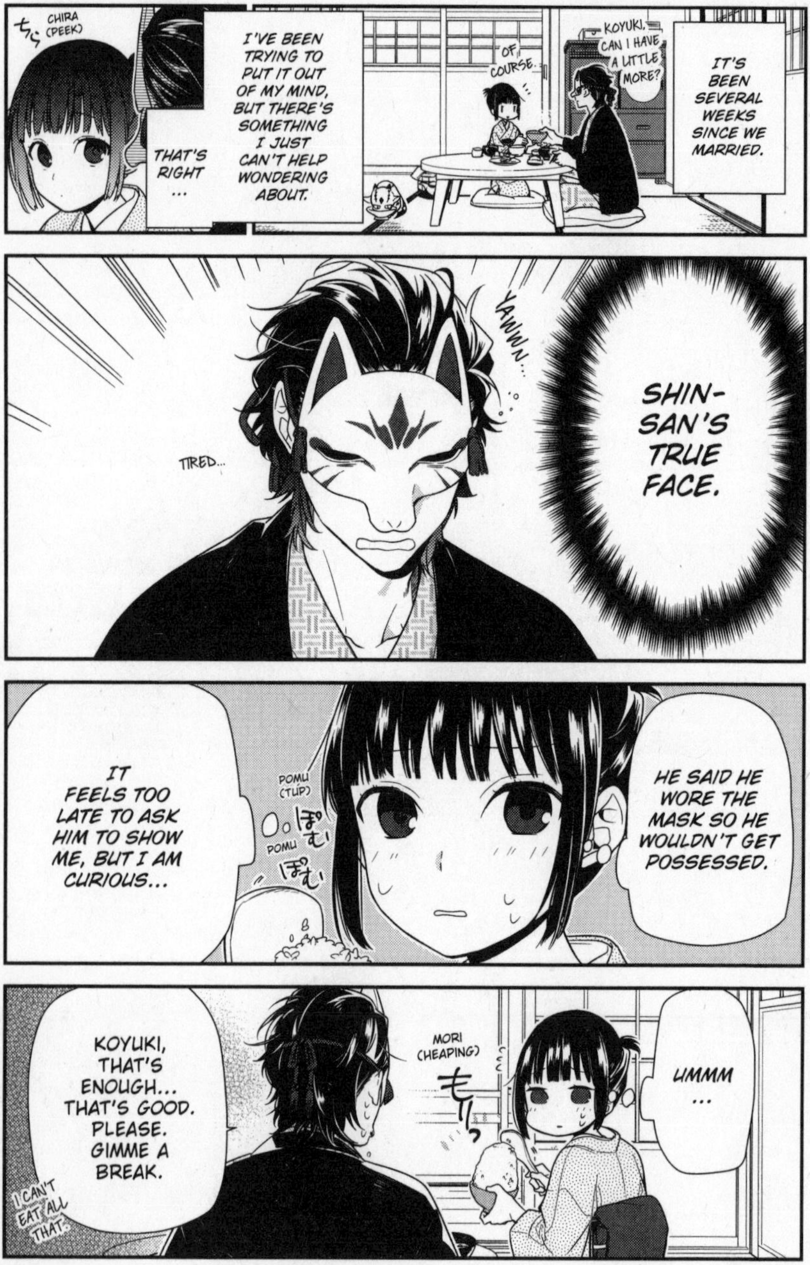
IT'S BEEN SEVERAL WEEKS SINCE WE MARRIED.
KOYUKI, CAN I HAVE A LITTLE MORE?
OF COURSE.
I'VE BEEN TRYING TO PUT IT OUT OF MY MIND, BUT THERE'S SOMETHING I JUST CAN'T HELP WONDERING ABOUT.
ちら
CHIRA (PEEK)
THAT'S RIGHT ...
SHIN-SAN'S TRUE FACE.
YAWWN...
TIRED...
HE SAID HE WORE THE MASK SO HE WOULDN'T GET POSSESSED.
ぽむ
POMU (TUP)
ぽむ
POMU
IT FEELS TOO LATE TO ASK HIM TO SHOW ME, BUT I AM CURIOUS...
UMMM ...
もりっ
MORI (HEAPING)
KOYUKI, THAT'S ENOUGH... THAT'S GOOD. PLEASE. GIMME A BREAK.
I CAN'T EAT ALL THAT.

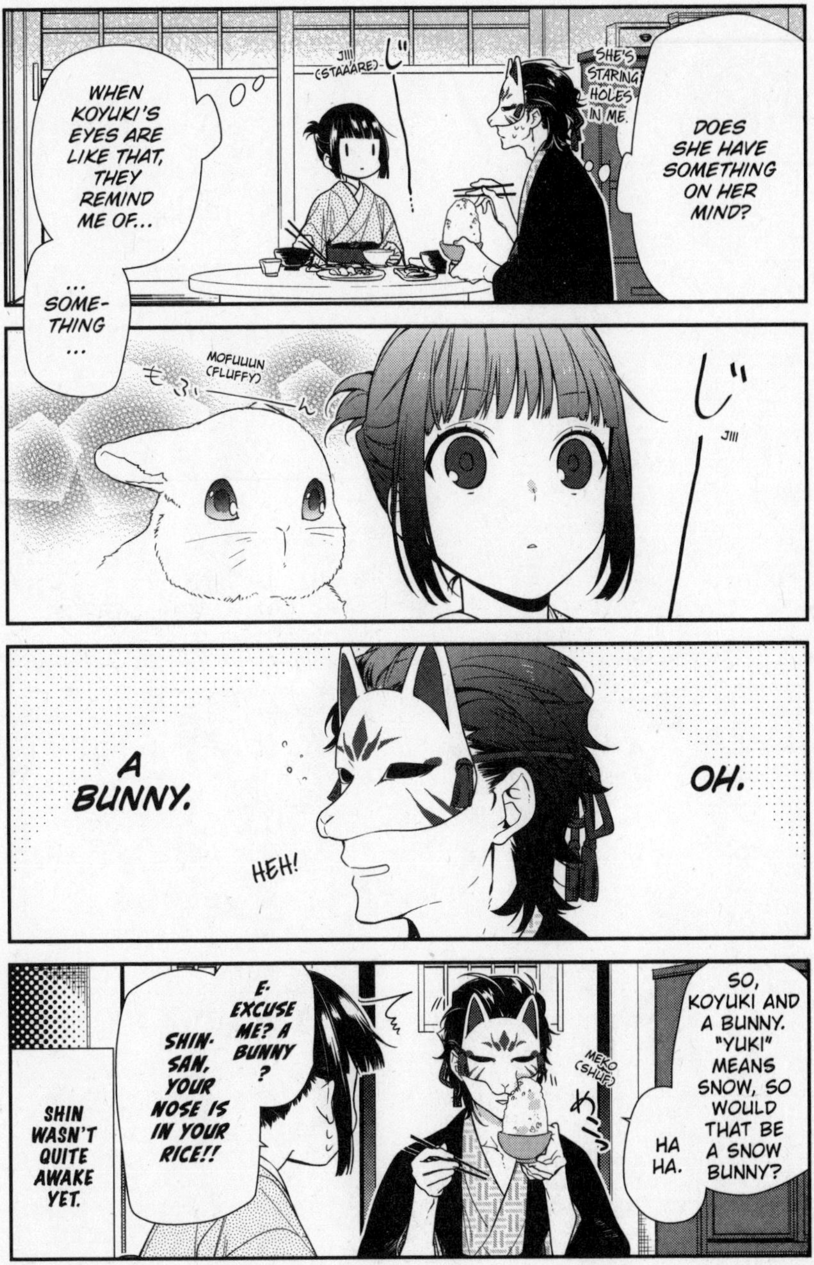
DOES SHE HAVE SOMETHING ON HER MIND?
SHE'S STARING HOLES IN ME.
JIII (STAAARE) じ
WHEN KOYUKI'S EYES ARE LIKE THAT, THEY REMIND ME OF...
...SOMETHING...
じ JIII
MOFUUUN (FLUFFY) もふーん
OH.
A BUNNY.
HEH!
SO, KOYUKI AND A BUNNY. "YUKI" MEANS SNOW, SO WOULD THAT BE A SNOW BUNNY?
HA HA.
MEKO (SHUF) めこっ
E-EXCUSE ME? A BUNNY?
SHIN-SAN, YOUR NOSE IS IN YOUR RICE!!
SHIN WASN'T QUITE AWAKE YET.

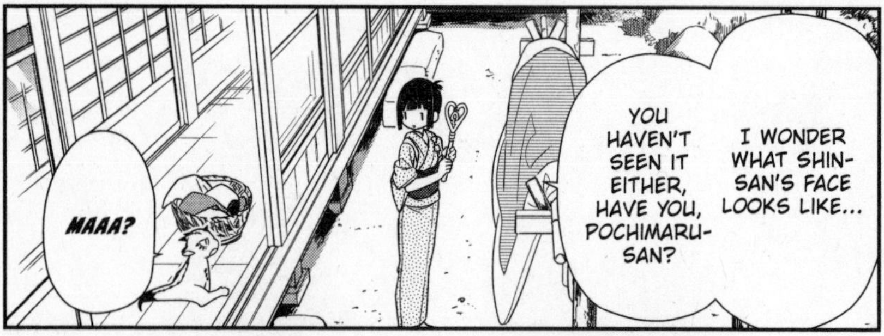
I WONDER WHAT SHIN-SAN'S FACE LOOKS LIKE...
YOU HAVEN'T SEEN IT EITHER, HAVE YOU, POCHIMARU-SAN?
MAAA?

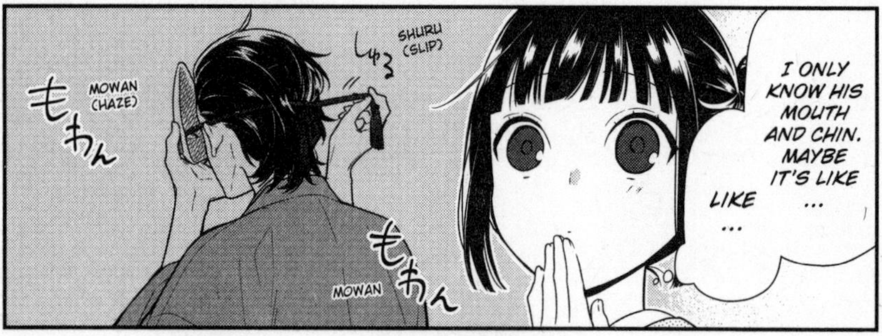
I ONLY KNOW HIS MOUTH AND CHIN. MAYBE IT'S LIKE ... LIKE ...
しゅる
SHURU (SLIP)
もわん
MOWAN (HAZE)
もわん
MOWAN

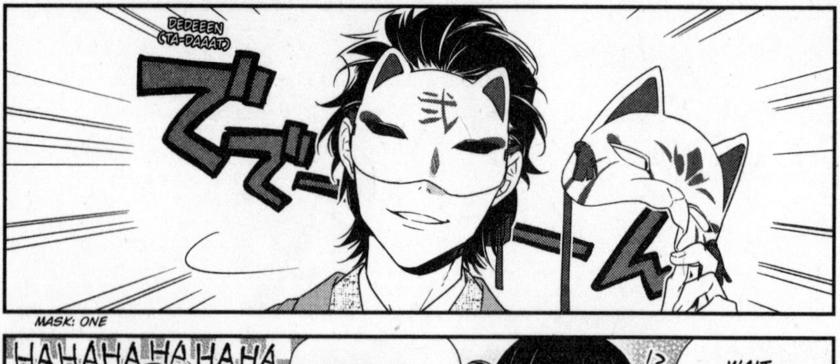
でで―ん
DEDEEEN (TA-DAAAT)
MASK: ONE

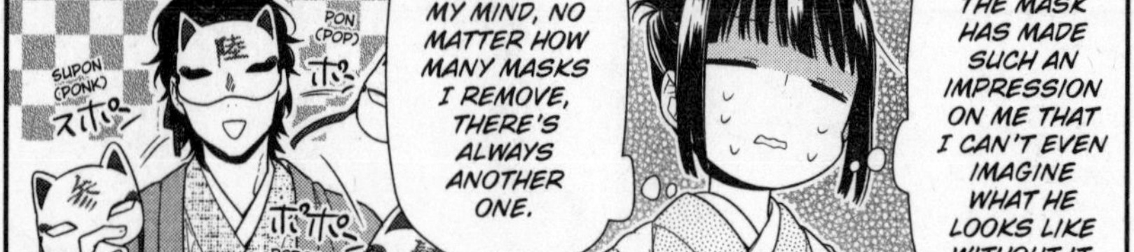
WAIT... THE MASK HAS MADE SUCH AN IMPRESSION ON ME THAT I CAN'T EVEN IMAGINE WHAT HE LOOKS LIKE WITHOUT IT.
!?
EVEN IN MY MIND, NO MATTER HOW MANY MASKS I REMOVE, THERE'S ALWAYS ANOTHER ONE.
HAHAHA HA HAHA
ポン
PON (POP)
スポン
SUPON (PONK)
ポポン
POPON (PAPOP)
MASKS (L TO R): THREE, SIX, FOUR

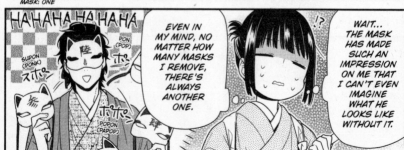

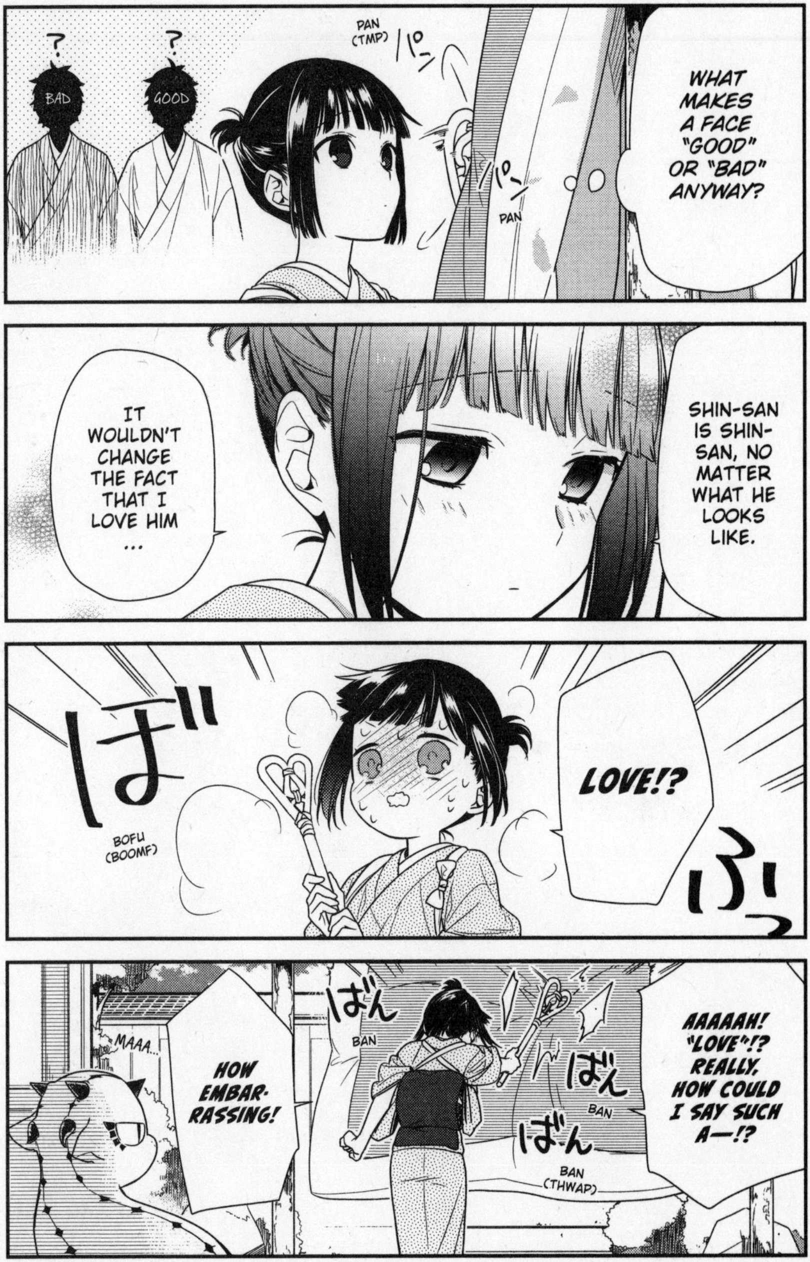
WHAT MAKES A FACE "GOOD" OR "BAD" ANYWAY?
PAN (TMP)
PAN
GOOD
BAD
SHIN-SAN IS SHIN-SAN, NO MATTER WHAT HE LOOKS LIKE.
IT WOULDN'T CHANGE THE FACT THAT I LOVE HIM ...
LOVE!?
BOFU (BOOMF)
AAAAAH! "LOVE"!? REALLY, HOW COULD I SAY SUCH A—!?
BAN
BAN
BAN (THWAP)
HOW EMBAR-RASSING!
MAAA...

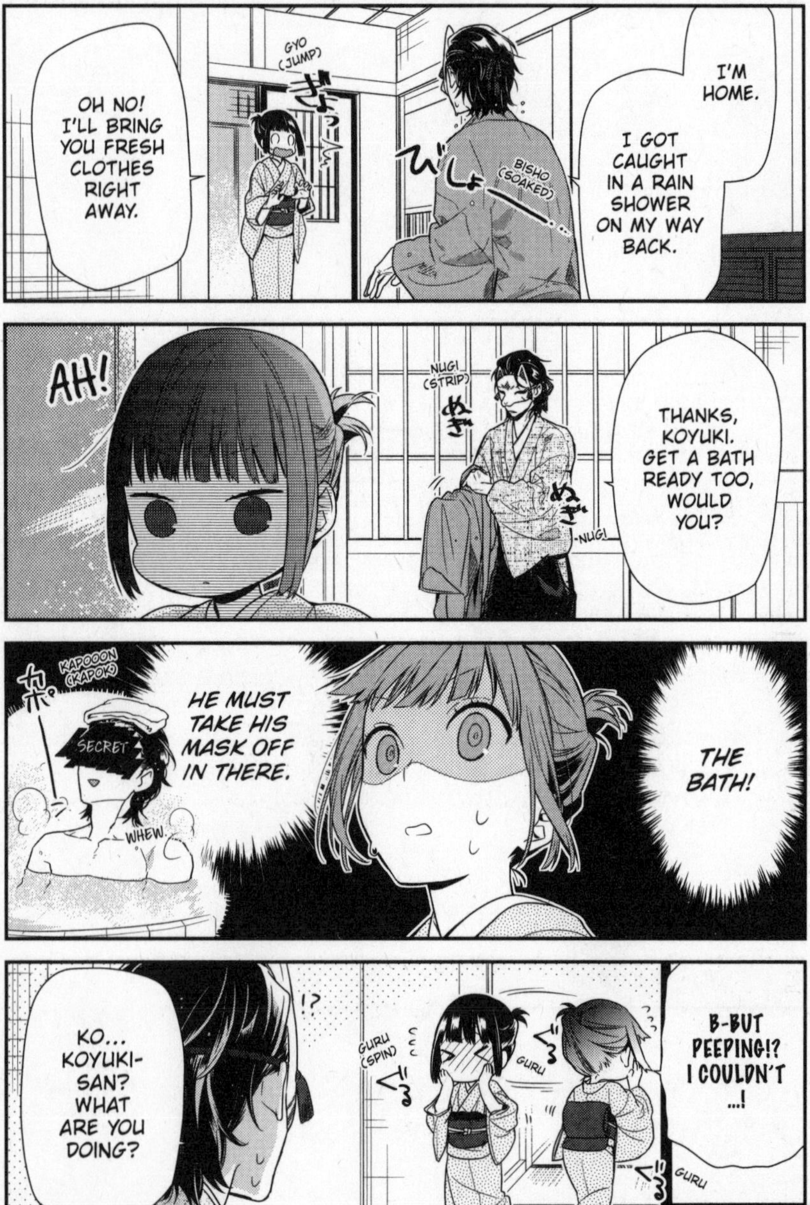

I'M HOME.
I GOT CAUGHT IN A RAIN SHOWER ON MY WAY BACK.
BISHO (SOAKED)
GYO (JUMP)
OH NO! I'LL BRING YOU FRESH CLOTHES RIGHT AWAY.
THANKS, KOYUKI. GET A BATH READY TOO, WOULD YOU?
NUGI (STRIP)
-NUGI!
AH!
THE BATH!
HE MUST TAKE HIS MASK OFF IN THERE.
KAPOOON (KAPOK)
SECRET
WHEW.
B-BUT PEEPING!? I COULDN'T ...!
GURU
GURU
GURU (SPIN)
!?
KO... KOYUKI-SAN? WHAT ARE YOU DOING?

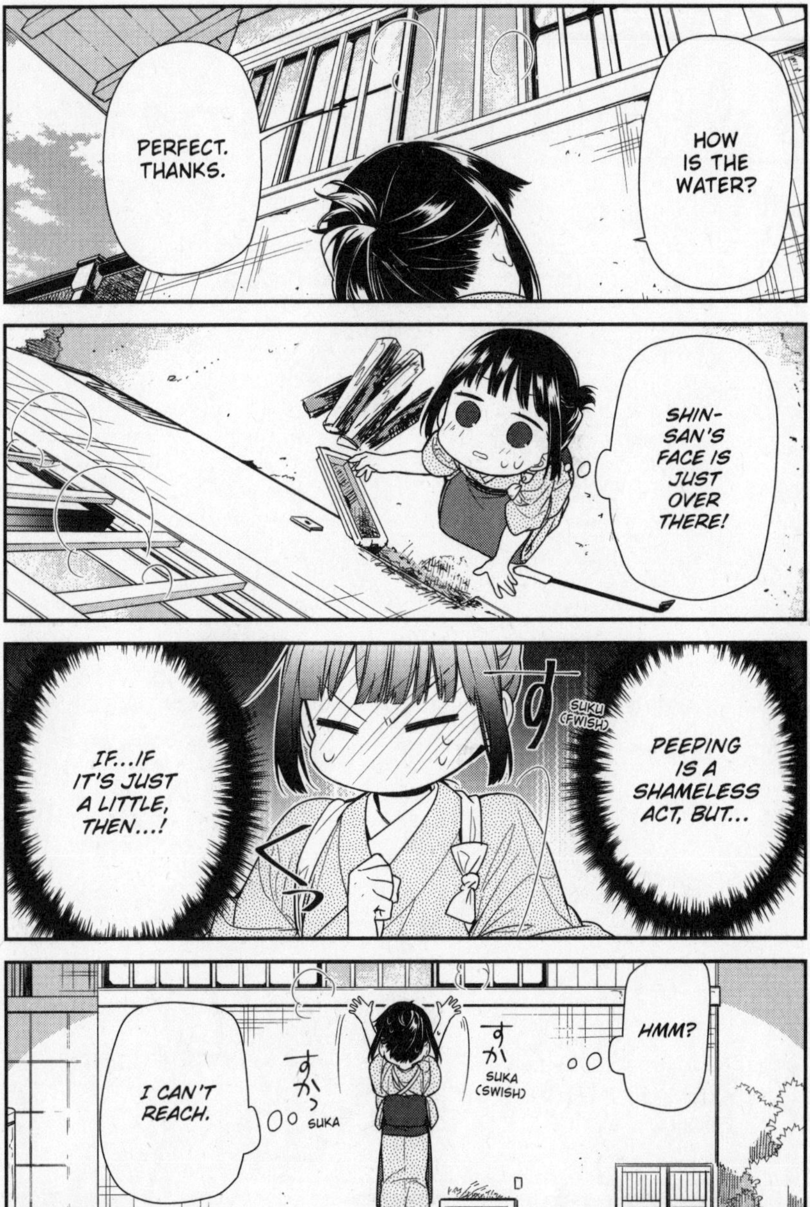
HOW IS THE WATER?
PERFECT. THANKS.
SHIN-SAN'S FACE IS JUST OVER THERE!
す
SUKU (FWISH)
PEEPING IS A SHAMELESS ACT, BUT...
IF...IF IT'S JUST A LITTLE, THEN...!
HMM?
すか
SUKA (SWISH)
すかっ
SUKA
I CAN'T REACH.

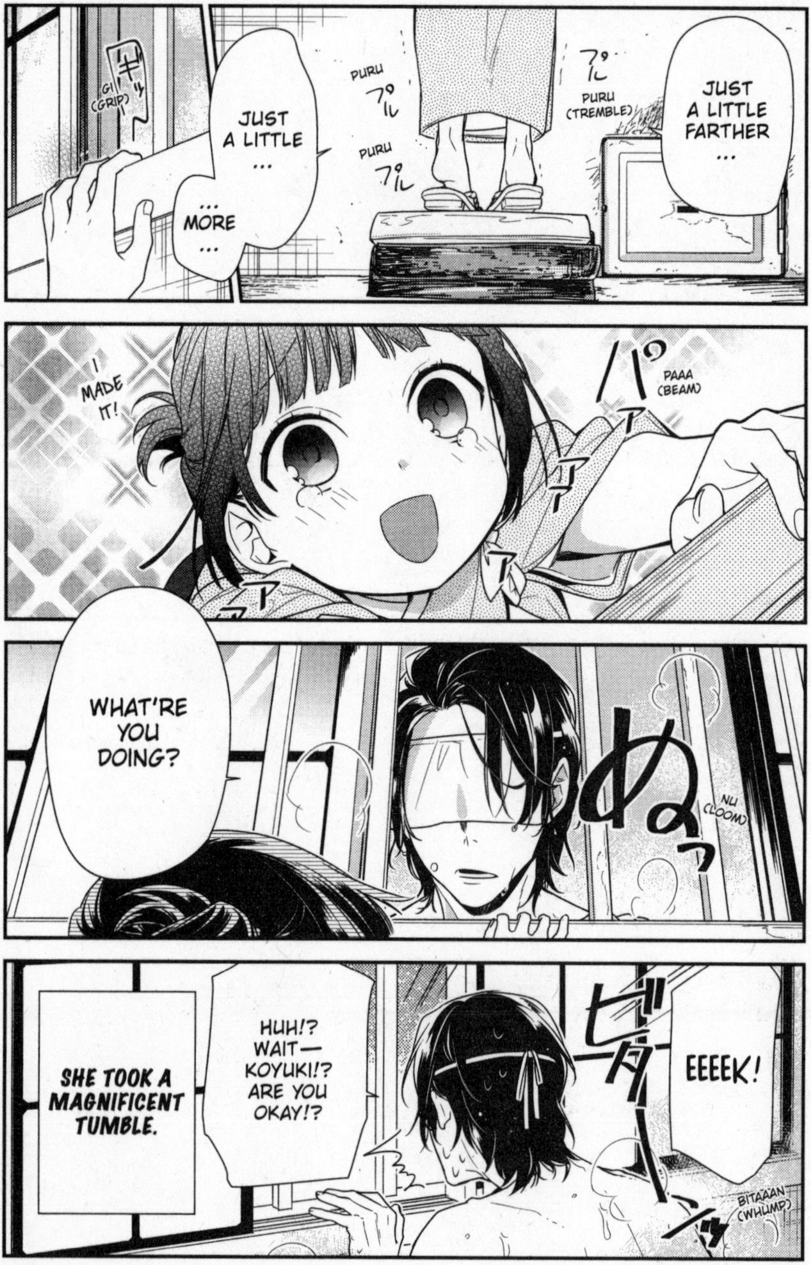
JUST A LITTLE FARTHER ...
PURU (TREMBLE)
PURU
PURU
JUST A LITTLE ...
... MORE ...
GI (GRIP)
PAAA (BEAM)
I MADE IT!
NU (LOOM)
WHAT'RE YOU DOING?
BITAAAN (WHUMP)
EEEEK!
HUH!? WAIT— KOYUKI!? ARE YOU OKAY!?
SHE TOOK A MAGNIFICENT TUMBLE.

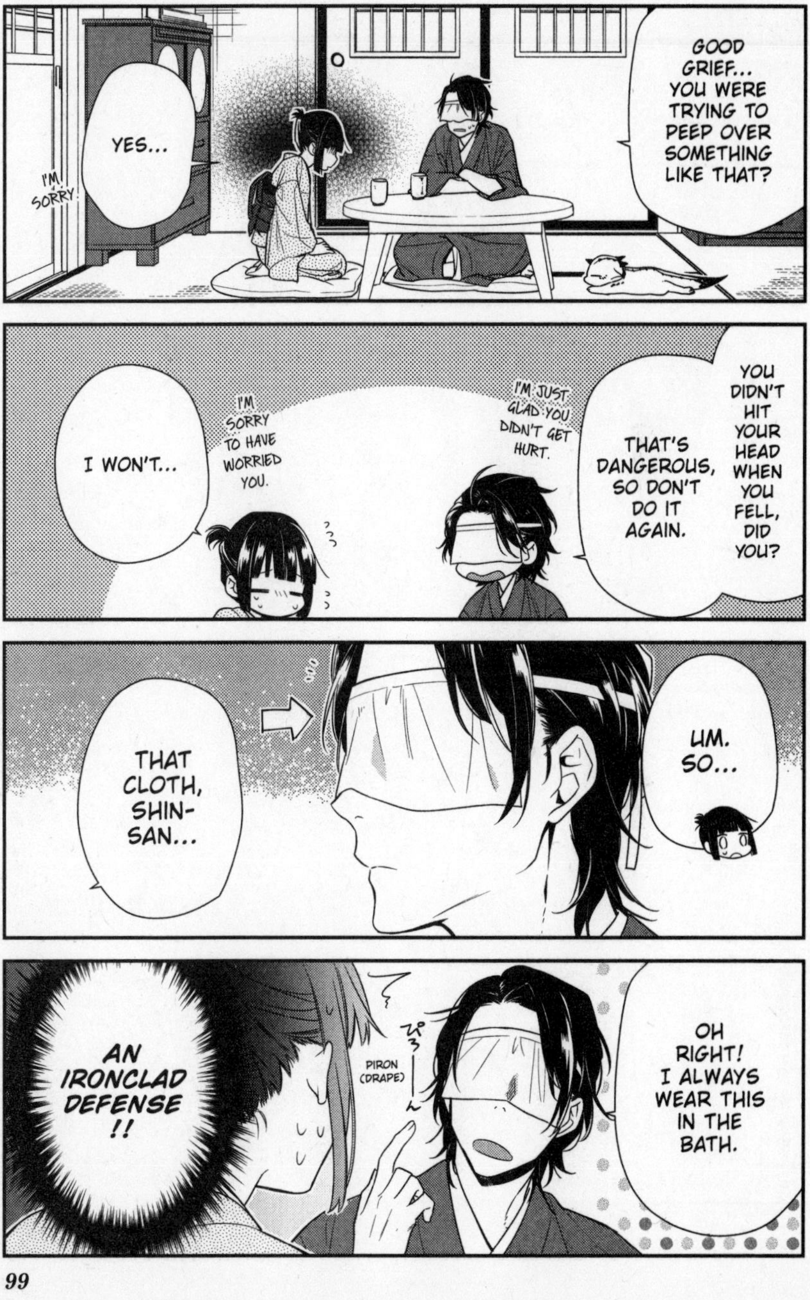
GOOD GRIEF... YOU WERE TRYING TO PEEP OVER SOMETHING LIKE THAT?
YES...
I'M SORRY.
YOU DIDN'T HIT YOUR HEAD WHEN YOU FELL, DID YOU?
THAT'S DANGEROUS, SO DON'T DO IT AGAIN.
I'M JUST GLAD YOU DIDN'T GET HURT.
I'M SORRY TO HAVE WORRIED YOU.
I WON'T...
UM. SO...
THAT CLOTH, SHIN-SAN...
OH RIGHT! I ALWAYS WEAR THIS IN THE BATH.
ぴろ～ん
PIRON (DRAPE)
AN IRONCLAD DEFENSE!!

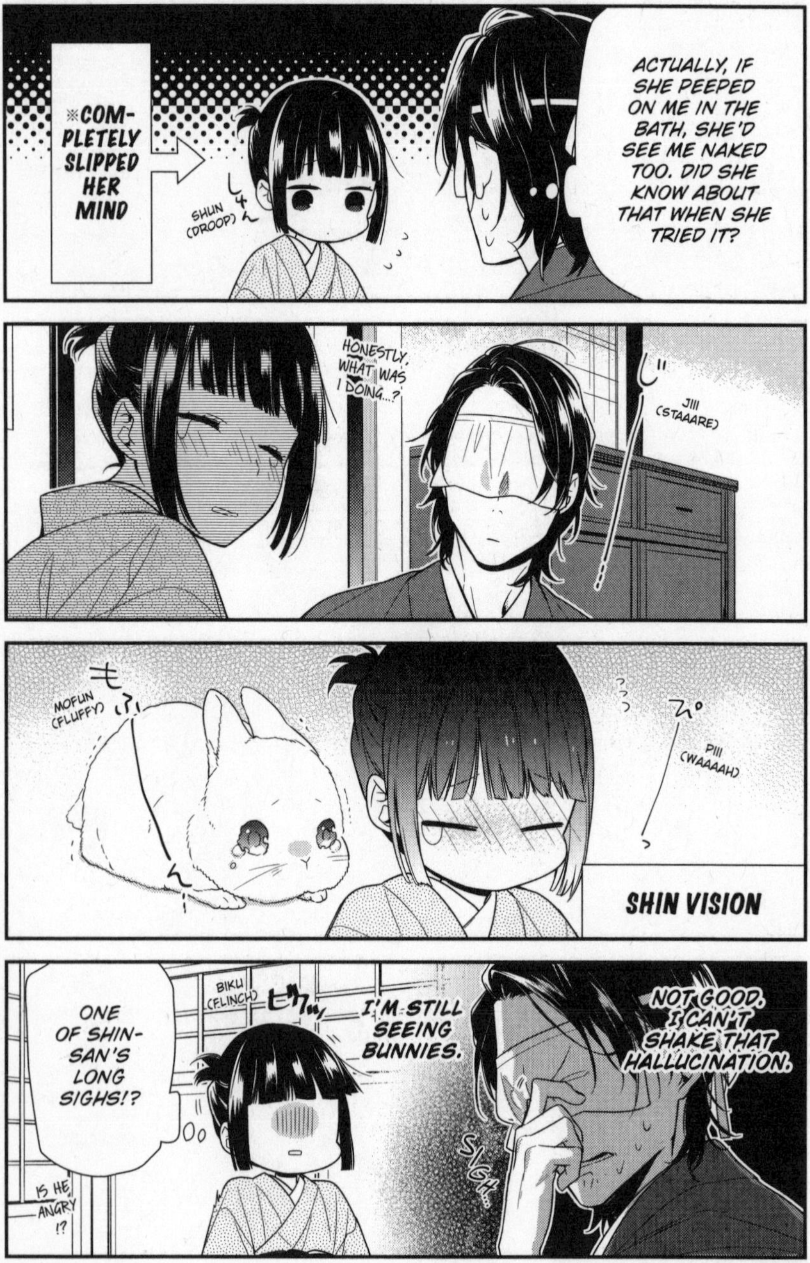
ACTUALLY, IF SHE PEEPED ON ME IN THE BATH, SHE'D SEE ME NAKED TOO. DID SHE KNOW ABOUT THAT WHEN SHE TRIED IT?
SHUN (DROOP)
※COMPLETELY SLIPPED HER MIND
JIII (STAAARE)
HONESTLY, WHAT WAS I DOING...?
SHIN VISION
PIII (WAAAAH)
MOFUN (FLUFFY)
NOT GOOD. I CAN'T SHAKE THAT HALLUCINATION.
SIGH...
I'M STILL SEEING BUNNIES.
BIKU (FLINCH)
ONE OF SHIN-SAN'S LONG SIGHS!?
IS HE ANGRY!?

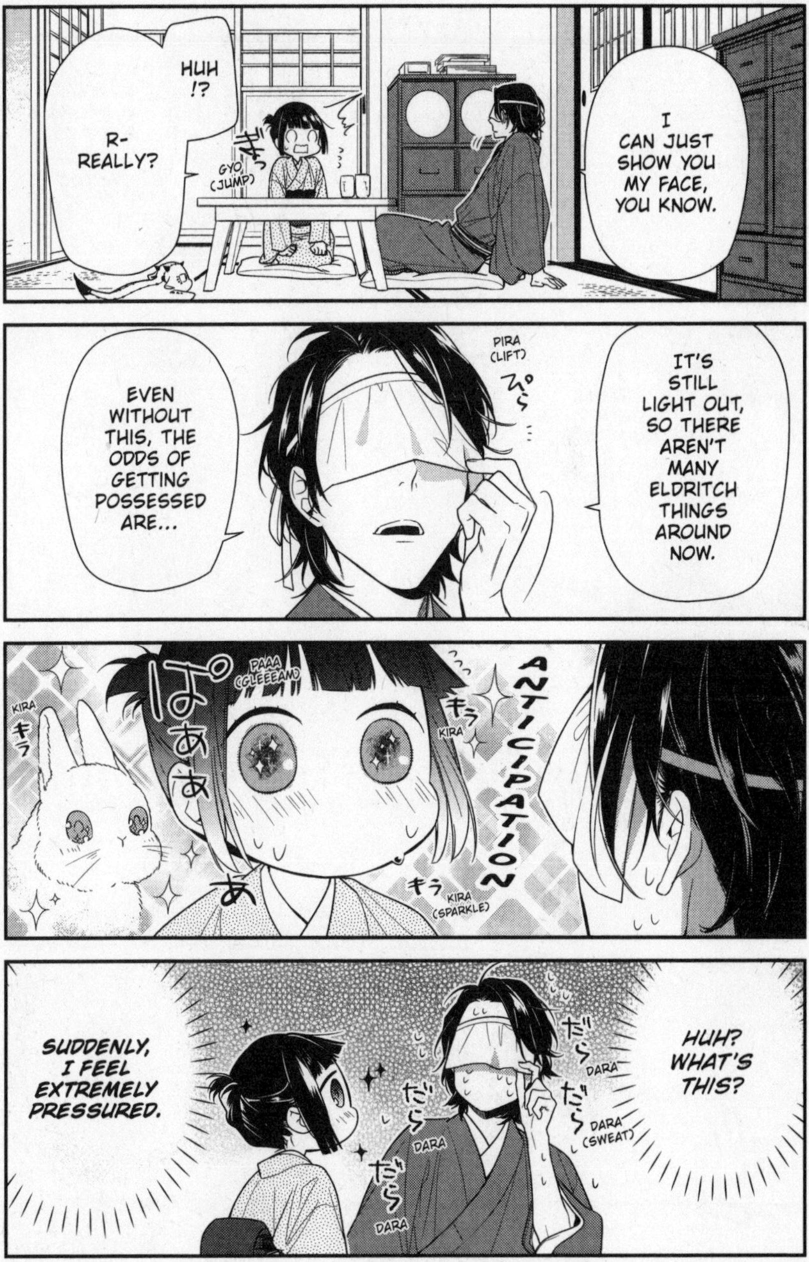

I CAN JUST SHOW YOU MY FACE, YOU KNOW.
ぎょっ
GYO (JUMP)
HUH!?
R-REALLY?
IT'S STILL LIGHT OUT, SO THERE AREN'T MANY ELDRITCH THINGS AROUND NOW.
ぴら
PIRA (LIFT)
EVEN WITHOUT THIS, THE ODDS OF GETTING POSSESSED ARE...
ANTICIPATION
キラ
KIRA
キラ
KIRA (SPARKLE)
ぱあああ
PAAA (GLEEEAM)
キラ
KIRA
HUH? WHAT'S THIS?
だら
DARA
だら
DARA (SWEAT)
だら
DARA
だら
DARA
SUDDENLY, I FEEL EXTREMELY PRESSURED.

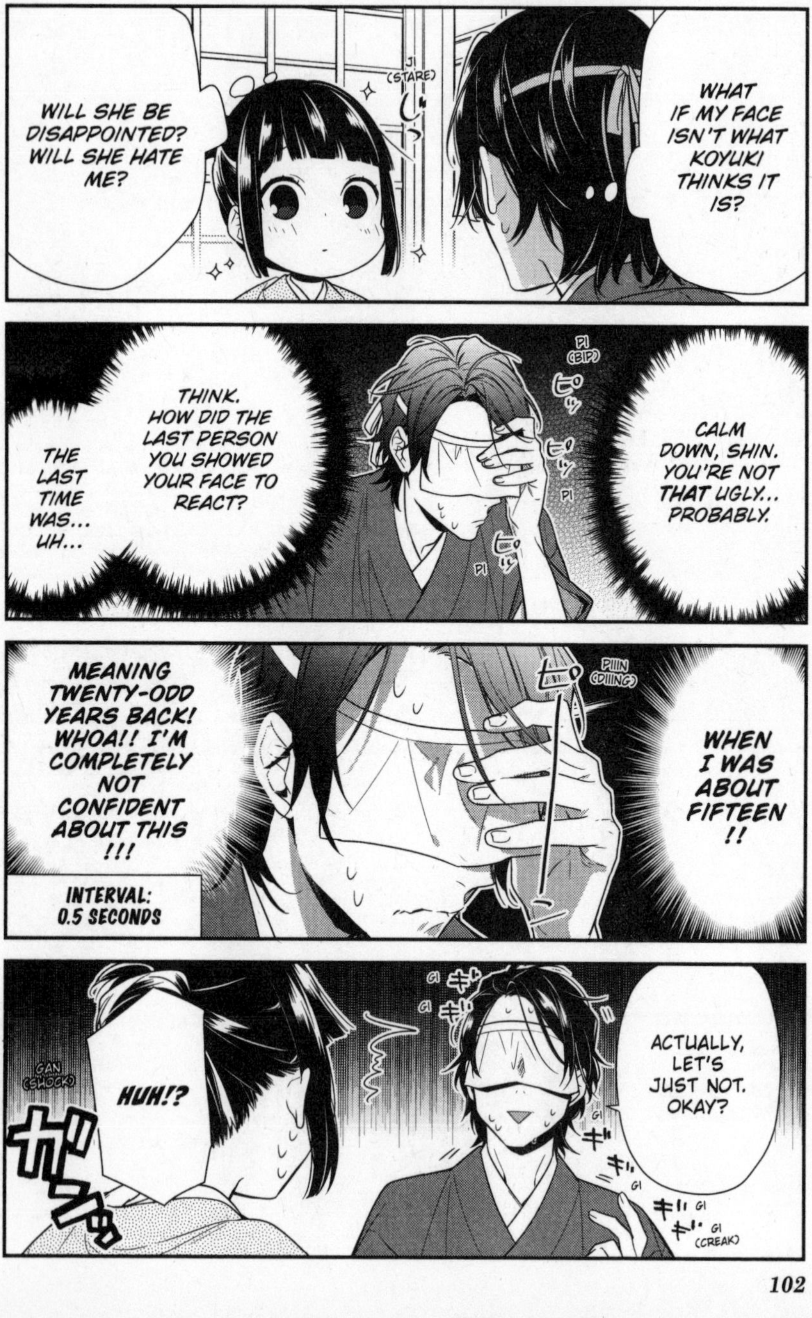
WHAT IF MY FACE ISN'T WHAT KOYUKI THINKS IT IS?
JI (STARE)
WILL SHE BE DISAPPOINTED? WILL SHE HATE ME?
CALM DOWN, SHIN. YOU'RE NOT THAT UGLY... PROBABLY.
PI (BIP)
PI
PI
THINK. HOW DID THE LAST PERSON YOU SHOWED YOUR FACE TO REACT?
THE LAST TIME WAS... UH...
WHEN I WAS ABOUT FIFTEEN !!
PIIIN (DIIING)
MEANING TWENTY-ODD YEARS BACK! WHOA!! I'M COMPLETELY NOT CONFIDENT ABOUT THIS !!!
INTERVAL: 0.5 SECONDS
GI
GI
ACTUALLY, LET'S JUST NOT. OKAY?
GI
GI
GI
GI (CREAK)
HUH!?
GAN (SHOCK)

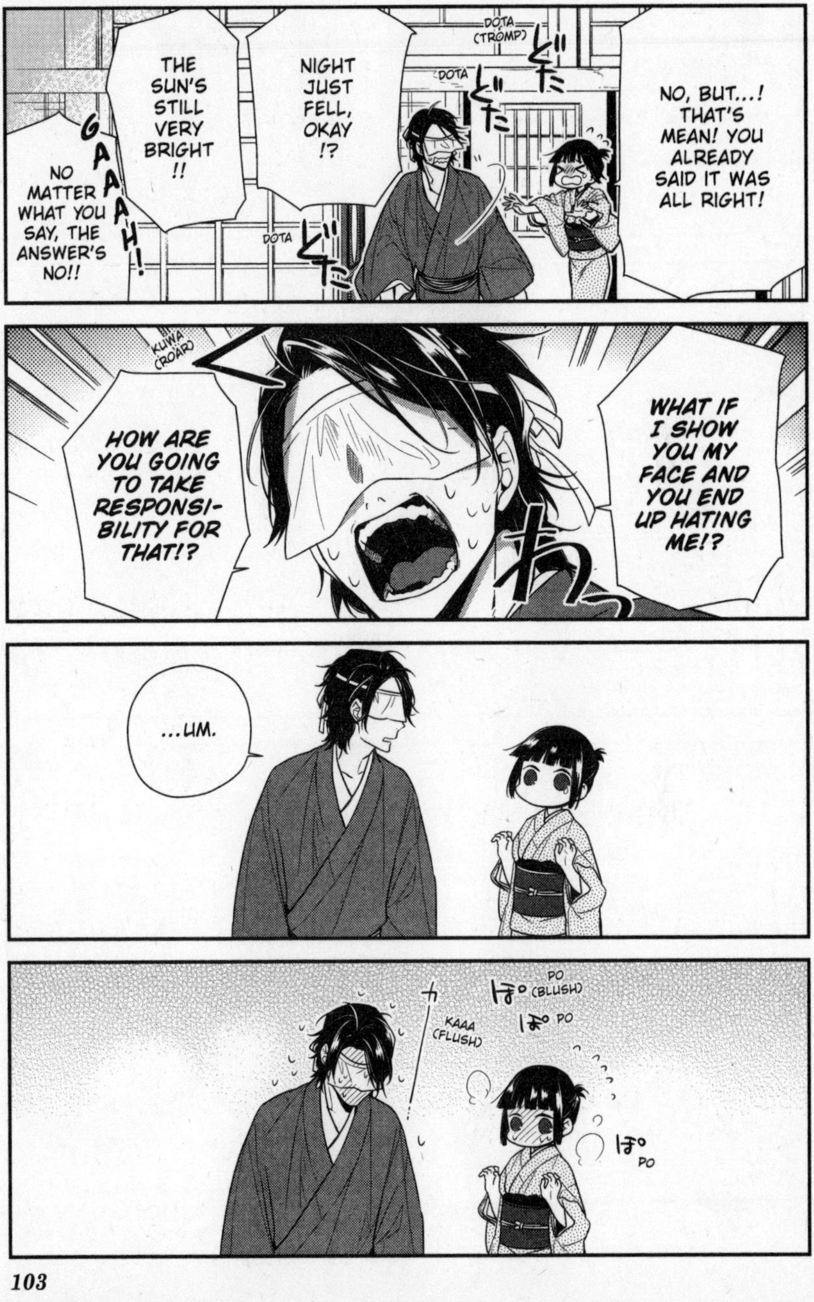
NO, BUT...! THAT'S MEAN! YOU ALREADY SAID IT WAS ALL RIGHT!
DOTA (TROMP)
DOTA
NIGHT JUST FELL, OKAY!?
THE SUN'S STILL VERY BRIGHT!!
GAAAH!
NO MATTER WHAT YOU SAY, THE ANSWER'S NO!!
DOTA
WHAT IF I SHOW YOU MY FACE AND YOU END UP HATING ME!?
KUWA (ROAR)
HOW ARE YOU GOING TO TAKE RESPONSIBILITY FOR THAT!?
...UM.
PO (BLUSH)
PO
KAAA (FLUSH)
PO

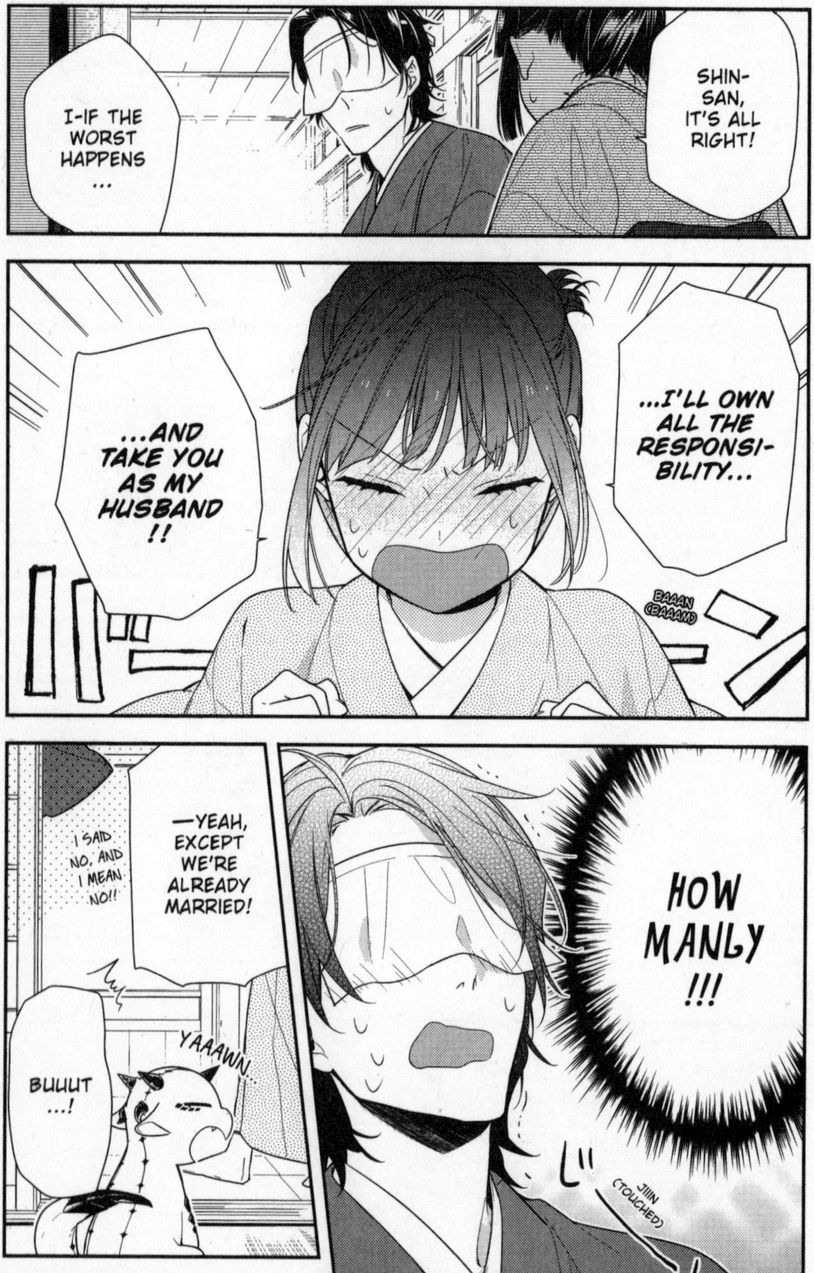
SHIN-SAN, IT'S ALL RIGHT!
I-IF THE WORST HAPPENS ...
...I'LL OWN ALL THE RESPONSI-BILITY...
BAAAN (BAAAN)
...AND TAKE YOU AS MY HUSBAND !!
HOW MANLY !!!
JIIIN (TOUCHED)
—YEAH, EXCEPT WE'RE ALREADY MARRIED!
I SAID NO, AND I MEAN NO!!
YAAAWN...
BUUUT ...!

Ne Ne Ne

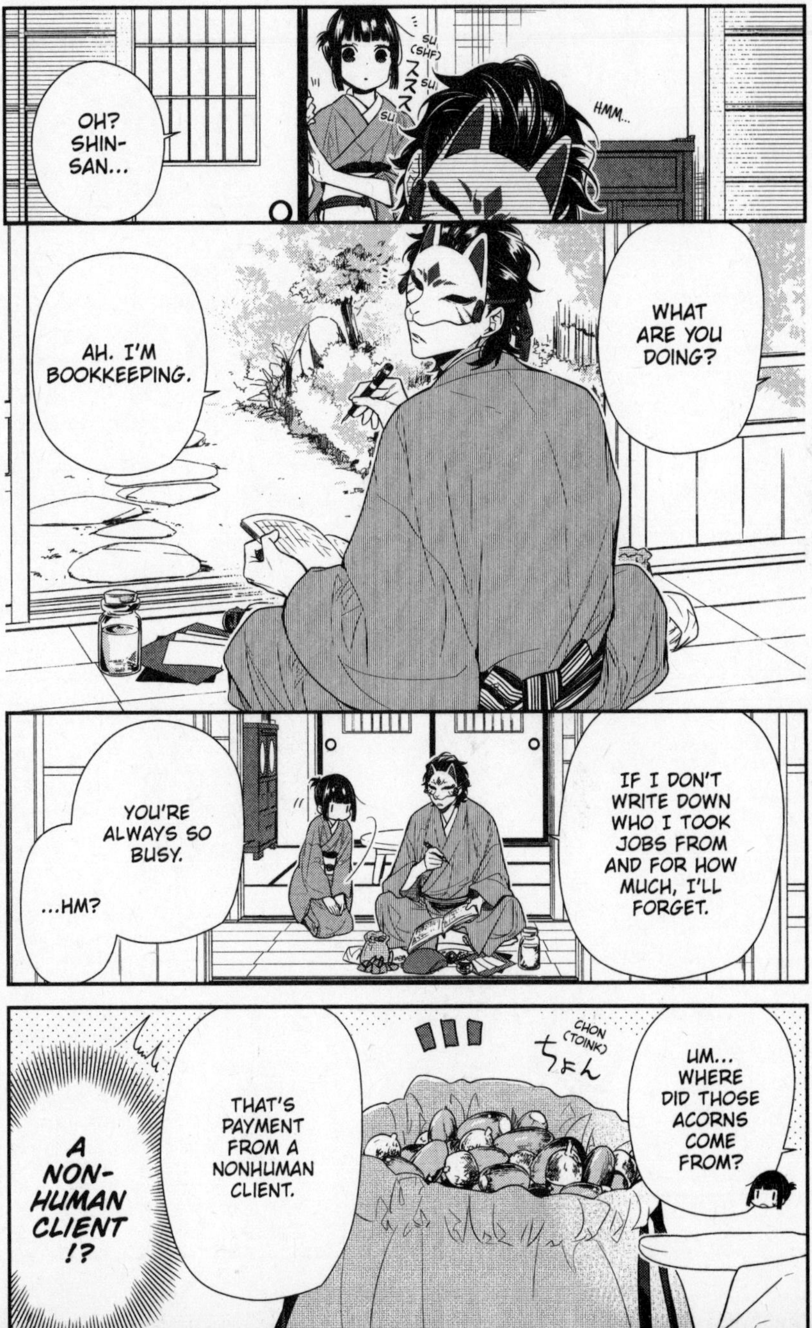
HMM...
SU (SHF) ススス SU SU
OH? SHIN-SAN...
WHAT ARE YOU DOING?
AH. I'M BOOKKEEPING.
IF I DON'T WRITE DOWN WHO I TOOK JOBS FROM AND FOR HOW MUCH, I'LL FORGET.
YOU'RE ALWAYS SO BUSY.
...HM?
UM... WHERE DID THOSE ACORNS COME FROM?
CHON (TOINK) ちょん
THAT'S PAYMENT FROM A NONHUMAN CLIENT.
A NON-HUMAN CLIENT!?

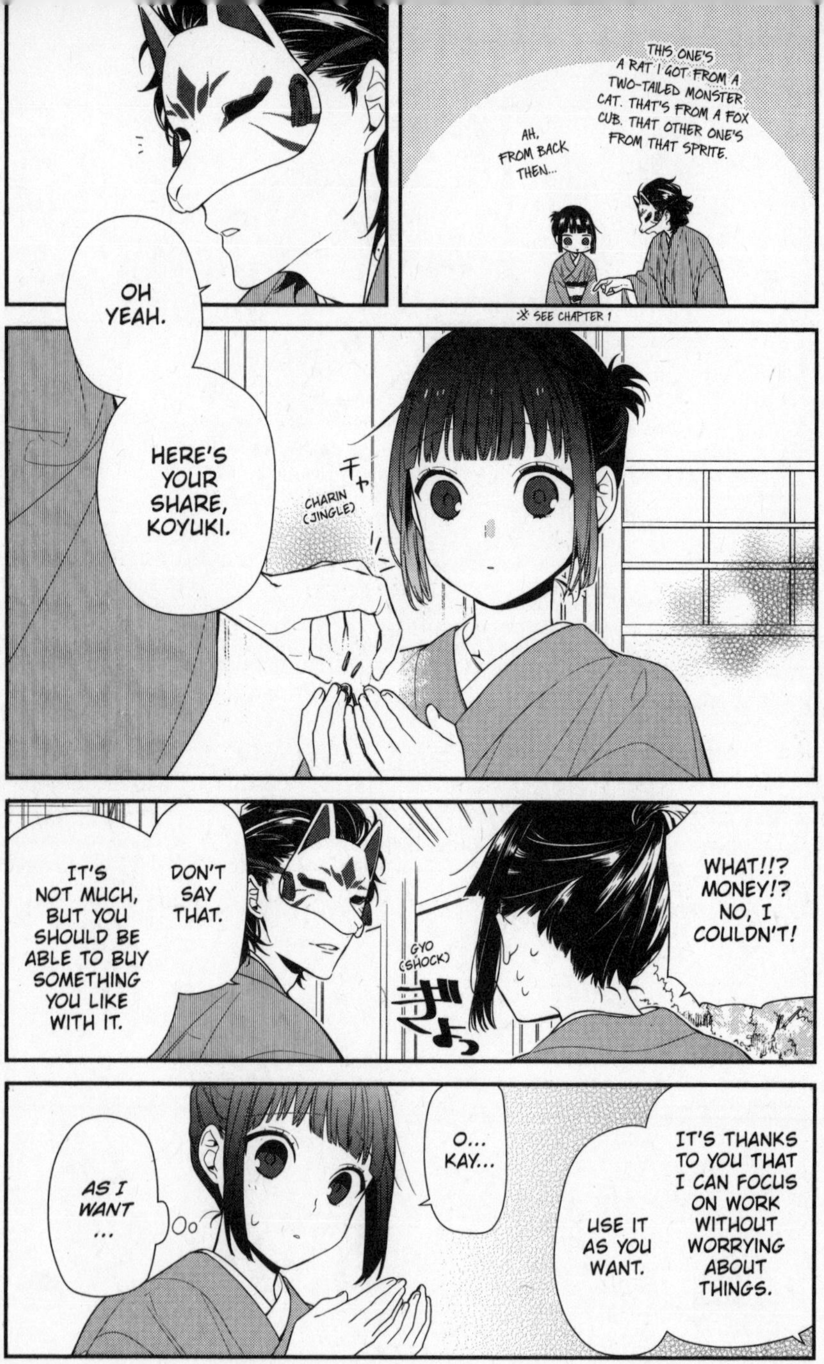
THIS ONE'S A RAT I GOT FROM A TWO-TAILED MONSTER CAT. THAT'S FROM A FOX CUB. THAT OTHER ONE'S FROM THAT SPRITE.
AH, FROM BACK THEN...
※ SEE CHAPTER 1
OH YEAH.
HERE'S YOUR SHARE, KOYUKI.
CHARIN (JINGLE)
WHAT!!? MONEY!? NO, I COULDN'T!
GYO (SHOCK)
DON'T SAY THAT.
IT'S NOT MUCH, BUT YOU SHOULD BE ABLE TO BUY SOMETHING YOU LIKE WITH IT.
IT'S THANKS TO YOU THAT I CAN FOCUS ON WORK WITHOUT WORRYING ABOUT THINGS.
USE IT AS YOU WANT.
O... KAY...
AS I WANT...

Chapter 6

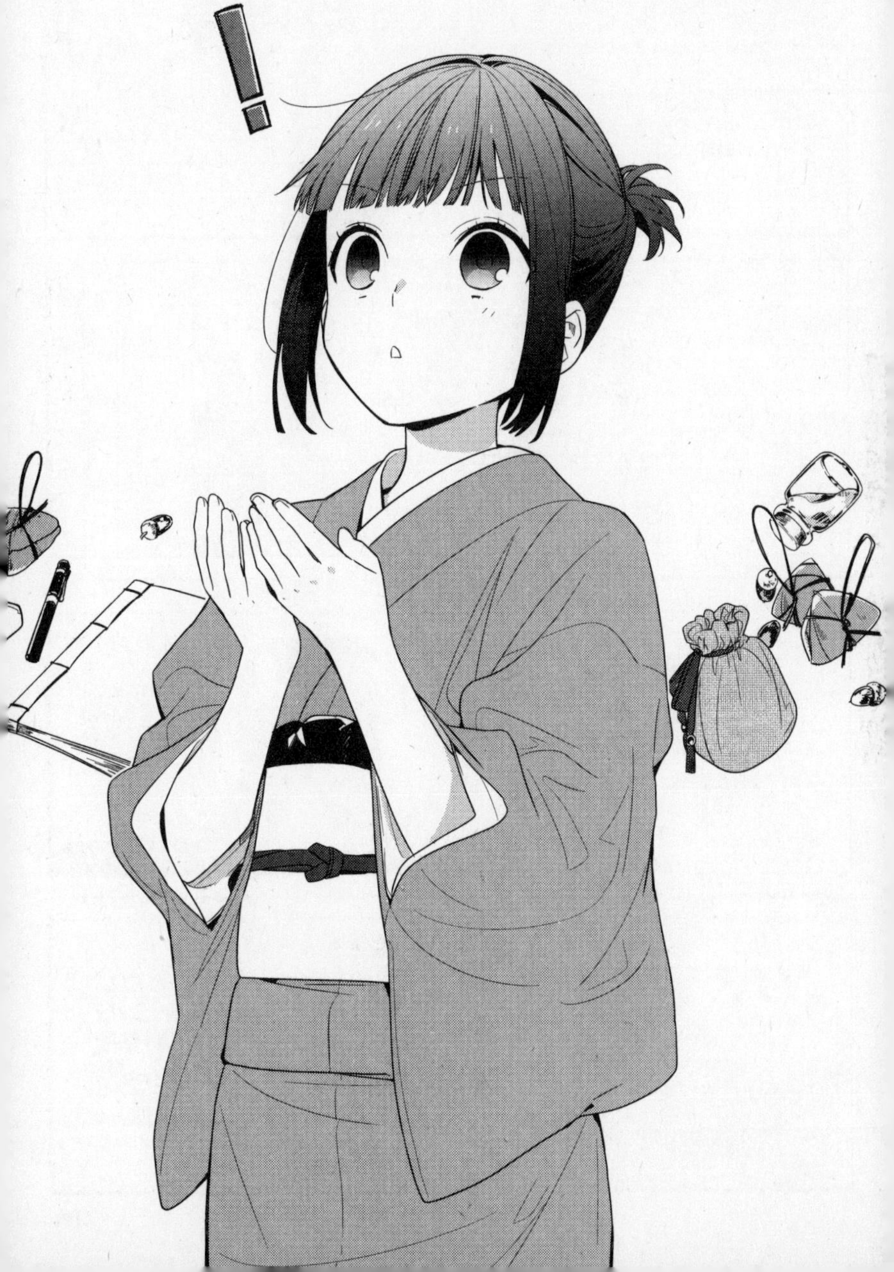
!

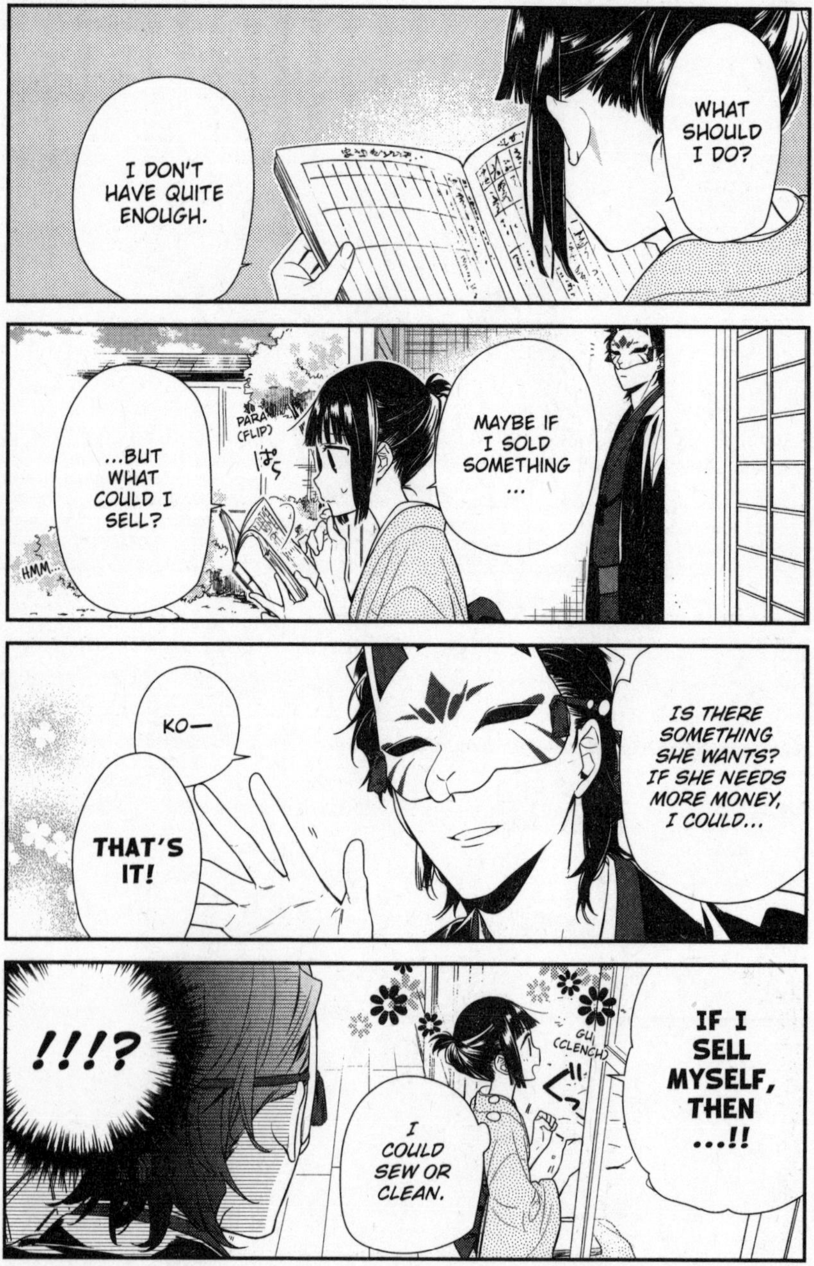
WHAT SHOULD I DO?
I DON'T HAVE QUITE ENOUGH.
MAYBE IF I SOLD SOMETHING ...
PARA (FLIP)
...BUT WHAT COULD I SELL?
HMM...
IS THERE SOMETHING SHE WANTS? IF SHE NEEDS MORE MONEY, I COULD...
KO—
THAT'S IT!
IF I SELL MYSELF, THEN ...!!
GU (CLENCH)
I COULD SEW OR CLEAN.
!!!?

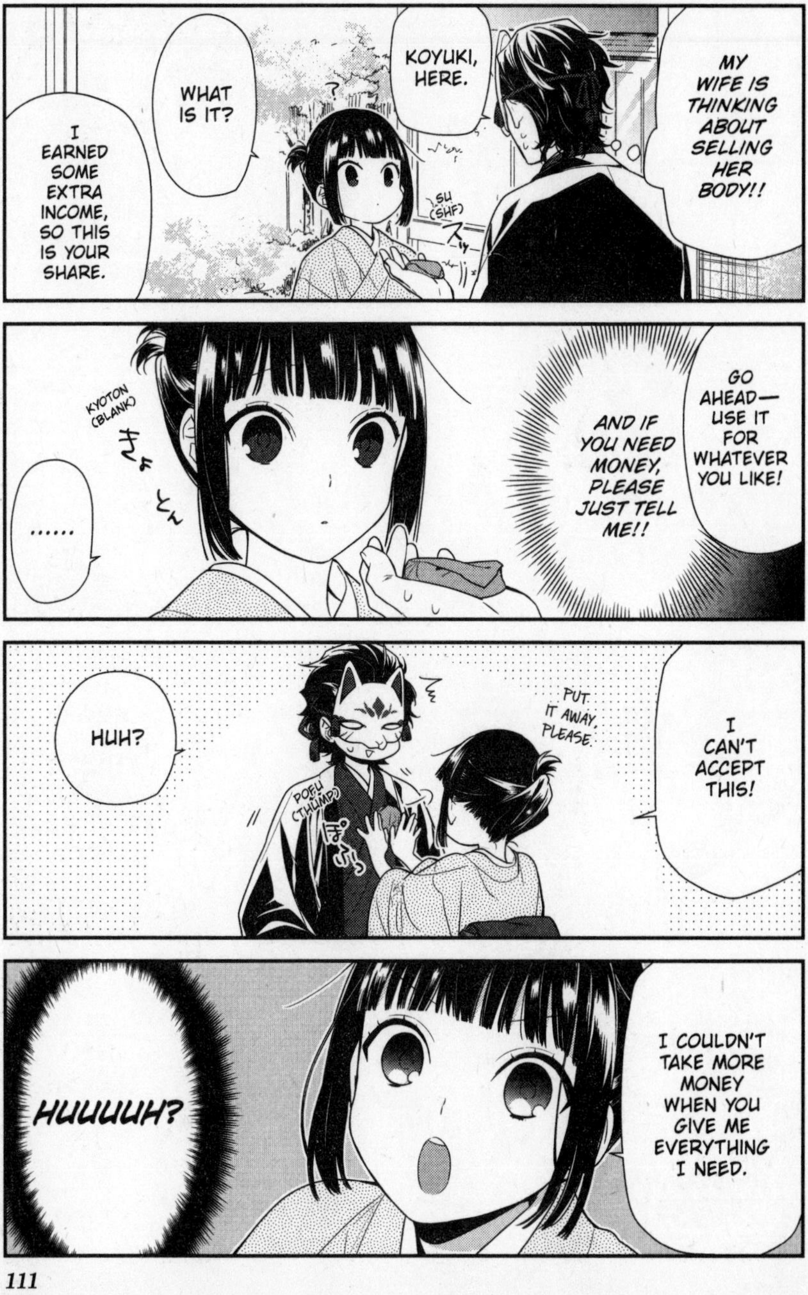
MY WIFE IS THINKING ABOUT SELLING HER BODY!!
KOYUKI, HERE.
WHAT IS IT?
SU (SHF)
I EARNED SOME EXTRA INCOME, SO THIS IS YOUR SHARE.
GO AHEAD— USE IT FOR WHATEVER YOU LIKE!
AND IF YOU NEED MONEY, PLEASE JUST TELL ME!!
KYOTON (BLANK)
......
I CAN'T ACCEPT THIS!
PUT IT AWAY, PLEASE.
POFU (THUMP)
HUH?
I COULDN'T TAKE MORE MONEY WHEN YOU GIVE ME EVERYTHING I NEED.
HUUUUH?

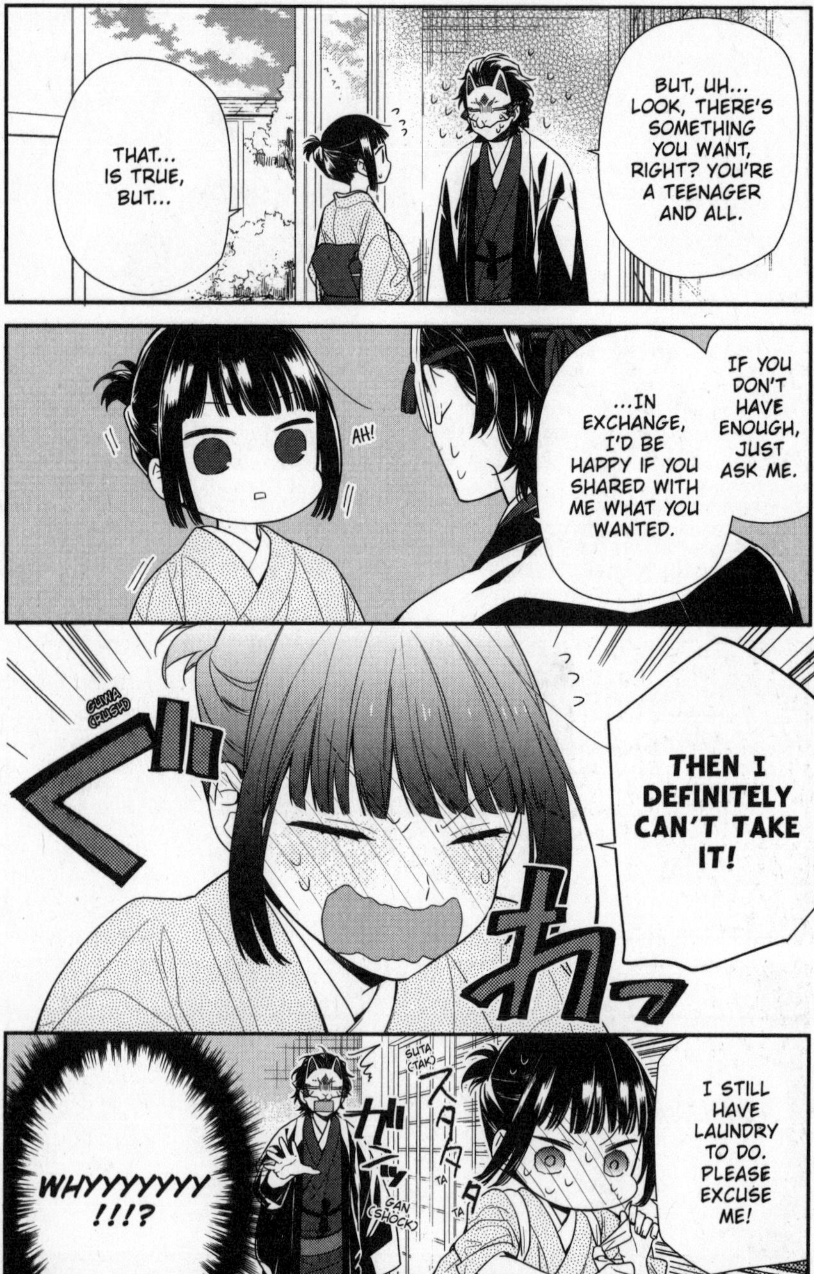
BUT, UH... LOOK, THERE'S SOMETHING YOU WANT, RIGHT? YOU'RE A TEENAGER AND ALL.
THAT... IS TRUE, BUT...
IF YOU DON'T HAVE ENOUGH, JUST ASK ME.
...IN EXCHANGE, I'D BE HAPPY IF YOU SHARED WITH ME WHAT YOU WANTED.
AH!
THEN I DEFINITELY CAN'T TAKE IT!
GUWA (CRUSH)
I STILL HAVE LAUNDRY TO DO. PLEASE EXCUSE ME!
SUTA (TAK)
TA
TA
GAN (SHOCK)
WHYYYYYYYY !!!?
TA
TA

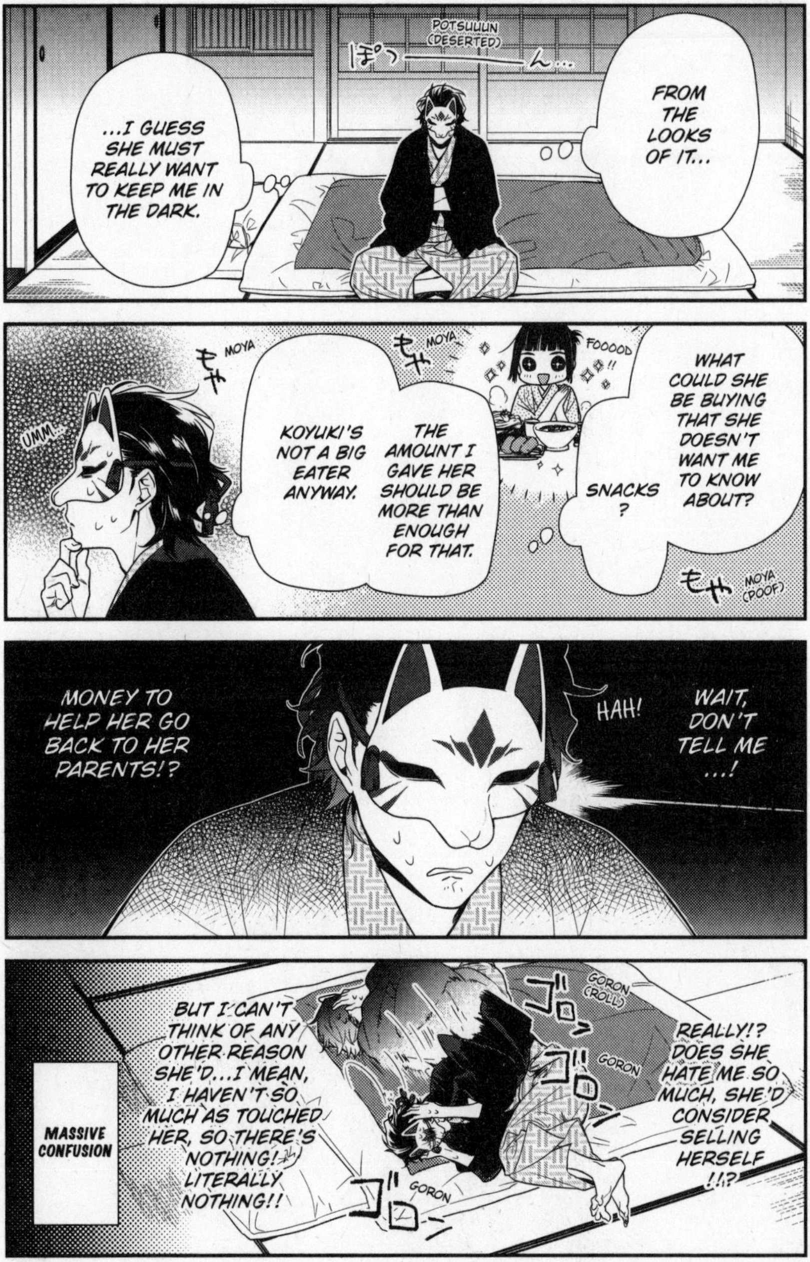
POTSUUUN (DESERTED)
FROM THE LOOKS OF IT...
...I GUESS SHE MUST REALLY WANT TO KEEP ME IN THE DARK.
WHAT COULD SHE BE BUYING THAT SHE DOESN'T WANT ME TO KNOW ABOUT?
SNACKS?
MOYA (POOF)
FOOOOD!!
THE AMOUNT I GAVE HER SHOULD BE MORE THAN ENOUGH FOR THAT.
KOYUKI'S NOT A BIG EATER ANYWAY.
MOYA
MOYA
UMM...
WAIT, DON'T TELL ME ...!
HAH!
MONEY TO HELP HER GO BACK TO HER PARENTS!?
GORON (ROLL)
REALLY!? DOES SHE HATE ME SO MUCH, SHE'D CONSIDER SELLING HERSELF!!?
GORON
BUT I CAN'T THINK OF ANY OTHER REASON SHE'D...I MEAN, I HAVEN'T SO MUCH AS TOUCHED HER, SO THERE'S NOTHING! LITERALLY NOTHING!!
GORON
MASSIVE CONFUSION

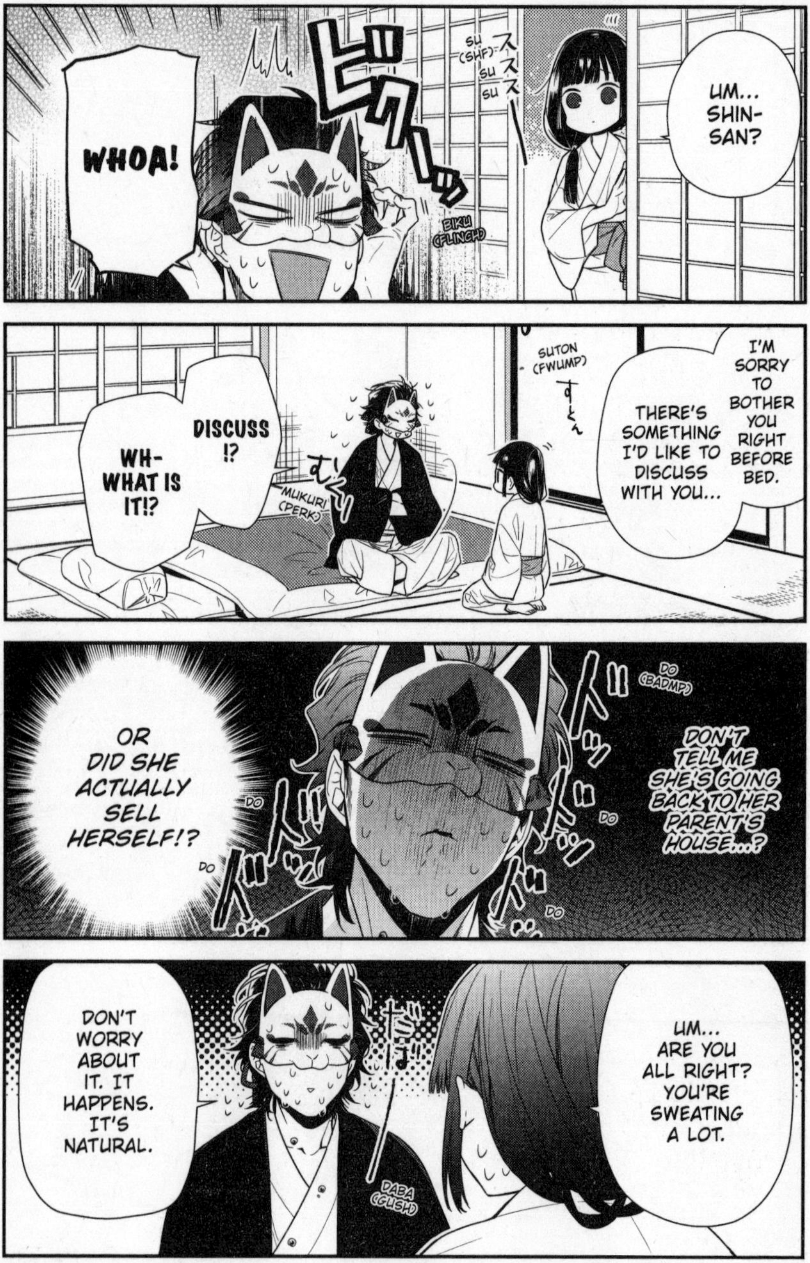
UM... SHIN-SAN?
SU (SHF) SU SU
BIKU (FLINCH)
WHOA!
I'M SORRY TO BOTHER YOU RIGHT BEFORE BED.
THERE'S SOMETHING I'D LIKE TO DISCUSS WITH YOU...
SUTON (FWUMP)
MUKURI (PERK)
DISCUSS!?
WH-WHAT IS IT!?
DO (BADMP)
DON'T TELL ME SHE'S GOING BACK TO HER PARENT'S HOUSE...?
DO
OR DID SHE ACTUALLY SELL HERSELF!?
DO
DO
DO
UM... ARE YOU ALL RIGHT? YOU'RE SWEATING A LOT.
DABA (GUSH)
DON'T WORRY ABOUT IT. IT HAPPENS. IT'S NATURAL.

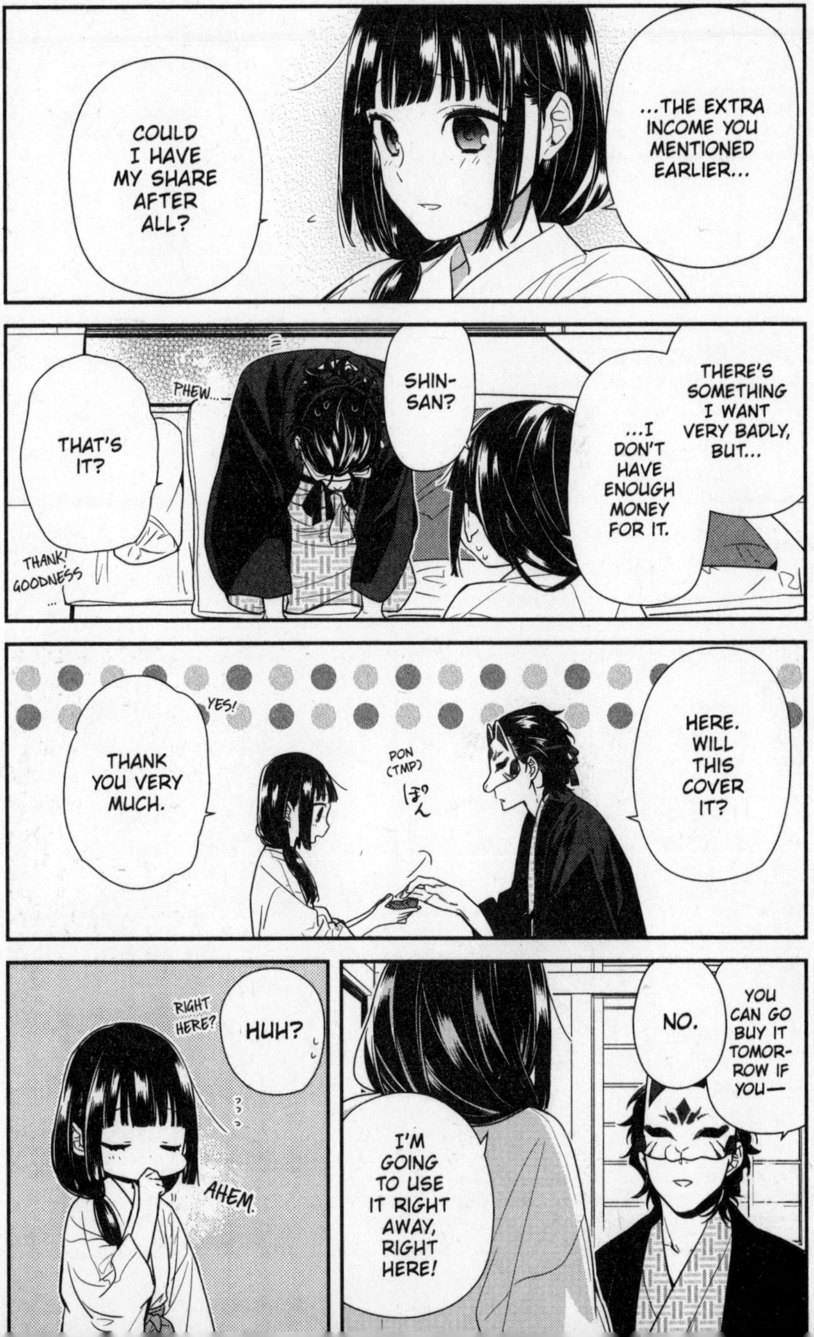
...THE EXTRA INCOME YOU MENTIONED EARLIER...
COULD I HAVE MY SHARE AFTER ALL?
THERE'S SOMETHING I WANT VERY BADLY, BUT...
...I DON'T HAVE ENOUGH MONEY FOR IT.
SHIN-SAN?
PHEW...
THAT'S IT?
THANK GOODNESS...
HERE. WILL THIS COVER IT?
PON (TMP)
ぽん
YES!
THANK YOU VERY MUCH.
YOU CAN GO BUY IT TOMORROW IF YOU—
NO.
I'M GOING TO USE IT RIGHT AWAY, RIGHT HERE!
HUH?
RIGHT HERE?
AHEM.

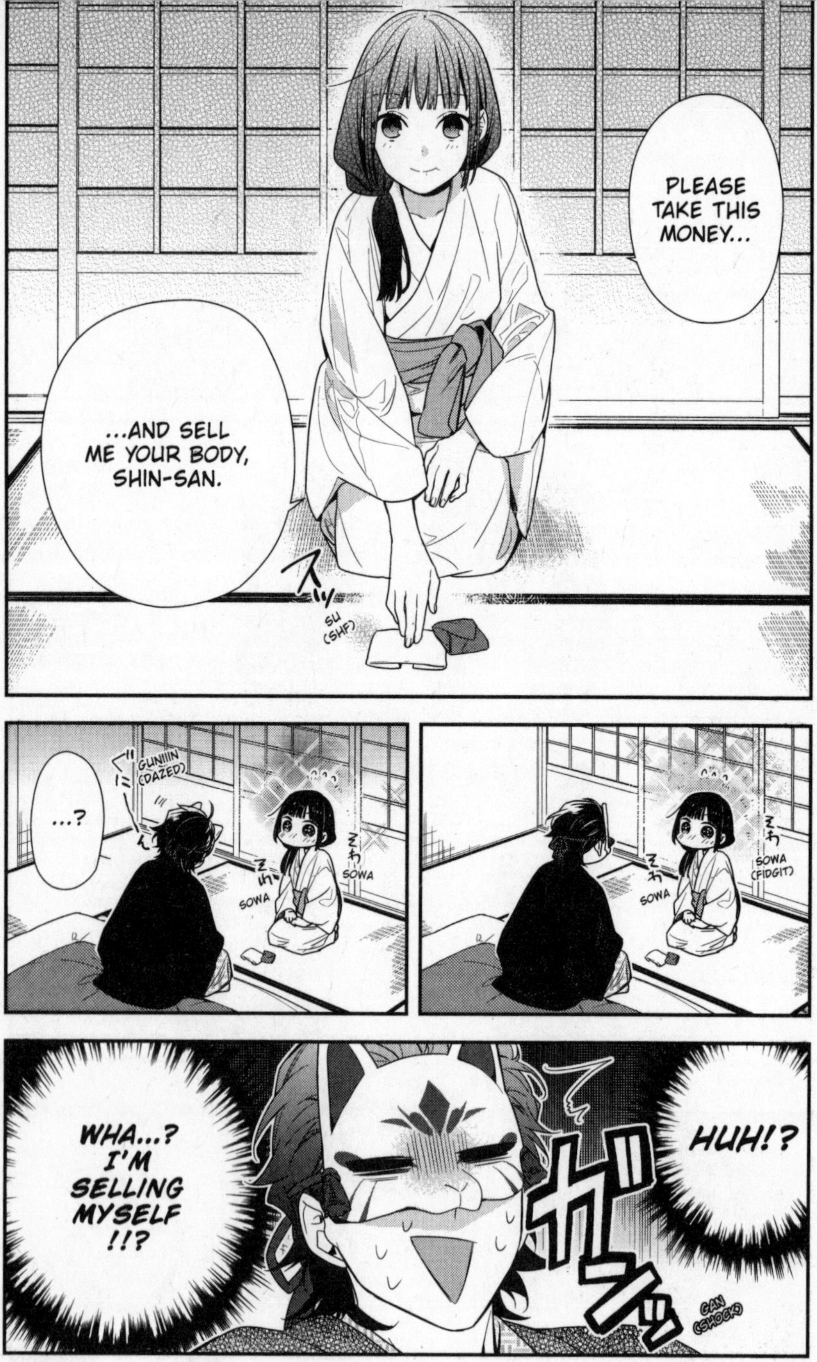
PLEASE TAKE THIS MONEY...
...AND SELL ME YOUR BODY, SHIN-SAN.
SU (SHF)
SOWA (FIDGIT)
SOWA
GUNIIIN (DAZED)
...?
SOWA
SOWA
HUH!?
GAN (SHOCK)
WHA...? I'M SELLING MYSELF!!?

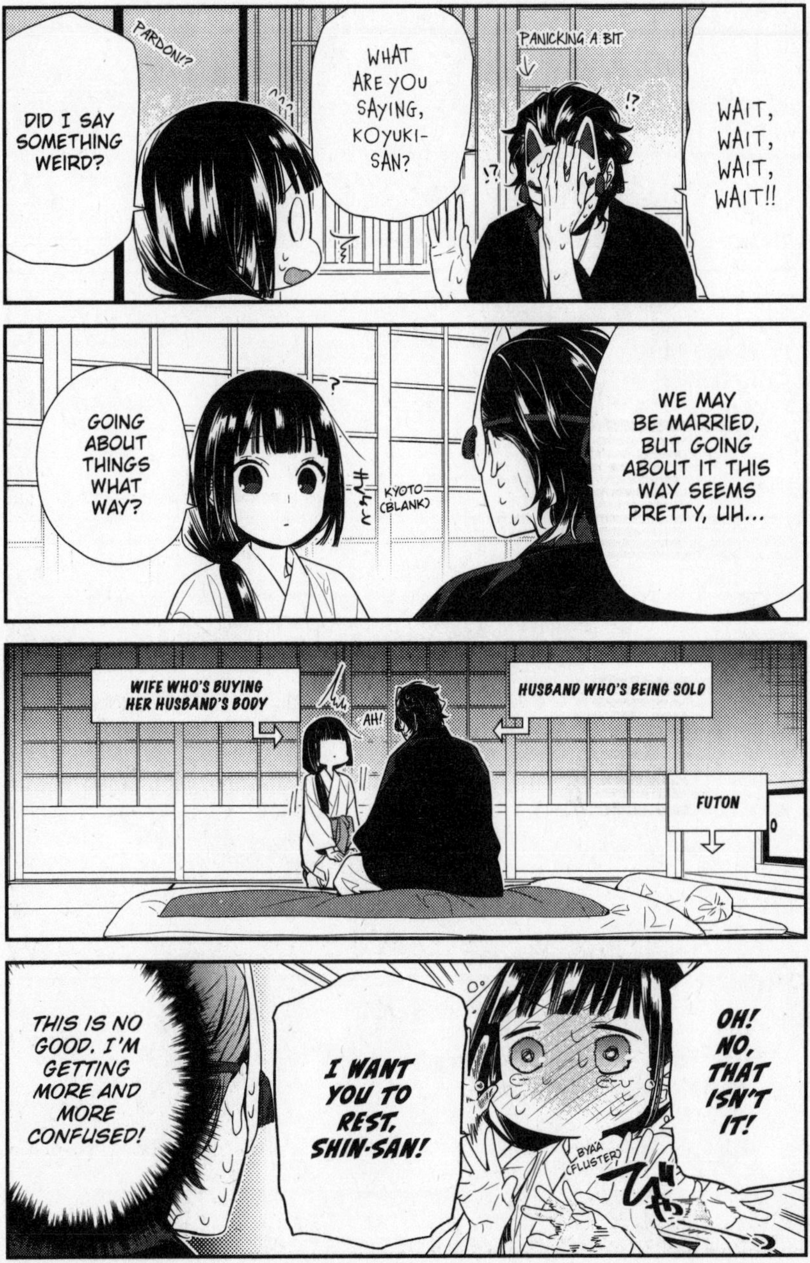
WAIT, WAIT, WAIT, WAIT!!
PANICKING A BIT
!?
!?
WHAT ARE YOU SAYING, KOYUKI-SAN?
PARDON!?
DID I SAY SOMETHING WEIRD?
WE MAY BE MARRIED, BUT GOING ABOUT IT THIS WAY SEEMS PRETTY, UH...
KYOTO (BLANK)
?
GOING ABOUT THINGS WHAT WAY?
HUSBAND WHO'S BEING SOLD
AH!
WIFE WHO'S BUYING HER HUSBAND'S BODY
FUTON
OH! NO, THAT ISN'T IT!
BYAA (FLUSTER)
I WANT YOU TO REST, SHIN-SAN!
THIS IS NO GOOD. I'M GETTING MORE AND MORE CONFUSED!

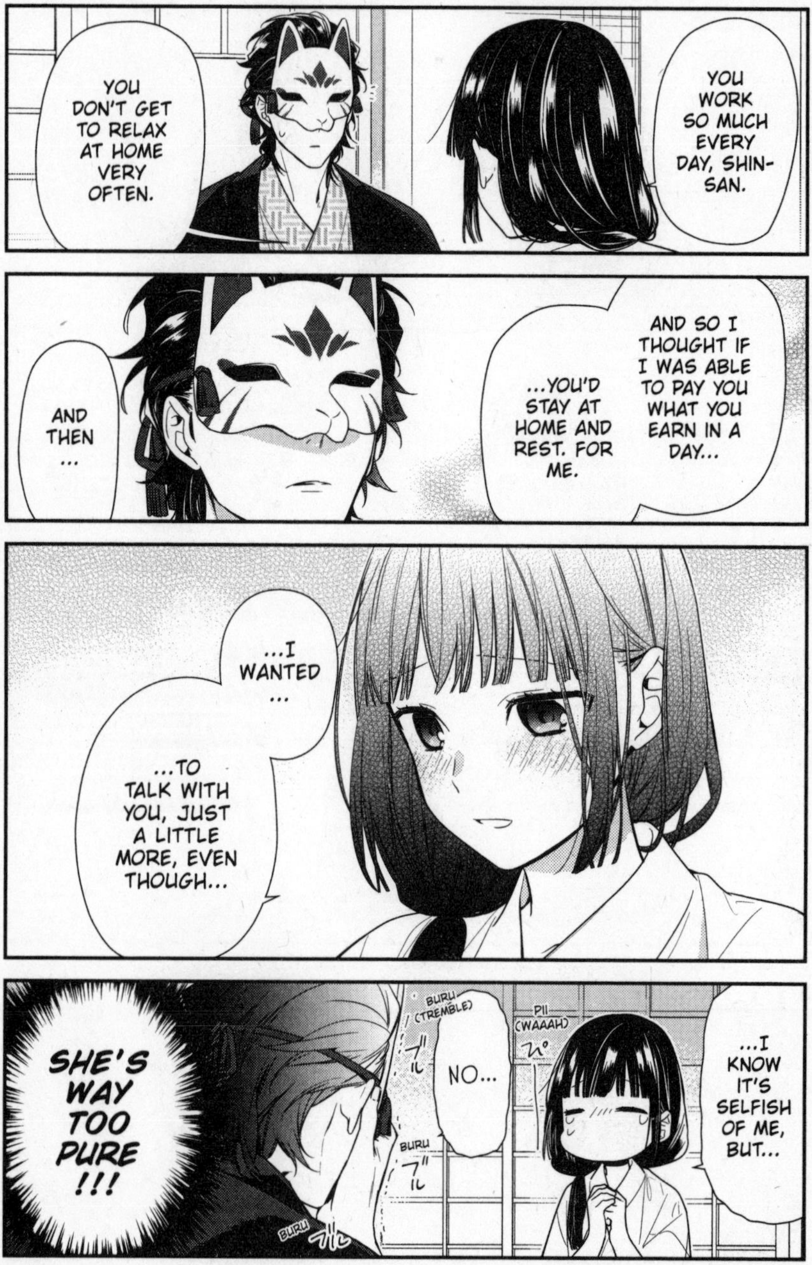
YOU WORK SO MUCH EVERY DAY, SHIN-SAN.
YOU DON'T GET TO RELAX AT HOME VERY OFTEN.
AND SO I THOUGHT IF I WAS ABLE TO PAY YOU WHAT YOU EARN IN A DAY...
...YOU'D STAY AT HOME AND REST. FOR ME.
AND THEN ...
...I WANTED ...
...TO TALK WITH YOU, JUST A LITTLE MORE, EVEN THOUGH...
...I KNOW IT'S SELFISH OF ME, BUT...
PII (WAAAH)
BURU (TREMBLE)
NO...
BURU
BURU
SHE'S WAY TOO PURE!!!

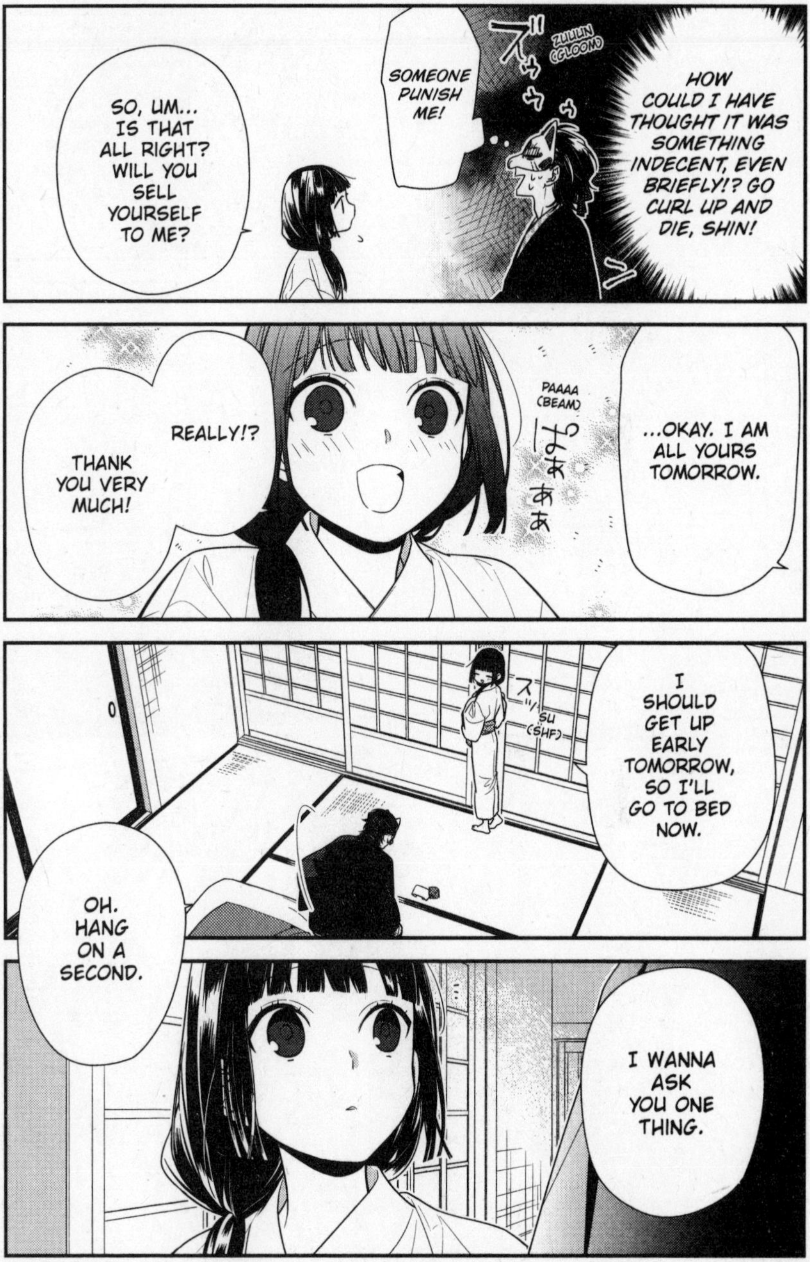
HOW COULD I HAVE THOUGHT IT WAS SOMETHING INDECENT, EVEN BRIEFLY!? GO CURL UP AND DIE, SHIN!
ZUUUN (GLOOM)
SOMEONE PUNISH ME!
SO, UM... IS THAT ALL RIGHT? WILL YOU SELL YOURSELF TO ME?
...OKAY. I AM ALL YOURS TOMORROW.
PAAAA (BEAM)
REALLY!?
THANK YOU VERY MUCH!
I SHOULD GET UP EARLY TOMORROW, SO I'LL GO TO BED NOW.
SU (SHF)
OH. HANG ON A SECOND.
I WANNA ASK YOU ONE THING.

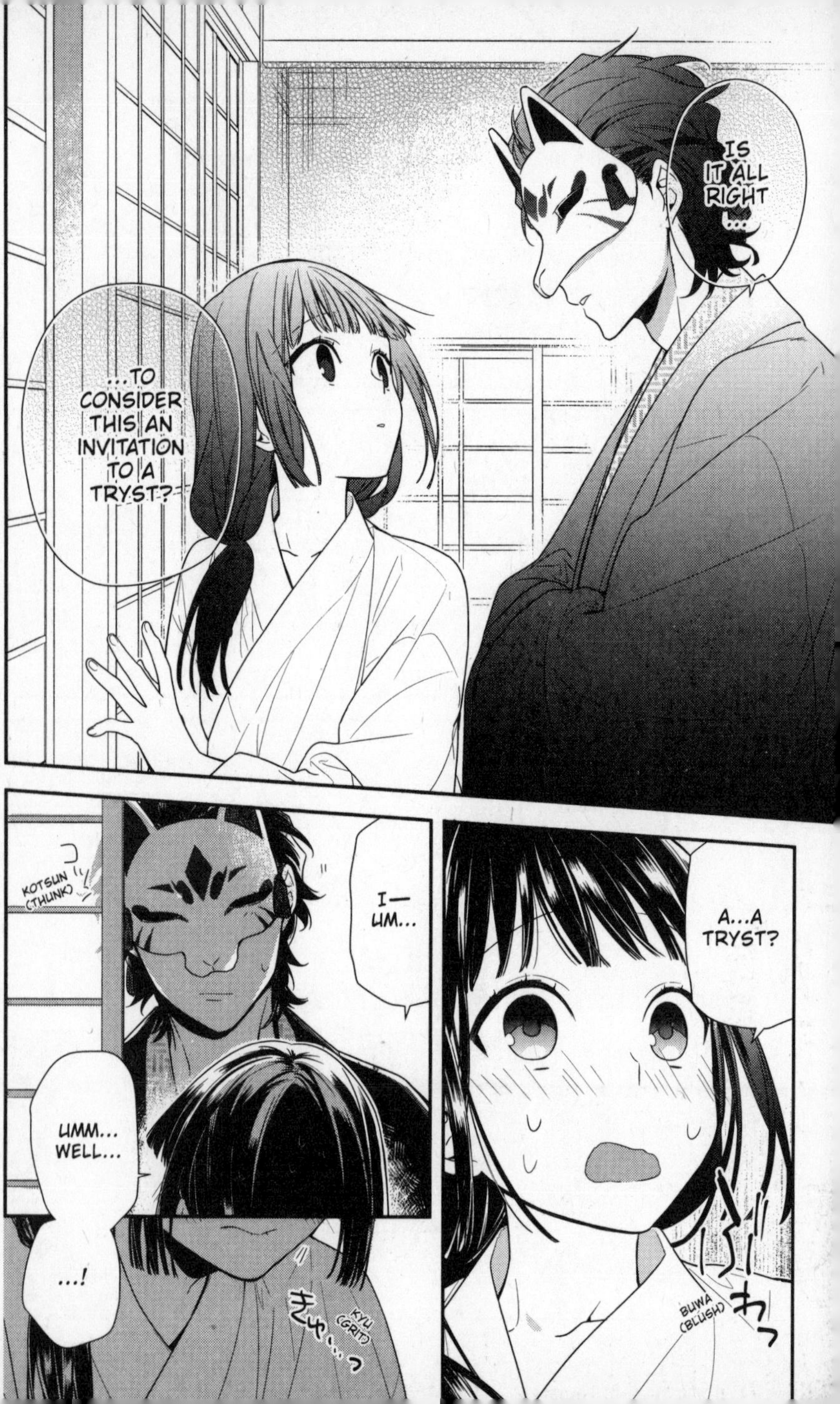
IS IT ALL RIGHT...
...TO CONSIDER THIS AN INVITATION TO A TRYST?
A...A TRYST?
BUWA (BLUSH)
I— UM...
KOTSUN (THUNK)
UMM... WELL...
...!
KYU (GRIT)

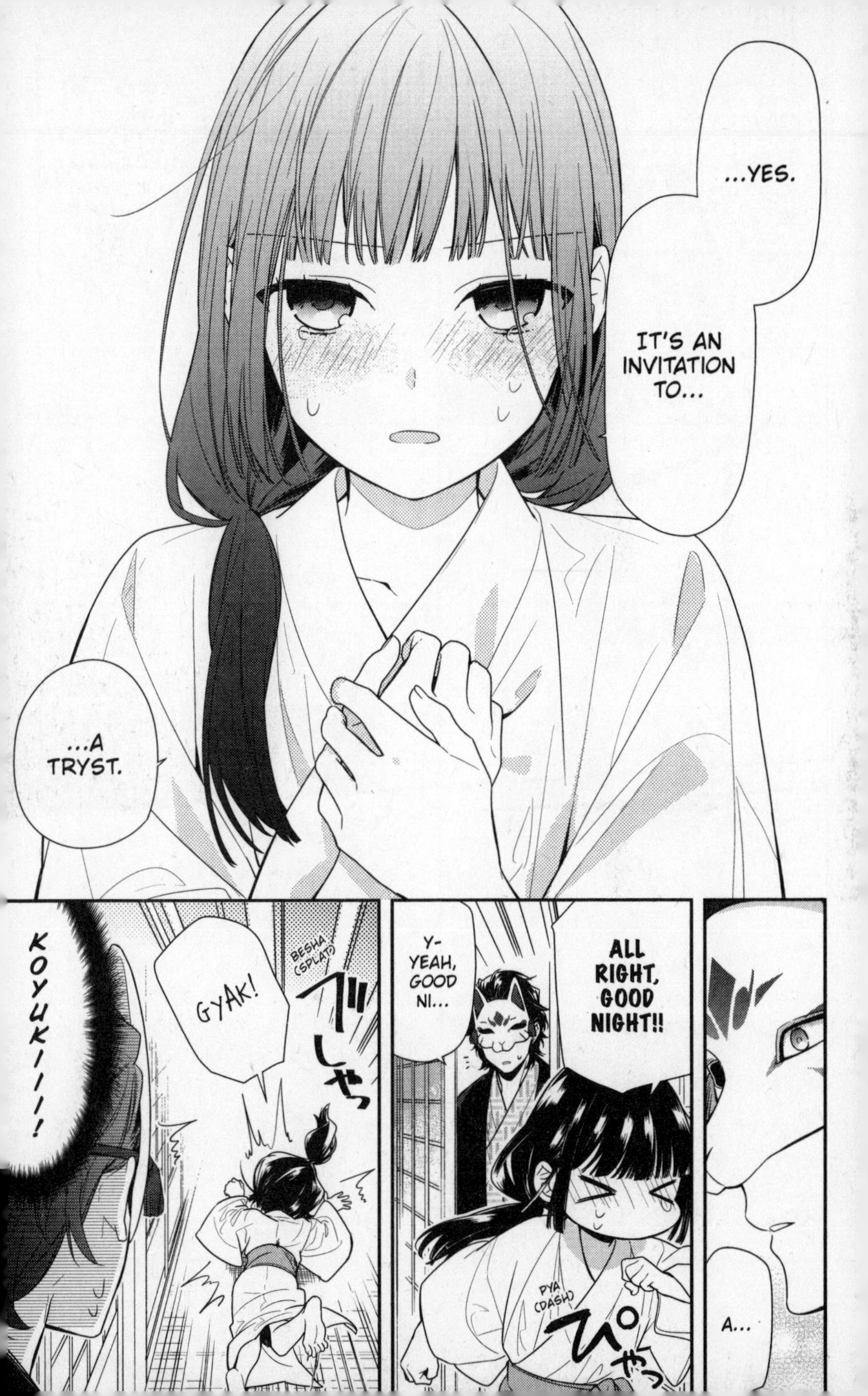
...YES.
IT'S AN INVITATION TO...
...A TRYST.
A...
ALL RIGHT, GOOD NIGHT!!
Y-YEAH, GOOD NI...
PYA (DASH)
BESHA (SPLAT)
GYAK!
KOYUKIIIII!

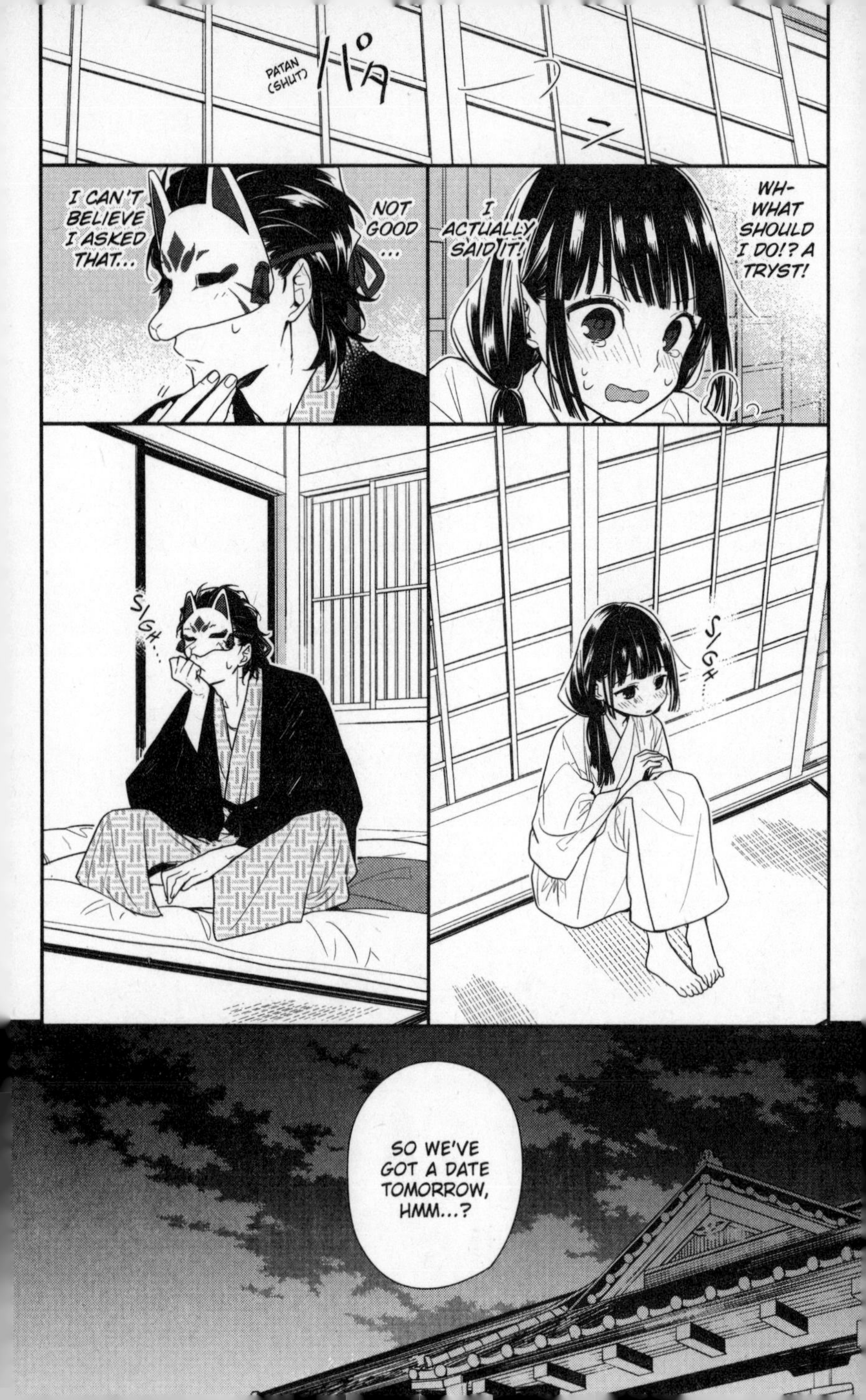
PATAN (SHUT)
WH-WHAT SHOULD I DO!? A TRYST!
I ACTUALLY SAID IT!
NOT GOOD...
I CAN'T BELIEVE I ASKED THAT...
SIGH...
SIGH...
SO WE'VE GOT A DATE TOMORROW, HMM...?

Ne Ne Ne

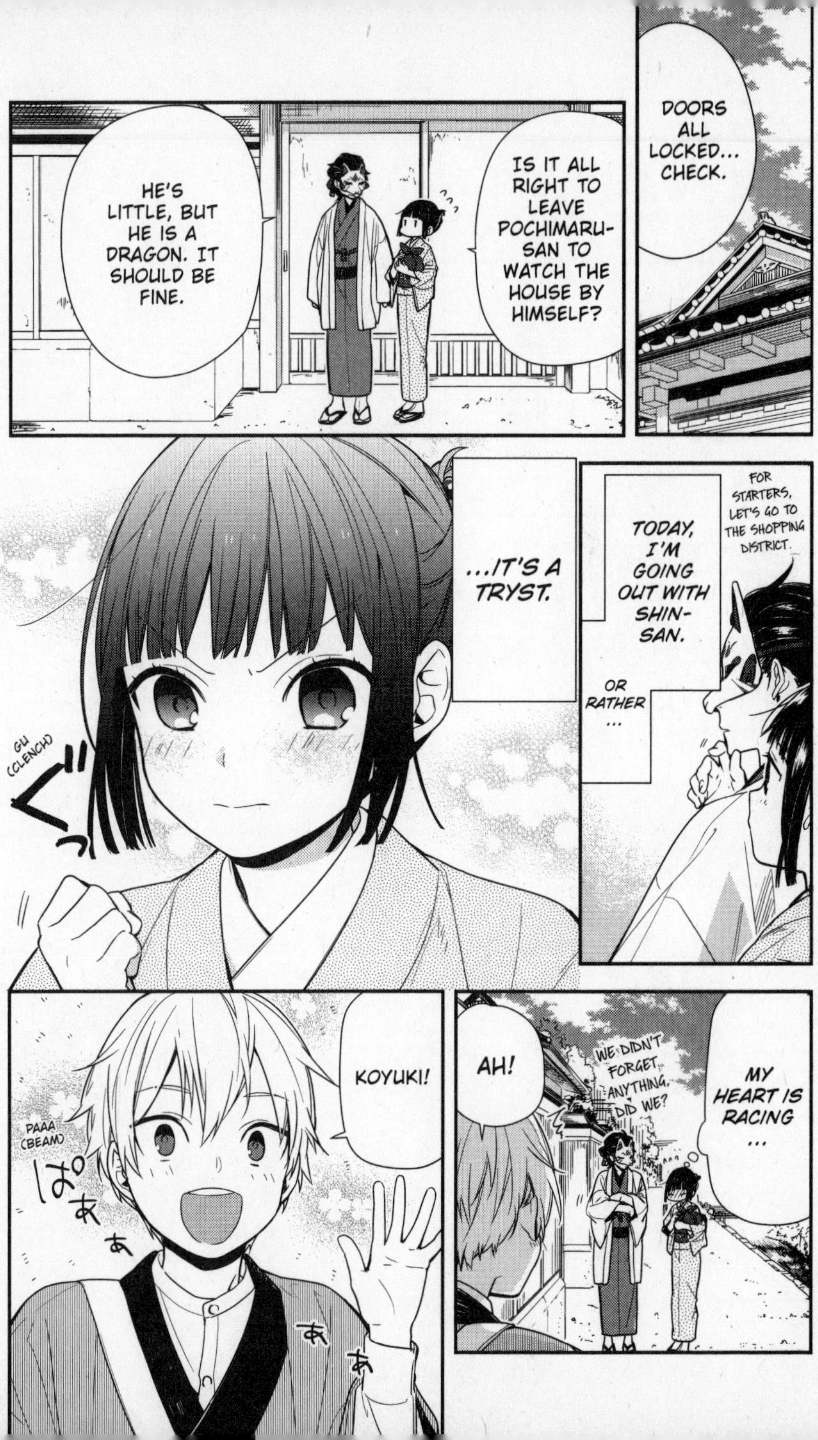
DOORS ALL LOCKED... CHECK.
IS IT ALL RIGHT TO LEAVE POCHIMARU-SAN TO WATCH THE HOUSE BY HIMSELF?
HE'S LITTLE, BUT HE IS A DRAGON. IT SHOULD BE FINE.
FOR STARTERS, LET'S GO TO THE SHOPPING DISTRICT.
TODAY, I'M GOING OUT WITH SHIN-SAN.
OR RATHER ...
...IT'S A TRYST.
GU (CLENCH)
MY HEART IS RACING ...
WE DIDN'T FORGET ANYTHING, DID WE?
AH!
KOYUKI!
PAAA (BEAM)

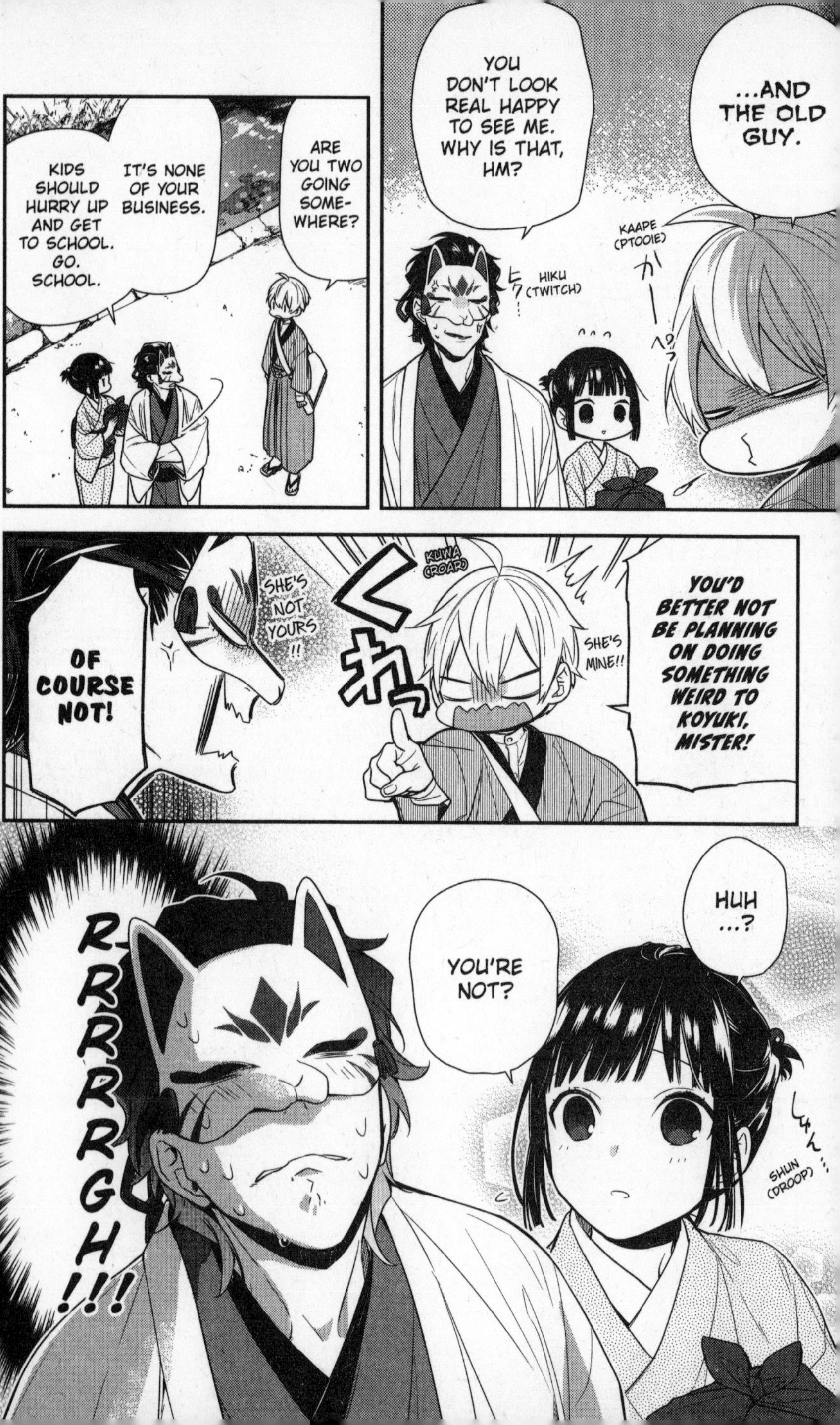
...AND THE OLD GUY.
YOU DON'T LOOK REAL HAPPY TO SEE ME. WHY IS THAT, HM?
KAAPE (PTOOIE)
HIKU (TWITCH)
ARE YOU TWO GOING SOME-WHERE?
IT'S NONE OF YOUR BUSINESS.
KIDS SHOULD HURRY UP AND GET TO SCHOOL. GO. SCHOOL.
YOU'D BETTER NOT BE PLANNING ON DOING SOMETHING WEIRD TO KOYUKI, MISTER!
SHE'S MINE!!
KUWA (ROAR)
SHE'S NOT YOURS!!
OF COURSE NOT!
HUH...?
SHUN (DROOP)
YOU'RE NOT?
R-RRRRRGH!!!

Chapter 7

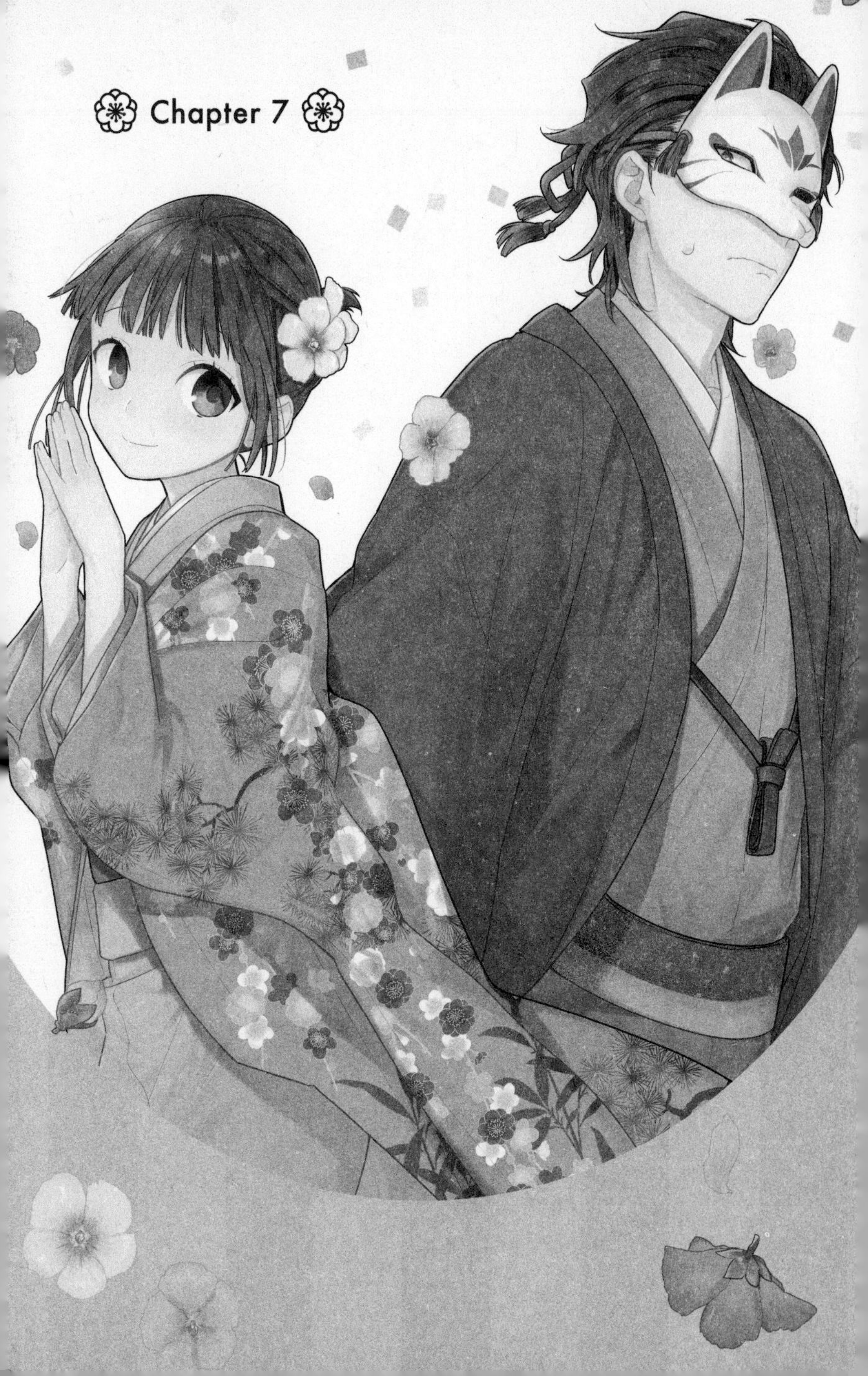

NE NE NE

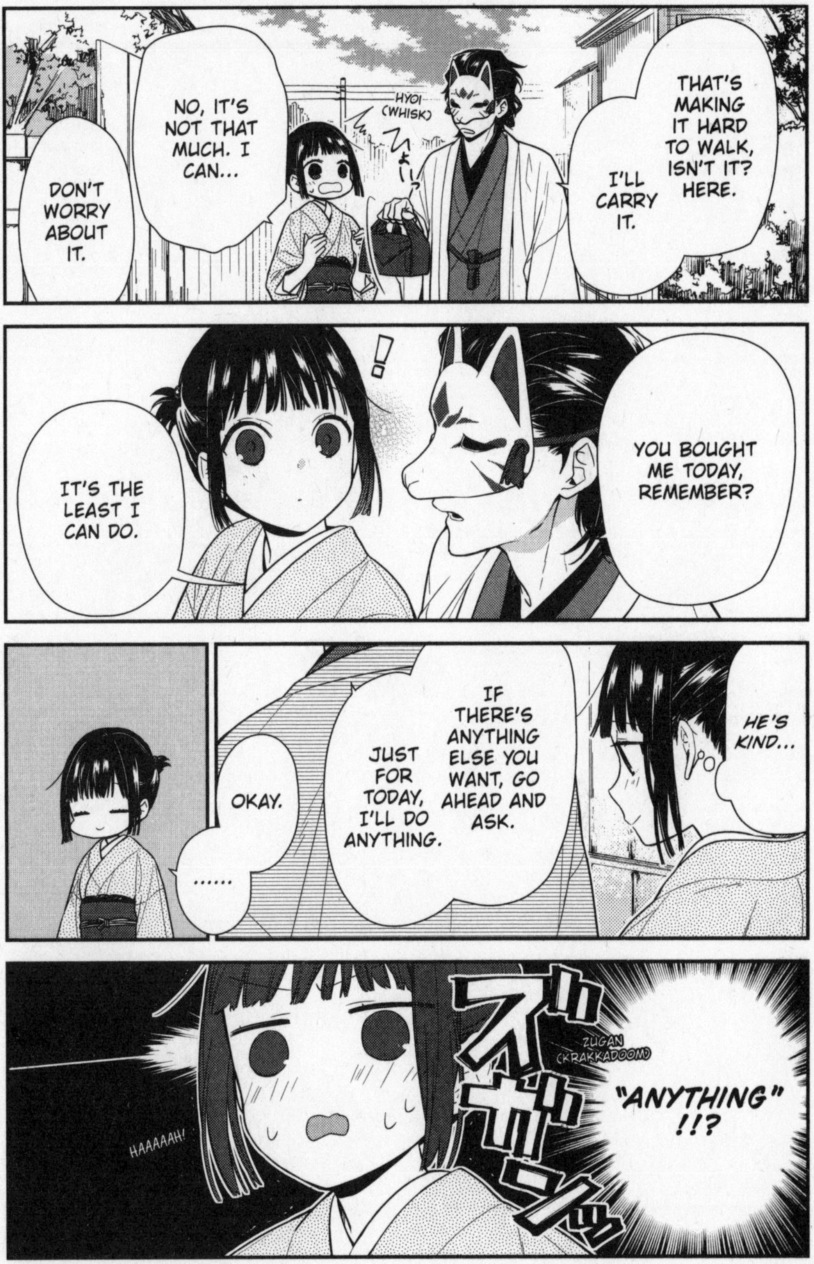
THAT'S MAKING IT HARD TO WALK, ISN'T IT? HERE.
I'LL CARRY IT.
HYOI (WHISK)
NO, IT'S NOT THAT MUCH. I CAN...
DON'T WORRY ABOUT IT.
YOU BOUGHT ME TODAY, REMEMBER?
!
IT'S THE LEAST I CAN DO.
HE'S KIND...
IF THERE'S ANYTHING ELSE YOU WANT, GO AHEAD AND ASK.
JUST FOR TODAY, I'LL DO ANYTHING.
OKAY.
......
"ANYTHING" !!?
ZUGAN (KRAKKADOOM)
HAAAAAH!

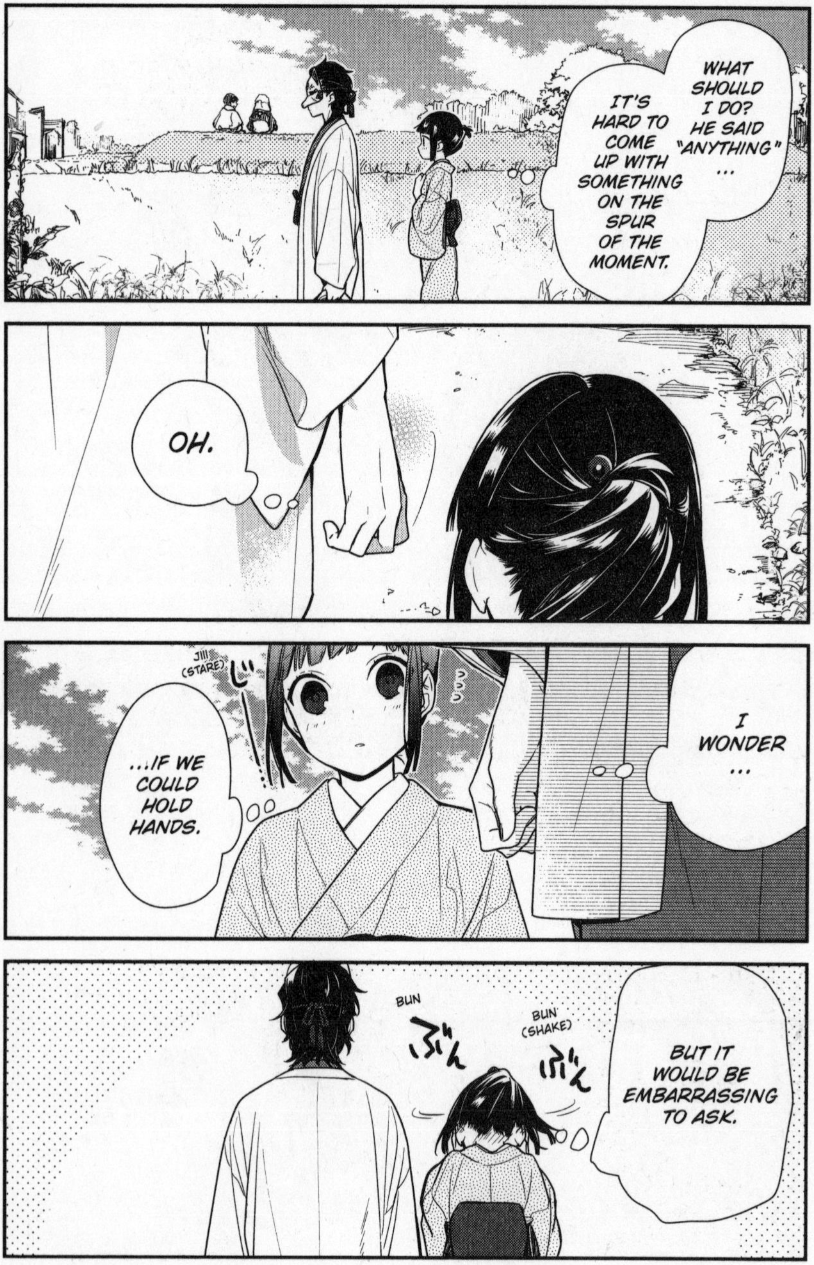
WHAT SHOULD I DO? HE SAID "ANYTHING"...
IT'S HARD TO COME UP WITH SOMETHING ON THE SPUR OF THE MOMENT.
OH.
I WONDER...
JIII (STARE)
...IF WE COULD HOLD HANDS.
BUT IT WOULD BE EMBARRASSING TO ASK.
BUN (SHAKE)
BUN

AT TIMES LIKE THIS, PEOPLE HOLD HANDS, DON'T THEY?

チラ CHIRA

UH...

チラ CHIRA (GLANCE)

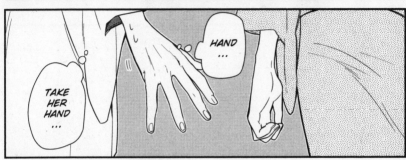

HAND ...

TAKE HER HAND ...

BIKUUU (FLINCH)

ビクッ

OH!

HYU (VWIP)

Y... YES, THEY ARE.

DO (BADMP)

DO

DO

DO

THOSE HOLLYHOCKS ARE BLOOMING. THEY'RE PRETTY, AREN'T THEY?

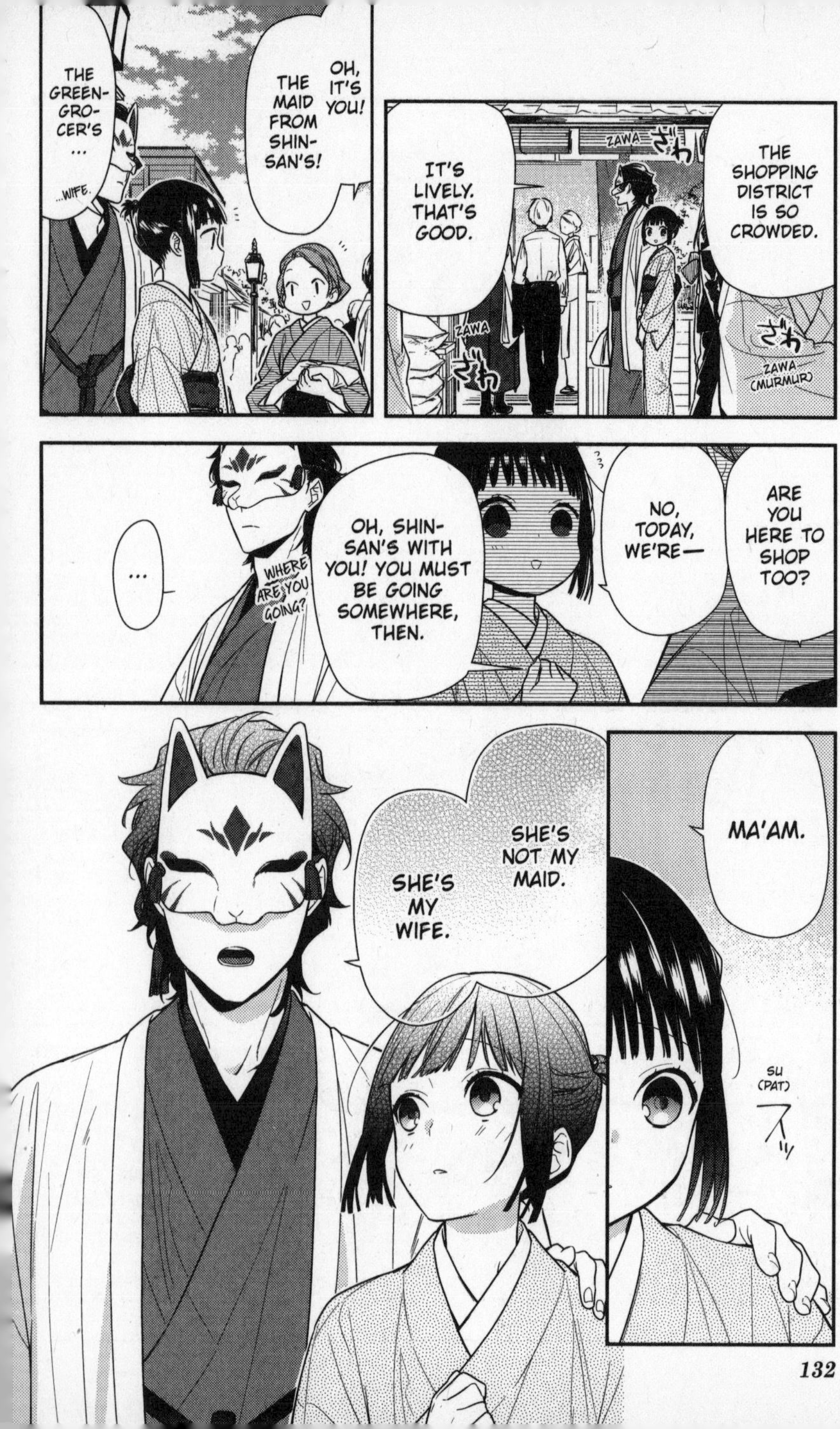
THE SHOPPING DISTRICT IS SO CROWDED.
ZAWA
ざわ
ZAWA (MURMUR)
ざわ
ZAWA
ざわ
IT'S LIVELY. THAT'S GOOD.
OH, IT'S YOU!
THE MAID FROM SHIN-SAN'S!
THE GREEN-GROCER'S...
...WIFE.
ARE YOU HERE TO SHOP TOO?
NO, TODAY, WE'RE—
OH, SHIN-SAN'S WITH YOU! YOU MUST BE GOING SOMEWHERE, THEN.
WHERE ARE YOU GOING?
...
MA'AM.
SU (PAT)
スッ
SHE'S NOT MY MAID.
SHE'S MY WIFE.

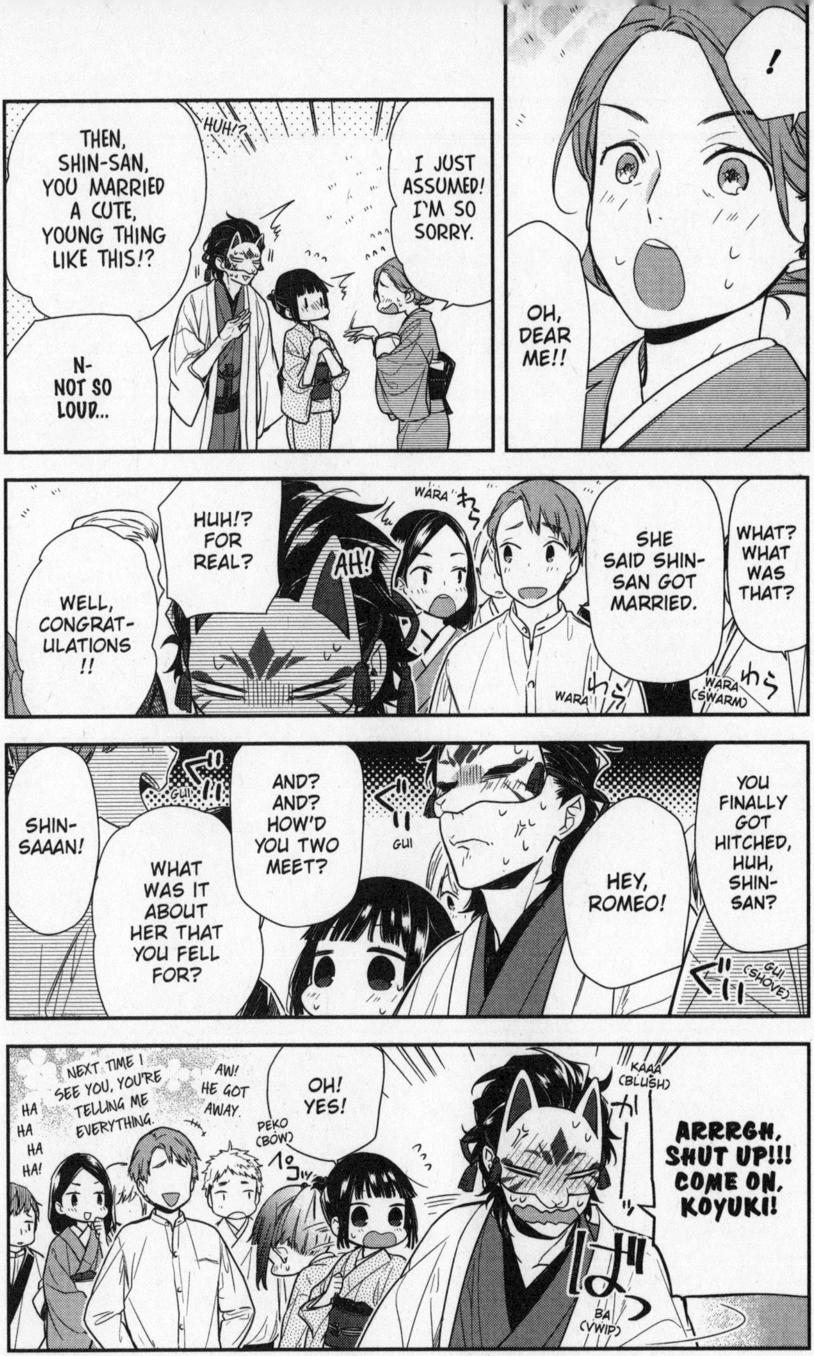
!
OH, DEAR ME!!
I JUST ASSUMED! I'M SO SORRY.
HUH!?
THEN, SHIN-SAN, YOU MARRIED A CUTE, YOUNG THING LIKE THIS!?
N-NOT SO LOUD...
WHAT? WHAT WAS THAT?
SHE SAID SHIN-SAN GOT MARRIED.
WARA
AH!
HUH!? FOR REAL?
WELL, CONGRAT-ULATIONS!!
WARA (SWARM)
WARA
YOU FINALLY GOT HITCHED, HUH, SHIN-SAN?
HEY, ROMEO!
GUI (SHOVE)
AND? AND? HOW'D YOU TWO MEET?
GUI
SHIN-SAAAN!
GUI
WHAT WAS IT ABOUT HER THAT YOU FELL FOR?
ARRRGH, SHUT UP!!! COME ON, KOYUKI!
KAAA (BLUSH)
BA (VWIP)
OH! YES!
PEKO (BOW)
AW! HE GOT AWAY.
NEXT TIME I SEE YOU, YOU'RE TELLING ME EVERYTHING.
HA HA HA HA!

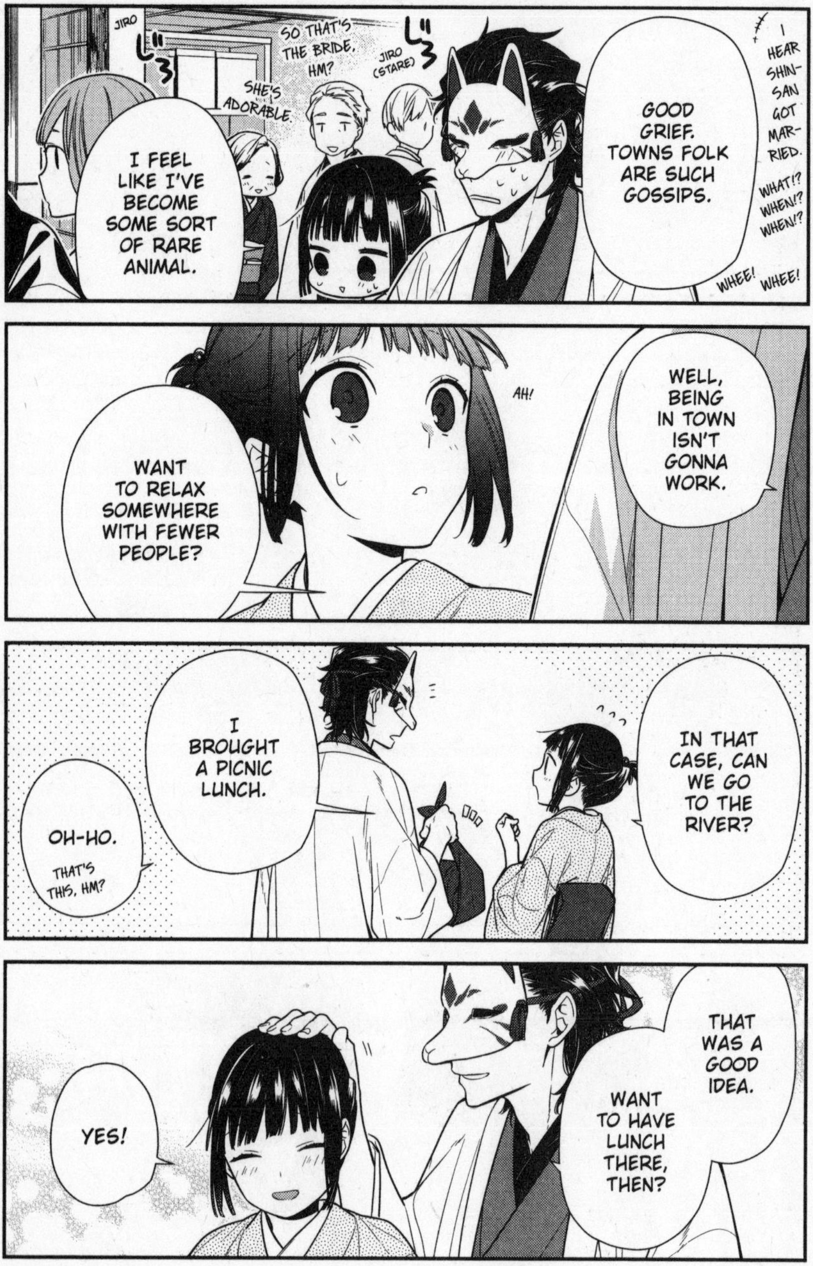
I HEAR SHIN-SAN GOT MARRIED.
WHAT!? WHEN!? WHEN!?
WHEE! WHEE!
GOOD GRIEF. TOWNS FOLK ARE SUCH GOSSIPS.
じろ
JIRO (STARE)
SO THAT'S THE BRIDE, HM?
SHE'S ADORABLE.
じろ
JIRO
I FEEL LIKE I'VE BECOME SOME SORT OF RARE ANIMAL.
WELL, BEING IN TOWN ISN'T GONNA WORK.
AH!
WANT TO RELAX SOMEWHERE WITH FEWER PEOPLE?
IN THAT CASE, CAN WE GO TO THE RIVER?
I BROUGHT A PICNIC LUNCH.
OH-HO.
THAT'S THIS, HM?
THAT WAS A GOOD IDEA.
WANT TO HAVE LUNCH THERE, THEN?
YES!

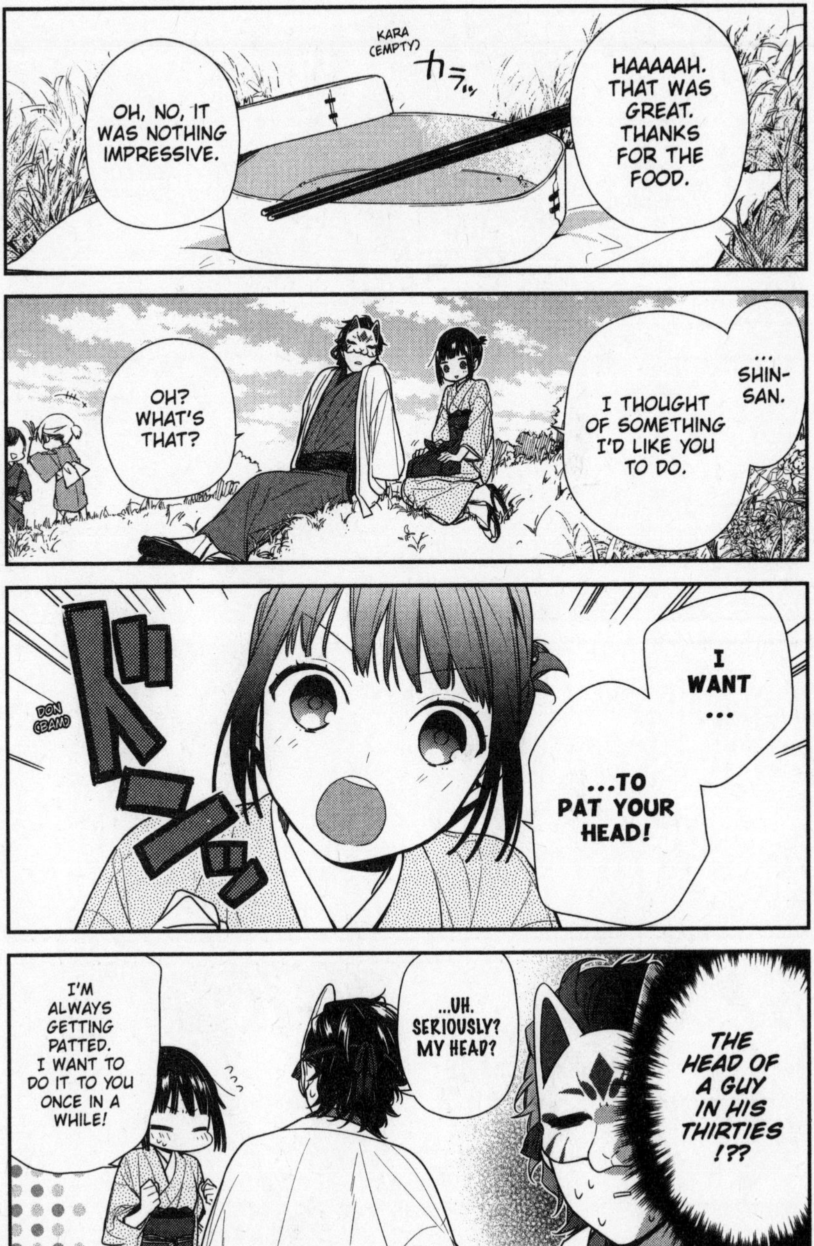
HAAAAAH. THAT WAS GREAT. THANKS FOR THE FOOD.
KARA (EMPTY)
OH, NO, IT WAS NOTHING IMPRESSIVE.
...SHIN-SAN.
I THOUGHT OF SOMETHING I'D LIKE YOU TO DO.
OH? WHAT'S THAT?
I WANT...
...TO PAT YOUR HEAD!
DON (BAM)
THE HEAD OF A GUY IN HIS THIRTIES !??
...UH. SERIOUSLY? MY HEAD?
I'M ALWAYS GETTING PATTED. I WANT TO DO IT TO YOU ONCE IN A WHILE!

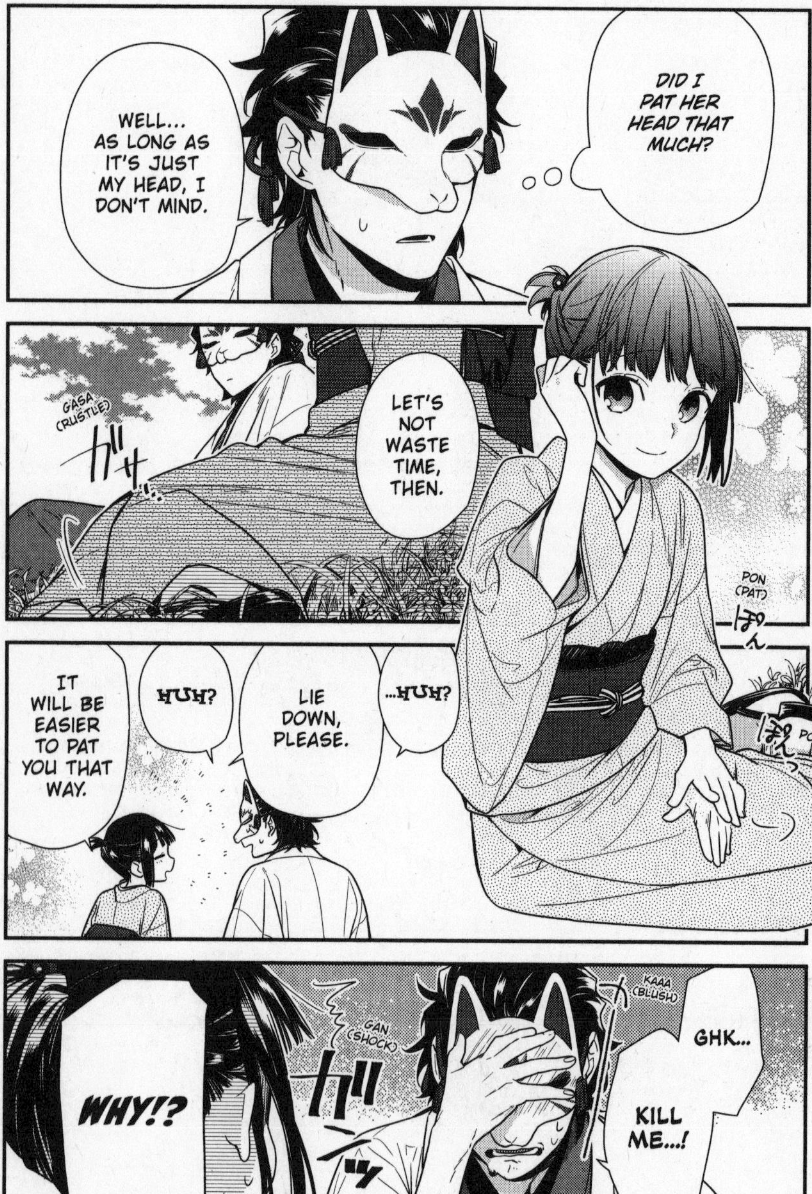
DID I PAT HER HEAD THAT MUCH?
WELL... AS LONG AS IT'S JUST MY HEAD, I DON'T MIND.
PON (PAT)
LET'S NOT WASTE TIME, THEN.
GASA (RUSTLE)
PON
...HUH?
LIE DOWN, PLEASE.
HUH?
IT WILL BE EASIER TO PAT YOU THAT WAY.
GHK...
KILL ME...!
KAAA (BLUSH)
GAN (SHOCK)
WHY!?

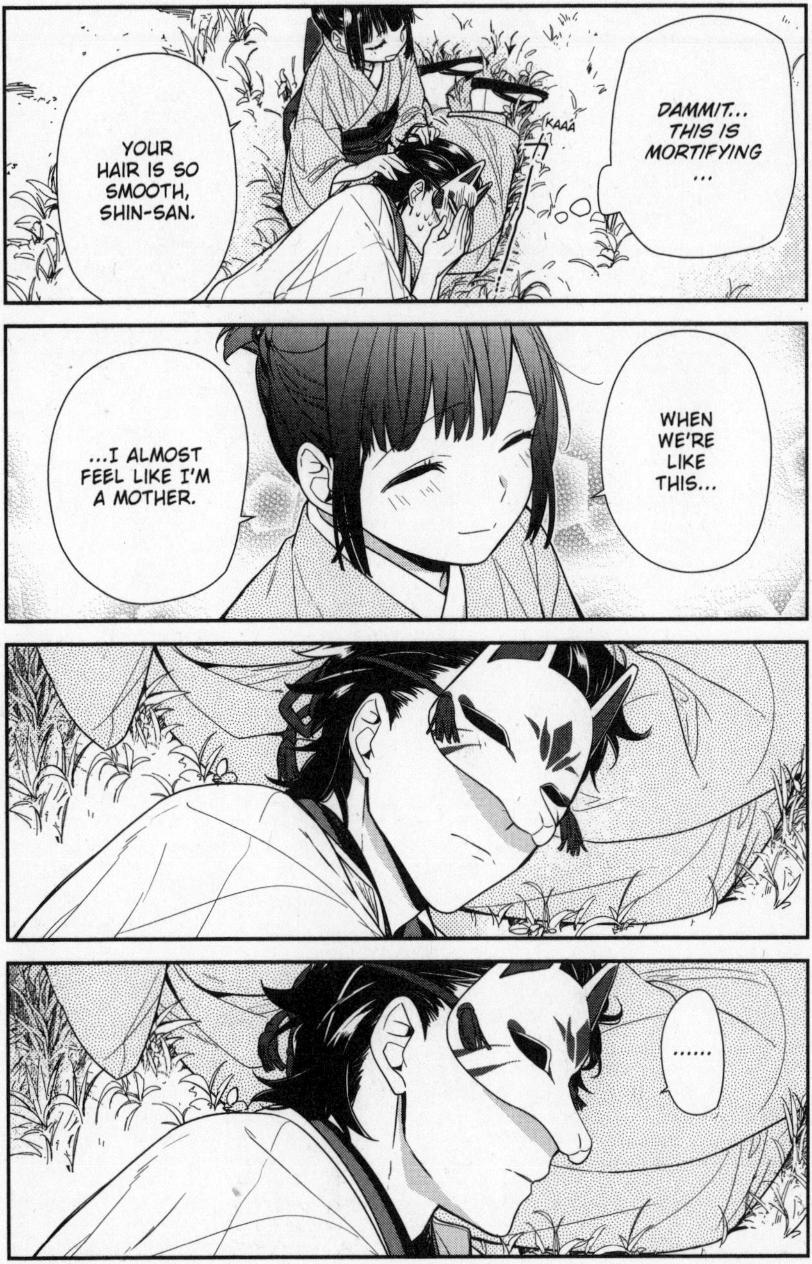
DAMMIT... THIS IS MORTIFYING ...
KAAA
YOUR HAIR IS SO SMOOTH, SHIN-SAN.
WHEN WE'RE LIKE THIS...
...I ALMOST FEEL LIKE I'M A MOTHER.
......

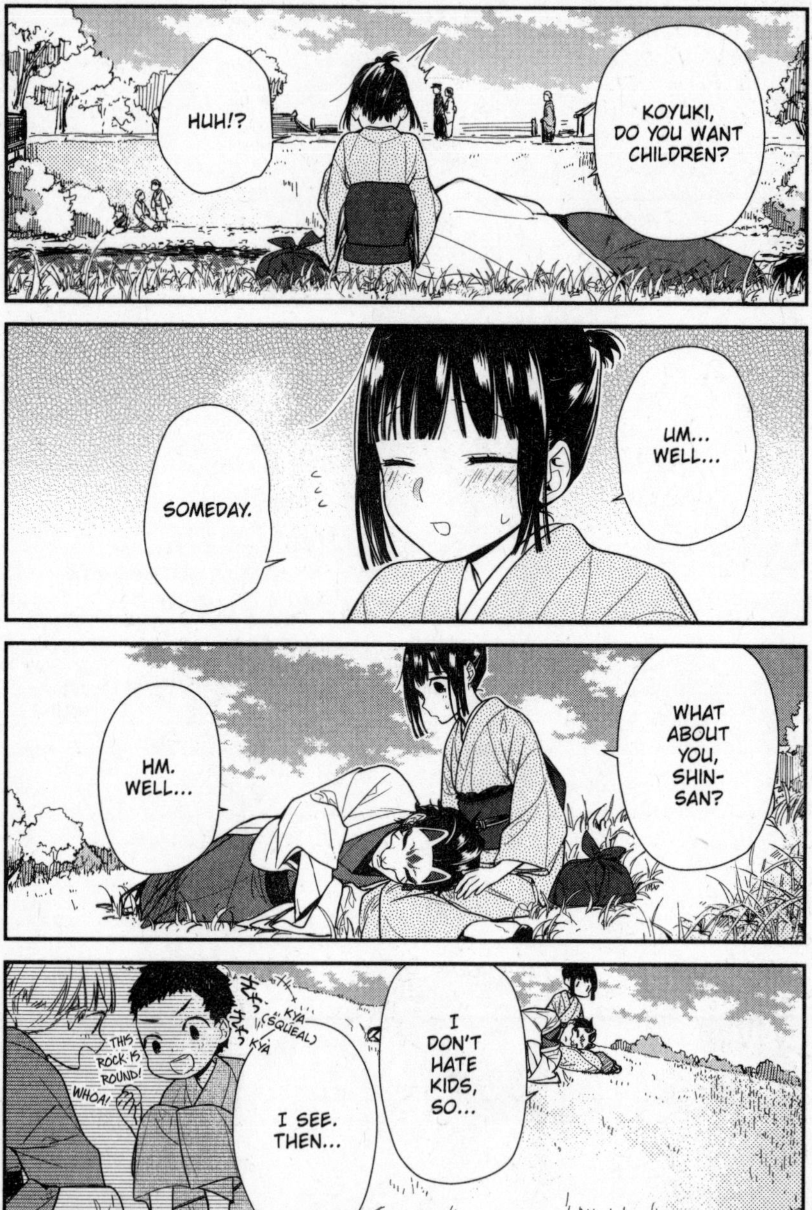
KOYUKI, DO YOU WANT CHILDREN?
HUH!?
UM... WELL...
SOMEDAY.
WHAT ABOUT YOU, SHIN-SAN?
HM. WELL...
I DON'T HATE KIDS, SO...
I SEE. THEN...
KYA (SQUEAL) KYA
THIS ROCK IS ROUND!
WHOA!

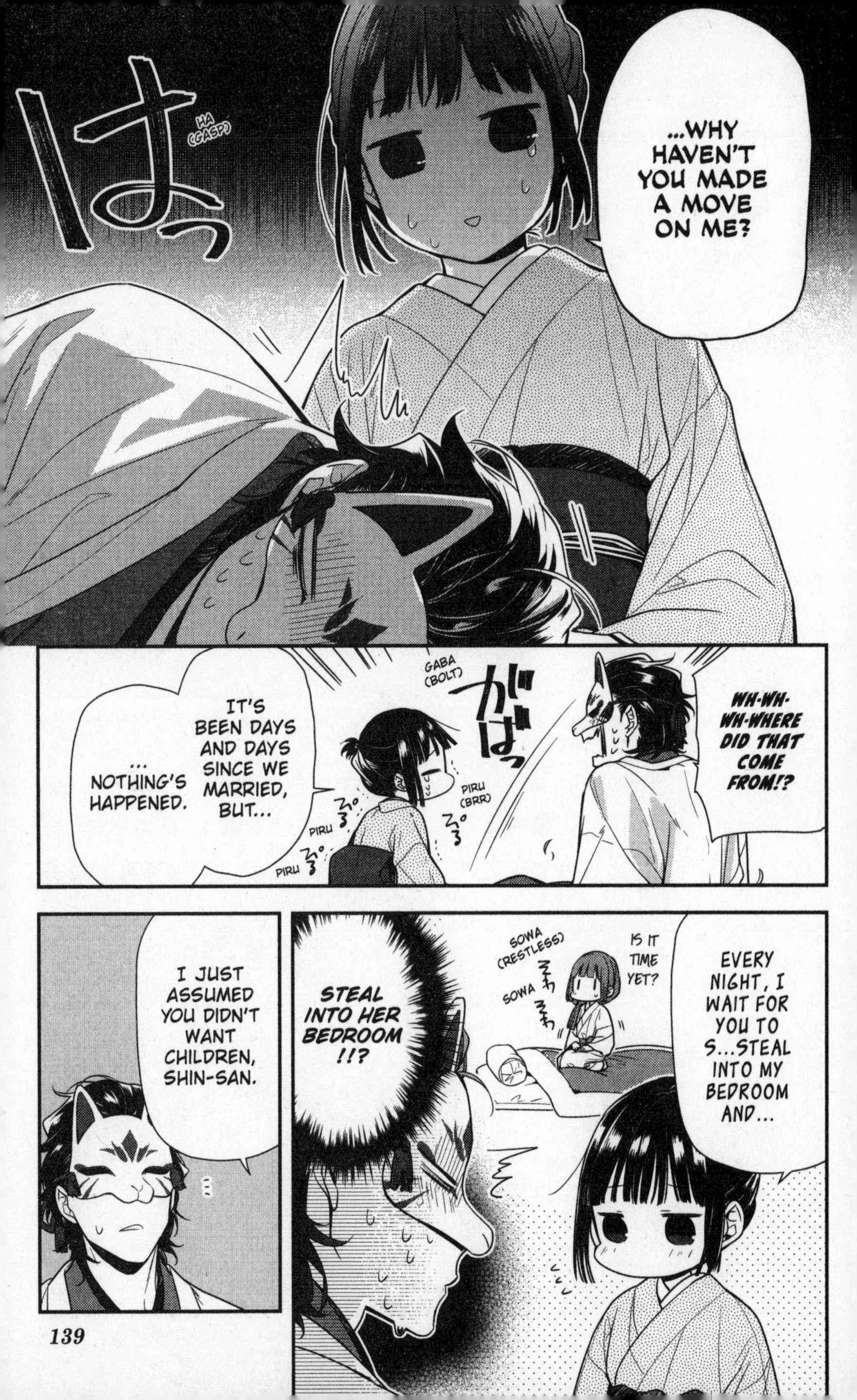
...WHY HAVEN'T YOU MADE A MOVE ON ME?
はっ
HA (GASP)
WH-WH-WH-WHERE DID THAT COME FROM!?
がばっ
GABA (BOLT)
PIRU (BRR)
PIRU
PIRU
IT'S BEEN DAYS AND DAYS SINCE WE MARRIED, BUT...
... NOTHING'S HAPPENED.
EVERY NIGHT, I WAIT FOR YOU TO S...STEAL INTO MY BEDROOM AND...
IS IT TIME YET?
SOWA (RESTLESS)
SOWA
STEAL INTO HER BEDROOM!!?
I JUST ASSUMED YOU DIDN'T WANT CHILDREN, SHIN-SAN.
...

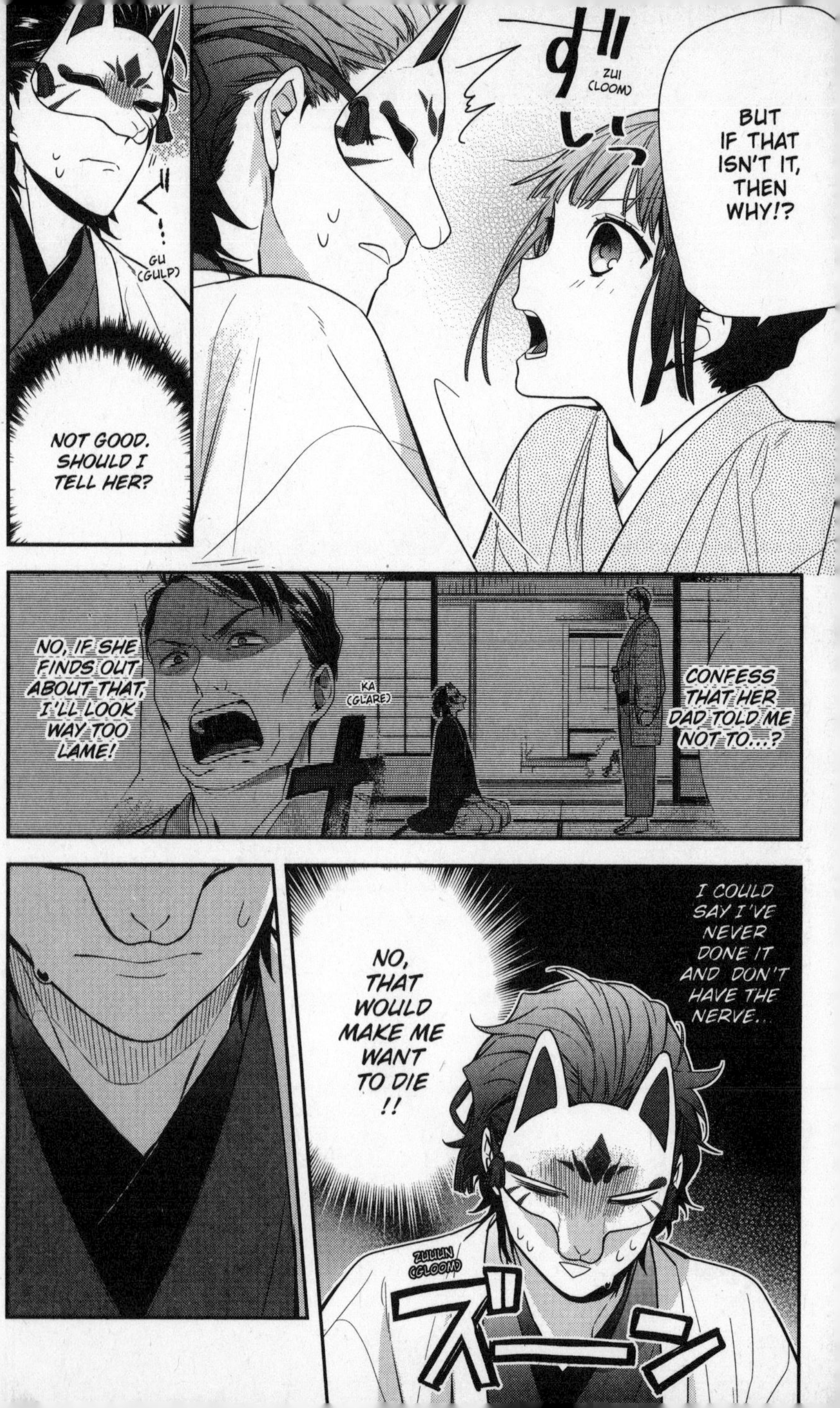

BUT IF THAT ISN'T IT, THEN WHY!?
ZUI (LOOM)
GU (GULP)
NOT GOOD. SHOULD I TELL HER?
CONFESS THAT HER DAD TOLD ME NOT TO...?
KA (GLARE)
NO, IF SHE FINDS OUT ABOUT THAT, I'LL LOOK WAY TOO LAME!
I COULD SAY I'VE NEVER DONE IT AND DON'T HAVE THE NERVE...
NO, THAT WOULD MAKE ME WANT TO DIE!!
ZUUUN (GLOOM)

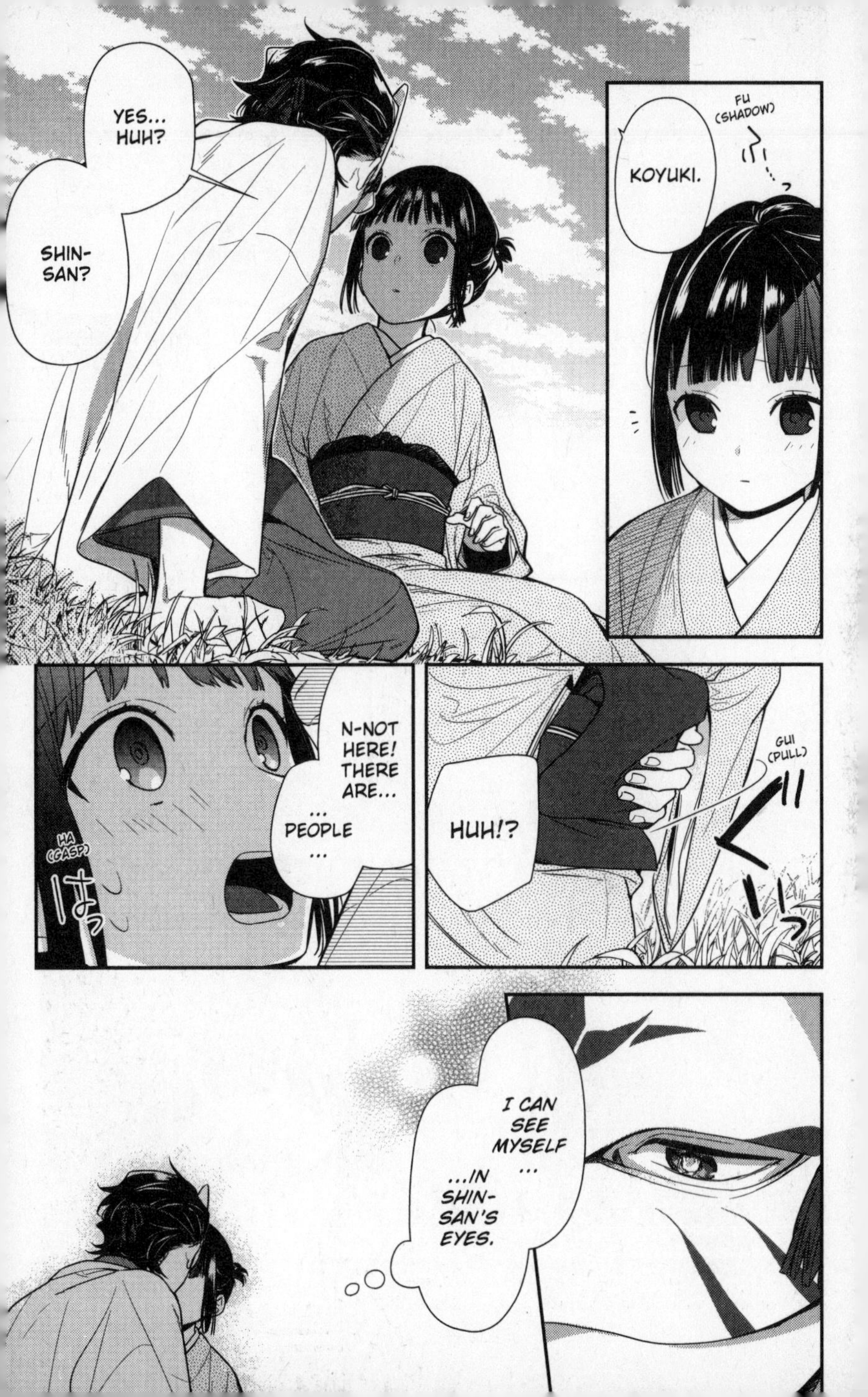
FU (SHADOW)
KOYUKI.
YES... HUH?
SHIN-SAN?
GUI (PULL)
HUH!?
N-NOT HERE! THERE ARE...
...PEOPLE...
HA (GASP)
I CAN SEE MYSELF...
...IN SHIN-SAN'S EYES.

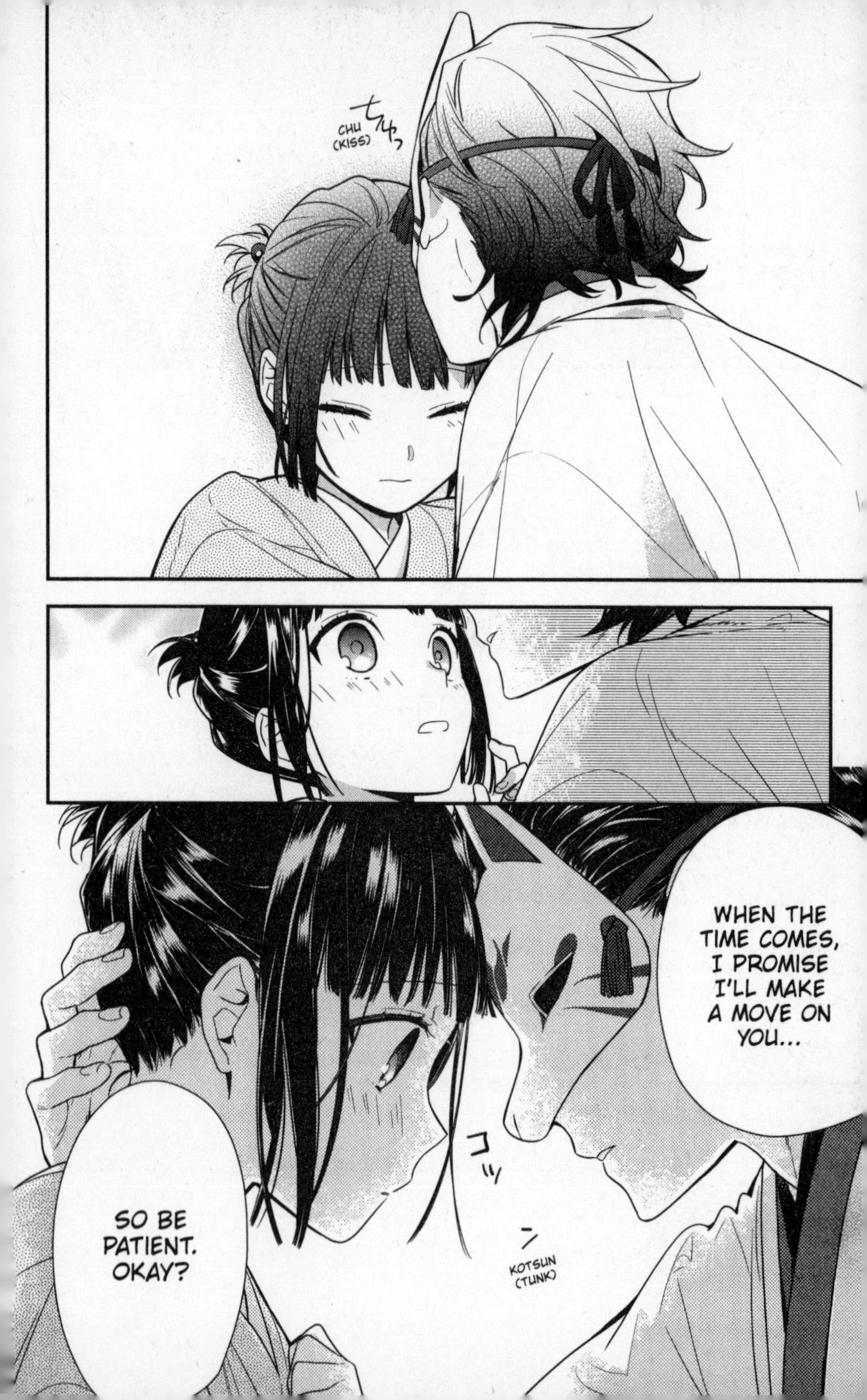
ちゅっ
CHU (KISS)
WHEN THE TIME COMES, I PROMISE I'LL MAKE A MOVE ON YOU...
SO BE PATIENT. OKAY?
コツン
KOTSUN (TUNK)

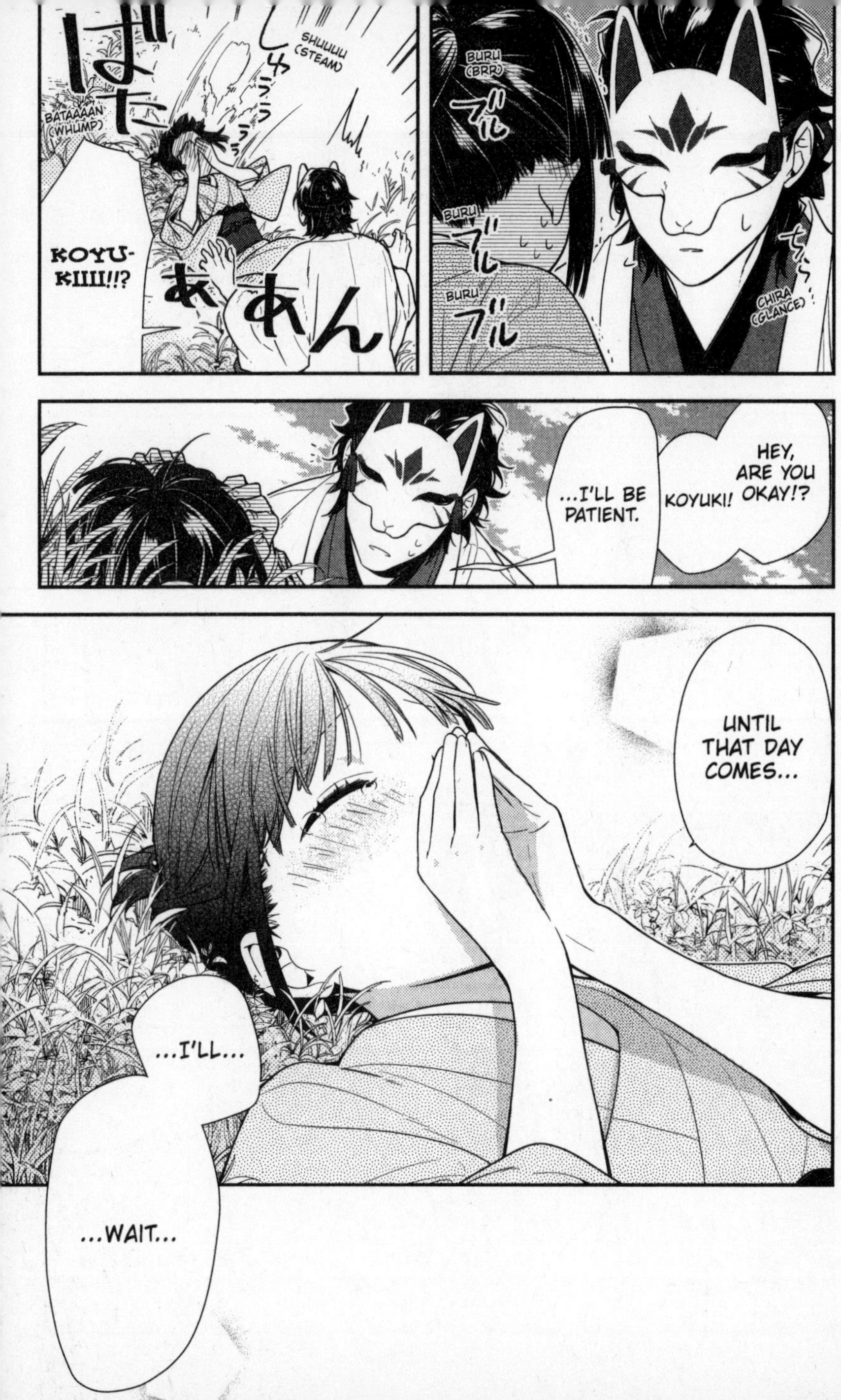
BURU (BRR)
BURU
BURU
CHIRA (GLANCE)
SHUUUU (STEAM)
BATAAAAN (WHUMP)
KOYUKIIII!!?
HEY, ARE YOU OKAY!?
KOYUKI!
...I'LL BE PATIENT.
UNTIL THAT DAY COMES...
...I'LL...
...WAIT...

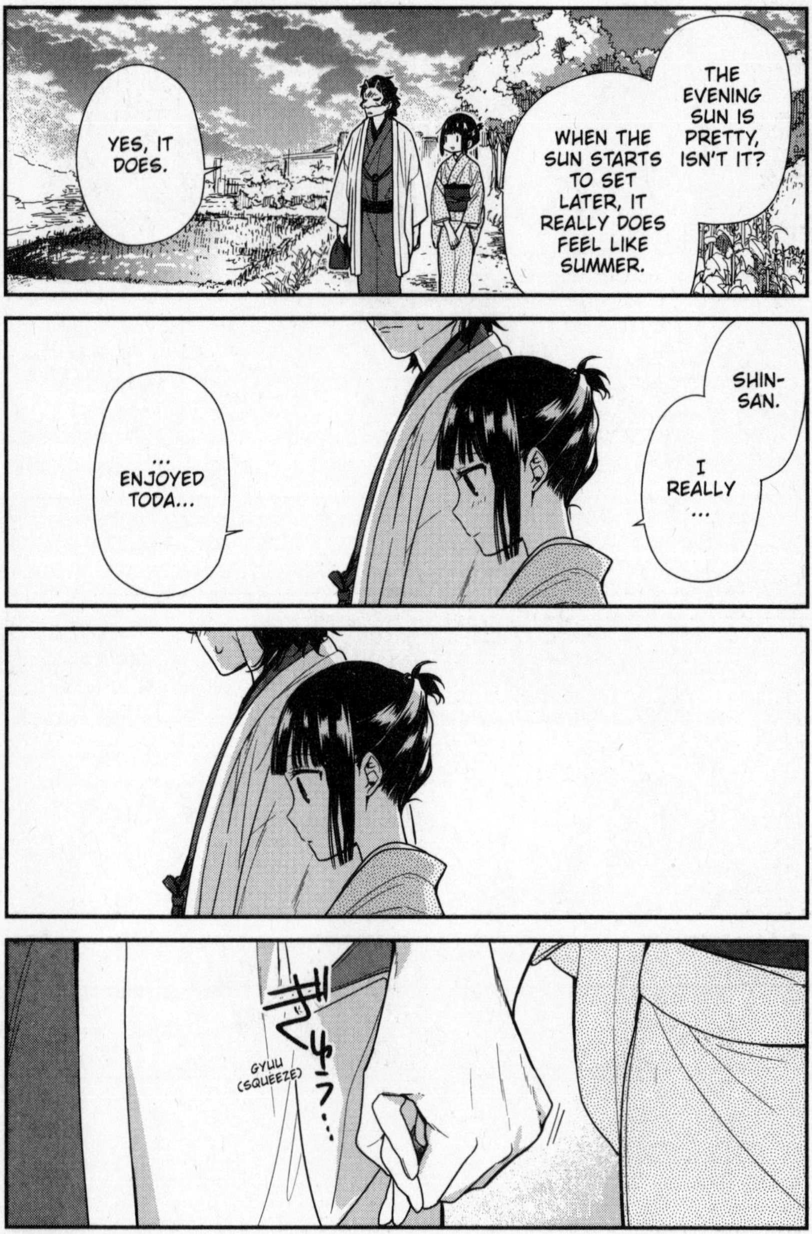
THE EVENING SUN IS PRETTY, ISN'T IT?
WHEN THE SUN STARTS TO SET LATER, IT REALLY DOES FEEL LIKE SUMMER.
YES, IT DOES.
SHIN-SAN.
I REALLY ...
... ENJOYED TODA...
GYUU (SQUEEZE)

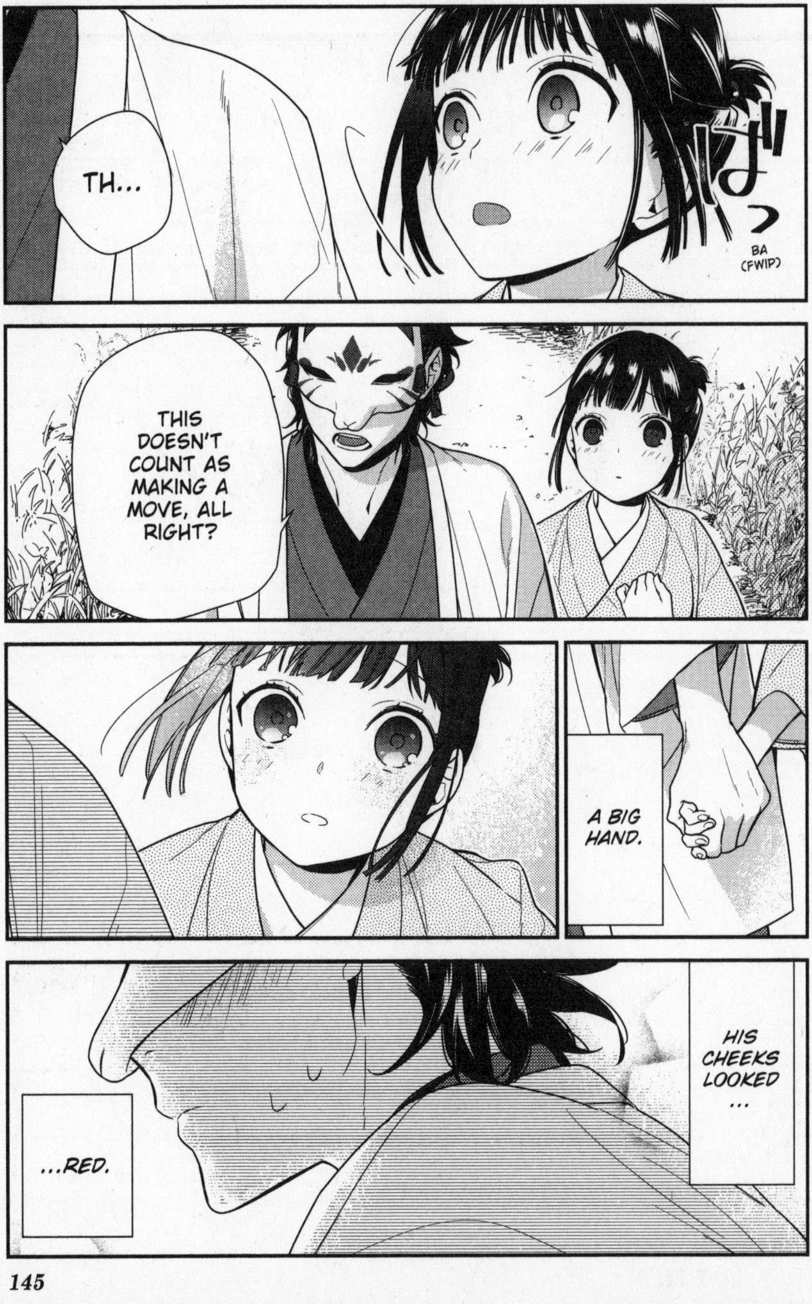
ばっ
BA (FWIP)
TH...
THIS DOESN'T COUNT AS MAKING A MOVE, ALL RIGHT?
A BIG HAND.
HIS CHEEKS LOOKED ...
...RED.

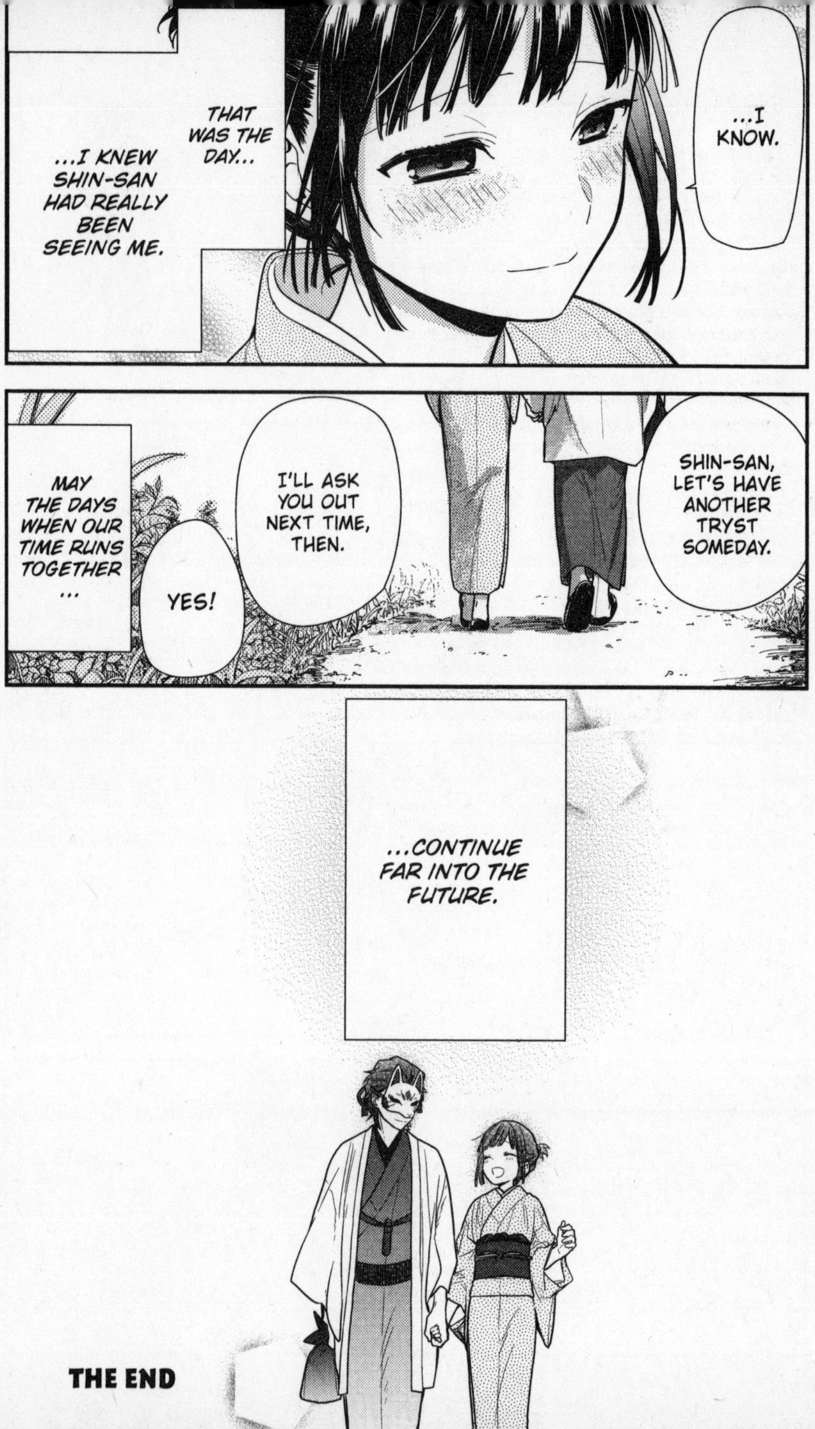
...I KNOW.
THAT WAS THE DAY...
...I KNEW SHIN-SAN HAD REALLY BEEN SEEING ME.
SHIN-SAN, LET'S HAVE ANOTHER TRYST SOMEDAY.
I'LL ASK YOU OUT NEXT TIME, THEN.
YES!
MAY THE DAYS WHEN OUR TIME RUNS TOGETHER...
...CONTINUE FAR INTO THE FUTURE.
THE END

Translation Notes

COMMON HONORIFICS
no honorific: Indicates familiarity or closeness; if used without permission or reason, addressing someone in this manner would constitute an insult.
-san: The Japanese equivalent of Mr./Mrs./Miss. If a situation calls for politeness, this is the fail-safe honorific.
-sama: Conveys great respect; may also indicate that the social status of the speaker is lower than that of the addressee.
-kun: Used most often when referring to boys, this indicates affection or familiarity. Occasionally used by older men among their peers, but it may also be used by anyone referring to a person of lower standing.
-chan: An affectionate honorific indicating familiarity used mostly in reference to girls; also used in reference to cute persons or animals of either gender.

Page 41
Chazuke: A simple dish made by pouring green tea over rice.

Page 74
Sake-pickled vegetables: *Narazuke* are a common type of pickle from Nara, made with the mash left over from making *sake*. This makes them slightly alcoholic, resulting in Koyuki's dazed state.

Page 90
Pochimaru: Pochi is a common dog's name, and *-maru* is a masculine-sounding ending that also means "round."

Page 93
Koyuki's name: The *yuki* in Koyuki's name means "snow."

Page 94
Shin's masks: The masks revealed when Koyuki tries to imagine Shin's face are marked with the old, traditional and more complicated kanji for the numbers "one," "three," "four," and "six."

THANK YOU VERY MUCH FOR READING THIS FAR. HAGIWARA-SENSEI DREW BEAUTIFUL ILLUSTRATIONS FOR THE FALTERING STORY I'D WRITTEN, AND THANKS TO THAT, IT WAS SUCCESSFULLY RELEASED AS A BOOK.

NE NE NE (ORIGINAL TITLE: *NEN NE NO NE*) CARRIES THE MEANING OF "*NENNE*" — IN OTHER WORDS, SOMEONE WHO'S YOUNG AND UNSOPHISTICATED, OR NAIVE ABOUT SEXUAL MATTERS AS WELL. I THINK IT'S A PERFECT TITLE FOR THESE TWO.

IN CLOSING, I HOPE WE'LL GET TO MEET KOYUKI AND SHIN AGAIN SOMEWHERE.

THANK YOU TO ALL THE READERS AND EVERYONE WHO WAS INVOLVED WITH THIS STORY!

THANK YOU VERY MUCH!!

SHIZUKU TOTONO
by 従々野雫

NENNE NO NE

STAFF

ORIGINAL WORK:
SHIZUKU TOTONO-SAMA
SUPERVISING EDITOR:
ISHIKAWA-SAMA

THANK YOU FOR EVERYTHING!!

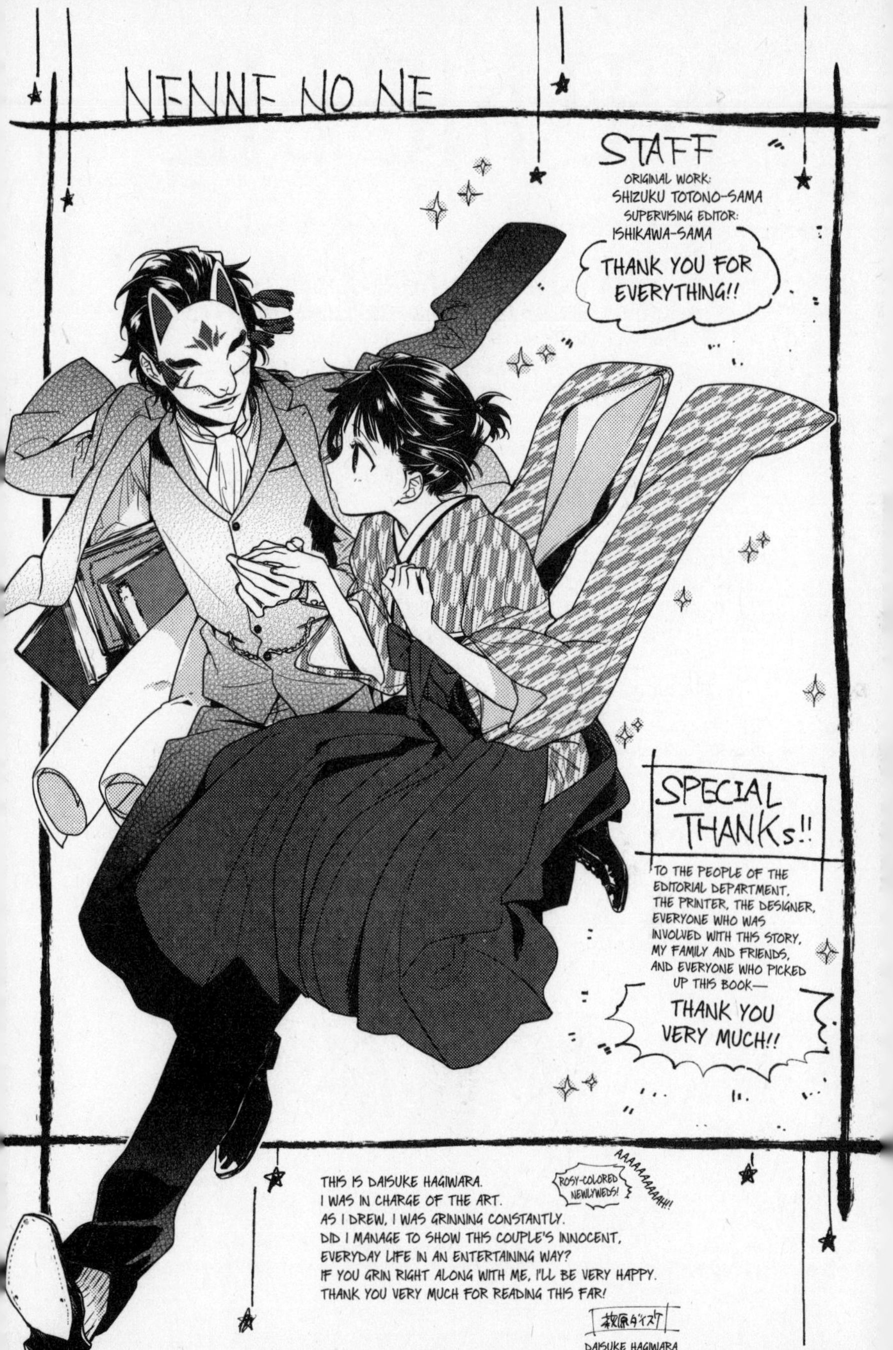

SPECIAL THANKs!!

TO THE PEOPLE OF THE EDITORIAL DEPARTMENT, THE PRINTER, THE DESIGNER, EVERYONE WHO WAS INVOLVED WITH THIS STORY, MY FAMILY AND FRIENDS, AND EVERYONE WHO PICKED UP THIS BOOK—

THANK YOU VERY MUCH!!

THIS IS DAISUKE HAGIWARA.
I WAS IN CHARGE OF THE ART.
AS I DREW, I WAS GRINNING CONSTANTLY.
DID I MANAGE TO SHOW THIS COUPLE'S INNOCENT, EVERYDAY LIFE IN AN ENTERTAINING WAY?
IF YOU GRIN RIGHT ALONG WITH ME, I'LL BE VERY HAPPY.
THANK YOU VERY MUCH FOR READING THIS FAR!

ROSY-COLORED NEWLYWEDS! AAAAAAAAAAAH!!

萩原ダイスケ
DAISUKE HAGIWARA

NE NE NE

STORY
Shizuku Totono

ART
Daisuke Hagiwara

TRANSLATION: TAYLOR ENGEL
LETTERING: BIANCA PISTILLO

NE NE NE © 2017 Shizuku Totono, Daisuke Hagiwara/SQUARE ENIX CO., LTD. First published in Japan in 2017 by SQUARE ENIX CO., LTD. English translation rights arranged with SQUARE ENIX CO., LTD. and Yen Press, LLC through Tuttle-Mori Agency, Inc.

English translation © 2018 by SQUARE ENIX CO., LTD.

Yen Press
1290 Avenue of the Americas
New York, NY 10104

Visit us at yenpress.com
facebook.com/yenpress twitter.com/yenpress
yenpress.tumblr.com
instagram.com/yenpress

First Yen Press Edition: December 2018
The chapters in this volume were originally published as ebooks by Yen Press.

Yen Press is an imprint of Yen Press, LLC.
The Yen Press name and logo are trademarks of Yen Press, LLC.

The publisher is not responsible for websites (or their content) that are not owned by the publisher.

Library of Congress Control Number: 2018953481

ISBNs: 978-1-9753-8103-5 (paperback)
978-1-9753-0420-1 (ebook)

10 9 8 7 6 5 4 3 2 1

WOR

Printed in the United States of America